CTET
English Grammar and Composition

For Competitive Examinations like CTET, UPSC, PSC, SSC, RRB, LIC and other Examinations

Chandan Sukumar Sengupta

Continuing Education Series

CTET English Grammar and Composition

Chandan Sukumar Sengupta.

Format of Publication: E Book, Workbook, Paperback and Hard Cover

There are millions of books available in market which can introduce a learner to English language and English grammar. More discussed theme of language learning is the English Grammar. This effort came in focus due to the increasing demand of people from different walks of life regarding the type of workbook which can equip a student in a specific way in terms of the enhancement of language related skills.

This workbook is designed to provide additional study materials to fellow students of High School standards. They equip themselves differently by making them fit for forthcoming examination. Learning by doing is the best way of acquiring such kinds of skills in stipulated time frame.

A language stands upon its rules of grammar and compositions. Similar mechanism is applicable to English also. It has such kinds of sets of rules through which one can aspire for the attainment of a perfectness in writing and expressions.

It is not merely for acquiring skills only in terms of speaking or writing. It has certain concern with quality writing. It is also equipped with more worksheets from the relevant topics with which one can enhance their skills within stipulated time frame. Most of the worksheets are taken up as per the prescribed format of examinations.

.

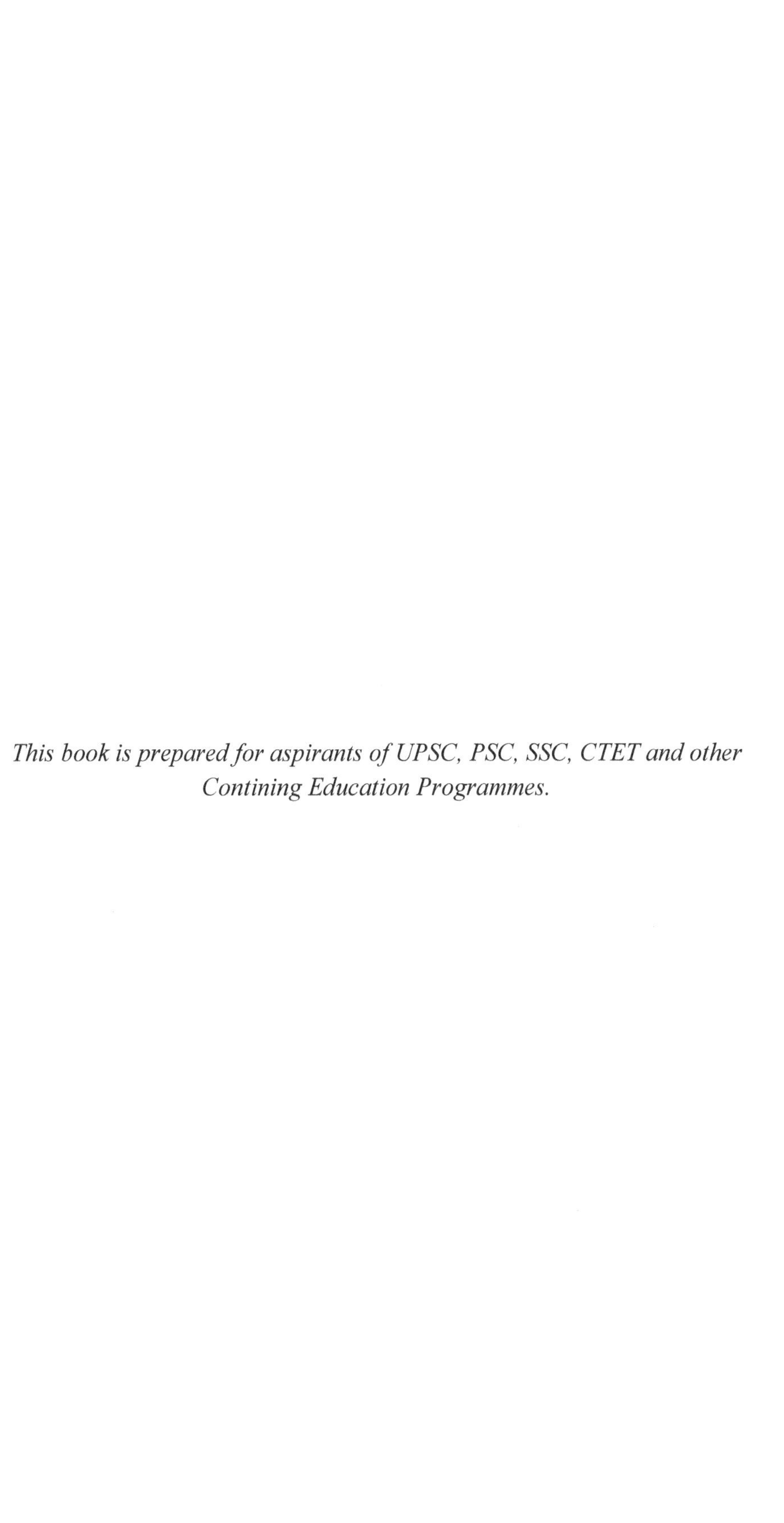

This book is prepared for aspirants of UPSC, PSC, SSC, CTET and other Contining Education Programmes.

Contents

Foreword

English as a language is not so difficult for any non-English person. The basic structure of English language is user friendly and is also of a comprehensive type. Modern instruments are also much friendly with this language. Because of this reason and some other, English as a user friendly language is becoming popular day by day. Number of people from non-English community who can read, write and speak English quite fluently are growing in number day by day. They are also taking different roles assigned to them in the cosmopolitan environment.

Non-English learners and aspirants often feel difficulties in pronounciating English words properly with needful tunings. These difficulties often become a serious obstacle while some English people go on trying to establish communication with them. Due to such difficulties also they often become disqualified in proving their capabilities of doing something fruitful.

This workbook and practice manual will provide an ample scope of gaining adequate skill and competence in linguistic communication. Stress is implied in the portions related to grammar and composition of the language so as to enhance the related skills and competences of the fellow learner.

It is also recommended that one should go on practicing related exercises alonside the referral readings for the purose of gaining proficiency. A discussion on the common mistakes related to the grammar and composition of this language is also included for the purpose of drawing attention of fellow students and aspirants towards the content areas of the communication techniques.

English as a language came to India along with the colonial rule. They people felt it necessary to educate a considerable part of Indian as well as Asian communities in English for ensuring their service lines in the colonies. It was more perfectly pitched in through religious propagations.

People of India accepted the language gladly and started getting adjusted with the cultural bands of English orientation. This West Germanic language is developed from Anglo-Frician dialects.[1] This dialect is brought to Britain during 6th to 7th Century by Anglo-Saxon[2] Migrants. In due course of time this language developed considerably and transformed into the dialect of modern time.[3]

Anglo –Saxon dialect was more commonly known as old-english.[4] Near about 400 Latin loan Words[5] were introduced in English alongside the advent of Christianity. During the development Middle English near about 10,000 loan words from French origin[6] entered the English dialect and made it an enriched one.

Fully developed English dictionary, the Dictionary of the English Language, was published by Samuel Johnson in 1755. English Grammar by Pristle[7] was an added contribution in the line of development of English Language. In modern time the total English speaking community

---

[1] *The Anglo-Frisian languages are the Anglic and Frisian varieties of West Germanic languages. The Northumbrian Language Society also considers Northumbrian a separate Anglic language.*

[2] *The Anglo-Saxon settlement of Britain is the process which changed the language and culture of most of what became England from Romano-British to Germanic. The Germanic-speakers in Britain, themselves of diverse origins, eventually developed a common cultural identity as Anglo-Saxons.*

[3] *Burke, Susan E (1998). ESL: Creating a quality English as a second language program: A guide for churches. Grand Rapids, Michigan: CRC Publications. ISBN 9781562123437.*

[4] *Shore, Thomas William (1906), Origin of the Anglo-Saxon Race - A Study of the Settlement of England and the Tribal Origin of the Old English People (1st ed.), London, pp. 3, 393*

[5] *English is a Germanic language, with a grammar and a core vocabulary inherited from Proto-Germanic. However, a significant portion of the English vocabulary comes from Romance and Latinate sources. A portion of these borrowings come directly from Latin,*

[6] *Baugh, Albert and Cable, Thomas. 2002. The History of the English Language. Upper Saddle River, New Jersey: Prentice Hall. pp. 158-178.*

[7] *Joseph Priestley was an English chemist, natural philosopher, separatist theologian, grammarian, multi-subject educator, and liberal political theorist who published over 150 works.*

worldwide may exceed 1.5 billion mark![8] There are several other instances to ascertain the fact regarding the ever increasing popularity of the International Language. It has also secured a propminent position in the international arena as a common dialect that people can opt with an ease.

After becoming assured about the ever increasing popularity of this language we can now imply adequate focus on the development of skills and competence of our fellow students and aspirants through exposing them to the horizon of interactives related to perfect and advanced English dialect. We also expect a timely participation of fellow scholars in this effort. They can continue evaluating their own skills through learning continuity supplemented with self paced evaluations.

Evolution of English Pronoun is another additional advantage of the modern English. Conflated forms of pronouns are also called an objective case. Development of such name is only because it is used only for objects of verbs. Once in old English there was distinct case system for both accusative and dative purposes. Later on such system collapsed into a single system of object (oblique) case having utility for objects of either a verb or a preposition. Studies in English were introduced in different universities during 19th and 20th Century because of its continuous developments in non-Europian continents. Development of such study was remarkably high in USA during 1970s. [9] It was also due to incorporation of English as another official language in most of the countries in the world.

Different courses in English are meant for different purposes. Studies in English are further accelerated with the advent of Informatics and allied fields. We consider English as a second language (a language study meant for non-English person). Errors in English are mainly observed from the field of syntax error, vocabulary error and error related to punctuations. Rules in English are periodically introduced by different

<hr>

[8] Algeo, John. 2010. *The Origins and Development of the English Language. Boston, MA: Wadsworth. pp. 182-187.*
[9] *National Center for Education Statistics (January 1993). "120 Years of American Education: A Statistical Portrait" (PDF). National Center for Education Statistics. Retrieved September 12, 2018.*

scholars time to time. Not to terminate a sentence by preposition, for an example, was the another rule introduced by *Robert Lowth*[10] .

Chandan Sukumar Sengupta

---

[10] *Robert Lowth (26 March 1794). A Short Introduction to English Grammar: With Critical Notes. Printed for J.J. Tourneisin – via Internet Archive.*

Revision Works

Practice Set 1

1. (A) They were/ (B) waiting for/(C) the train arrival. /(D) No error
2. (A) He is/(B) a student of three/(C) year's degree course. /(D) No error
3. (A) The two friends pointed out/ (B) each other merits and demerits/ (C) before the teacher./(D) No error
4. (A) None of the/(B) two sisters has/(C) paid her tuition fees. /(D) No error
5. (A) She was more/(B) beautiful than/(C) either of her three sisters. /(D) No error
6. (A) The hotels of/(B) Kolkata are cheaper/(C) than Patna./(D) No error
7. (A) The principal as well as/(B) the teachers /(C) absented themselves from the office./(D) No error
8. (A) I am sure that all my monthly/(B) expenses would exceed the income/(C) if I do not economise./ (D) No error
9. (A) When it comes to comparison between the two/(B) quality is most/(C) important than quantity./(D) No error
10. (A)Your over-dependent on others/(B) even for trivial matters/(C) may prove disadvantageous./(D) No error
11. (A) When I reminded of the mistake/(B) I had made/(C) I was struck with remorse. /(D) No error
12. (A) Mr. Mishra had/(B) to be operate on/(C) to cure him of the disease./(D) No error
13. (A) He overcame with sorrow/(B) when he heard the sad news/(C) of his failure./(D) No error
14. (A) The book on Political science brought/(B) in the market recently is really an asset/(C) for all college students./(D) No error

15. (A) You must not held in high esteem/(B) those who are dangerous/(C) to our society./(D) No error
16. (A) He read the message/(B) but he cannot/(C) understand it./(D) No error
17. (A) His mother thinks that/(B) somebody must have dared/(C) him steal the bicycle. /(D) No error
18. (A) Hard had he thrown the ball/(B) when it fell/(C) on the ground./(D) No error
19. (A) He ran so fastly that/(B) he reached the destination/(C) in just two minutes./(D) No error
20. (A) The old man continued live a hard life/(B) but he never asked for/(C) any help from neighbours./(D) No error

Practice Set 2
1. (A) Raman was one of those great/(B) sons of India who has earned everlasting/(C) fame for scientific researches/(D). No error
2. (A) Money which is a source/(B) of the happiness in life becomes/(C) a source of peril and confusion/(D) unless we control it/.(E) No error
3. (A) On almost every/(B) page there were/(C) announcements for/(D) cigarettes and tobacco/(E). No error
4. (A) The Cotton Textile Company/(B) cannot work properly unless/(C) it employs a talented/(D) sale representative/(E). No error
5. (A) The count/(B) married a rich heir/(C) a lass of fifteen/(D) who was a Jewess/(E). No error
6. (A) The eldest son/(B) of Mr. Thakur honours/(C) his senior's/(D) desires/.(E) No error
7. (A) One of them/(B) has given/(C) up one's/(D) studies/.(E) No error
8. (A) The more/(B) you read/(C) this book, the more/(D) you will like this/.(E) No error
9. (A) Some people have generously/(B) contributed to

the welfare/(C) fund, but they wanted/(D) there names
should be published/.(E) No error
10. (A) Lenin was greater/(B) than most/(C) other
revolutionary/(D) in the world/.(E) No error
Practice Set 3
1. The agitation by 1)/ municipal employees is 2)/
snowballing under 3)/ a crisis for the city. 4)/ No error 5)
2. The entire engineering 1)/ departments of the two
corporations 2)/ will also be 3)/ on an indefinite strike
from today. 4)/ No error 5)
3. The day is not father 1)/ when parents in the city 2)/
may have to send their children 3)/ abroad even for
nursery education. 4)/ No error 5)
4. After the incident, they 1)/ contact him and offered
him 2)/ a cash reward in exchange 3)/ for spotting the
error. 4)/ No error 5)
5. The follow-up surveys 1)/ are the only depended
source of information 2)/ on the unorganised sector 3)/
of non- agricultural production for the preparation of
the national accounts. 4)/ No error 5)
6. The major portion of 1)/ the Indian subcontinent was
2)/ in British rule 3)/ from 1857 to 1947. 4)/ No error 5)
7. He met the commissioners 1)/ of the three
corporations 2)/ and sought its support 3)/ for the drive.
4)/ No error 5)
8. To identify such a defaulters, 1)/ the department
tracks 2)/ data of 3)/ bank statements, 4)/ No error 5)
9. This is one of the 1)/ many bizarre anomaly 2)
noticed in the first semester results and confirmed 3)/
by the university's exam branch officials. 4)/ No error 5)
10. Teachers who figured 1)/ this out believe the
problem 2)/ may extended to 3)/ other subjects. 4)/ No
error 5)
Practice Set 4
1. 1) Producers must take/ 2) responsibility for/ 3) the

disposal of/ 4) end - to- life products./ 5) No error.

2. 1) Youngest of the group/ 2) thought/ 3) he had found/ 4) the perfect name./ 5) No error.

3. 1) GM app will help/ 2) small and medium businesses (SMBs) create/ 3) and manage their business information online across/ 4) Google in English and Hindi for free without having to invest in a website or a domain./ 5) No error.

4. 1) On reaching the beautiful city of Rajasthan,/ 2) the trainers/ 3) lay out a feast/ 4) for their new state elephant/ 5) No error.

5. 1) The children/ 2) came forward/ 3) one by one hold flowers/ 4) of different shades./ 5) No error.

6. 1) A welcome features of the new rules/ 2) are the emphasis/ 3) on extended/ 4) producer responsibility. / 5) No error

7. 1) Recycle of e-waste/ 2) is one/ 3) of the biggest/ 4) challenges today,/ 5) No error

8. I too became/ 2) quite found of/ 3) him and would wait/ 4)for him to come./ 5) No error

9. 1) He vowed never/ 2) to be lazy/ 3) and keep safe/ 4) the father's wealth./ 5) No error

10. 1) The woman picked up/ 2) the bell/ 3) quickly and rushed/ 4) toward the village./ 5) No error.

Practice Set 5

1. (A) Syrian government troops have captured almost 85 per cent of/(B) the eastern part of the city which fell over rebel/(C) hands in 2012 in one of the early setbacks to the regime of/(D) President Bashar al-Assad in the civil war./(E) No error

2. (A) The rebels accuse the regime for/(B) indiscriminate bombing and killing civilians/(C), while the government says it had no option/(D) but to move in as the city was controlled by terrorists./(E) No error

3. (A) Gen2 Core elevators/(B) attain a speed of 0.7

meters per second/(C) and provides options of machine room or/(D) machine-less room arrangements/(E). No error

4. (A) Affordable homes do not only mean the/(B) cost accessibility of the home also lower operational/(C) and maintenance costs. Sustainable features are/(D) key to any affordable housing project/.(E) No error

5. (A) Over the past 27 centuries, the average day has lengthen at a rate/(B) of about +1.8 milliseconds (ms) per century, a British/(C) research team concluded in the journal/(D) Proceedings of the Royal Society A/.(E) No error

6. (A) Factors which influences the Earth's rotation include/(B) the Moon's braking effect, Earth's altering shape due to/(C) shrinking polar ice caps since the last Ice Age/(D), electro-magnetic interactions between the mantle and core/.(E) No error

7. (A) The production of pepper and natural rubber/(B) contribute significantly to the total national output/(C). In the agricultural sector, coconut, tea/(D), coffee, cashew and spices are important. /(E) No error

8. (A) She has told me that her brother might/(B) have done much better at the university/(C) last year had he not given so much/(D) time to the students' union./(E) No error

9. (A) My wife often/(B) goes to the indoor's pool/(C) but I don't like/(D) going there./(E) No error

10. (A) Even though he found the/(B) subject rather interesting Raghu/(C) could not manage good marks/(D) in the examination./(E) No error

Practice Set 6

1. 1) Turnover of share trading/ 2) over mobile devices had increased/ 3) more than four times/ 4) in the last two years./ 5) No error.

2. 1) Cheating in the ongoing state/ 2) Board

matriculation exams in the UP/ 3) has literally scaled/ 4) new heights./ 5) No error.

3. 1) A day after, his father/ 2) apologised for hurting/ 3) the sentiments of people/ 4) in his last play./ 5) No error.

4. 1) Pledging himself to serving Gujarat for the next five years./ 2) she blamed any talk/ 3) by his party members of contesting election/ 4) elsewhere on arrogance./ 5) No error.

5. 1) Unlike conventional marketing channels./ 2) digital marketing allow/ 3) very little room/ 4) for errors./ 5) No error.

6. 1) Drinking too much/ 2) on a single occasion or over time/ 3) can take a serious toll/ 4) to your health/ 5) No error.

7. 1) Behind increasing interconnectedness/ 2) promised by globalisation/ 3) are global decisions, / 4) policies and practices/ 5) No error.

8. 1) The long delays in Air India flights/ 2) due to lack of trained crew/ 3) and maintenance staff evoke/ 4) major concern in the Rajya Sabha./ 5) No error.

9. 1) Rose McGowan is an American actress/ 2) and director/ 3) known for her contribution/ 4) to independent film/ 5) No error.

10. Still, even with a rising market/ 2) for socially responsible business,/ 3) issues like race relations are still/ 4) challenging for businesses to address/ 5) No error.

Practice Set 7

1. (A) An old man in the/(B) crowd warned Julius/(C) Caesar from the/(D) danger of death on certain day/(E). No error

2. (A) Mr. Parkash leads/(B) a very busy/(C) life so he goes/(D) everywhere by a scooter/(E). No error

3. (A) He does not like this/(B) type of a man who/(C)

does nothing but find/(D) fault with others/.(E) No error
4. (A) Now days workers are/(B) less interested in money as/(C) such and appear to be more concerned/(D) about opportunities for autonomy and freedom./(E) No error
5. (A) Knowledge of regional language is/(B) necessary for bank officers/(C) because they are to/ (D) understand what their customer say/(E). No error
6. (A) Having finished his breakfast/(B) he started working on/(C) the problem that had/(D) been awaiting disposal for the long time/.(E) No error
7. (A) Kabir and Rahim are/(B) great poets but the/(C) former is greater/(D) than latter/.(E) No error
8. (A) You have been learning Tamil/(B) for last one year but/(C) you show no/(D) improvement whatsoever/. (E) No error
9. (A) He has been sent to the prison /(B) several time but has/(C) shown no improvement/(D) in his conduct./(E) No error
10. (A) On my request/(B) Jatin introduced/(C) me to his friend who/(D) is singer and a scientist/.(E) No error

Practice Set 8

1. (A) The government contended/(B) that she could not be/(C) commissioned as she has/(D) rejected the offer earlier./(E) No Error
2. (A) The plane that crashed in Colombia/(B) was out of fuel, had no electric/(C) power and was preparing for an emergency/(D) landing when it crashed/.(E) No error
3. (A) The astronomical phenomena of Aurora Borealis/(B), commonly known as Northern Lights/(C), is caused when the Sun's energy/(D) produce a 'Solar Storm', spreading charged particles across space./(E) No error
4. (A) Dictionary has named 'Xenophobia' as Word/(B) of the Year for 2016. Xenophobia refers/(C) to the fear

or hatred for foreigners/(D), people from different cultures or strangers/(E). No error

5. (A) To the wake of demonetisation, a Noida-based/(B) startup named Tailmill is making home/ (C) deliveries of cash up to Rs. 1,000 per day/(D) per customer in valid currency notes./(E) No error

6. (A) This comes amid an ongoing territorial/(B) dispute among Israel and Palestine which started in/(C) 1948. Palestine has been a non-member/(D) 'Observer' state in the UN since 2012./ (E) No error

7. (A) A study on Mumbai parents have revealed nearly 75% /(B) mothers subject their children to helicopterstyle parenting/(C), characterised by tendencies of overseeing their/(D) child's life and rescuing them at the first sight of trouble./(E) No error

8. (A) Paragraph development continues with an /(B) expression of the rationale or the explanation that the/(C) writer gives for how the reader should/(D) interpret the informations presented in the idea statement or topic sentence of the paragraph./(E) No error

9. (A) The government said NGOs and/(B) voluntary organisations (VOs) need to /(C) register itself with NITI Aayog to receive/(D) grant-in-aid from the Centre./(E) No error

10. (A) Sambhaji Brigade, one of the group/(B) organising Maratha protests across/(C) Maharashtra, is set to become/(D) a political party, reports said./(E) No error

Practice Set 9

1. (A) Many a profound thinker/ (B) believes that/ (C) the march of civilization/ (D) has not coincided with real human progress. /(E) No error

2. (A) The Hindi and the Marathi are/(B) different forms of the Sanskrit language/(C) which were once

spoken/(D) in almost every part of India./(E) No error

3. (A) A pair of goggle was/(B) brought from the market/(C) for Vijay /(D) making him fit to a gentleman./(E) No error

4. (A) He would not have/(B) written this letter,/(C) if he would not /(D) have heard the news. / (E) No error

5. (A) The discrete enquiry revealed/(B) that his involvement in the/(C) fraud cases have been/ (D) more than what was first guessed. (E) No error

6. (A) Not any other /(B) fruit is as /(C) delicious as /(D) the mange/.(D) No error

7. (A) Some people have generously contributed/(B) to the welfare fund, but they/(C) wanted that there names should/(D) not be published./ (E) No error

8. (A) Although he is my /(B) bosom friend I cannot /(C) ask him for money without /(D) any vividly decision/.(E) No error

9. (A) The economical condition of /(B) our country is bad and /(C) unlikely to improve in /(D) the near future. /(E) No error

10. (A) Originally they had planned to buy /(B) an air conditioner but finally /(C) settled for an air cooler as /(D) the cost of the latter was very less./ (E) No error

Practice Set 10

1. (A) UIDAI efforts were undertaken by Government of India to provide an/(B) identity to residents first in 1993, with photo-identity/(C) cards tothe Election Commission and Further in/(D) 2003 with the approval of/(E) Multipurpose National Identity Card.

2. (A) He led a corrosive/ presidential campaign/(B), thumbing his nose on politically/(C) correct, conventional notions of all that/(D) it takes to be the President.

3. (A) The Vidhan Sabha Secretariat's/(B) action of paying the honorarium for its employees in/(C) currency

notes of Rs 1,000 denomination more than/(D) a week after Prime Minister Narendra Modi/(E) declared them invalid as legal tenders have raised questions.

4. (A) To encourage the generation of energy out of waste/(B), Himachal proposes to launch a pilot project in /(C) select cities where hotel clusters/(D) will be encouraged to take to biogas generation/(E) beside exploring the possibility of converting solid waste into fuel.

5. (A) In a major relief to students/(B), the government announced the mass/(C) promotion to students of Classes V to IX and Class XI/(D) in all government and private/(E) schools across the Valley.

6. (A) Banks still struggle to manage the huge rush/(B) of people thronging branches across/(C) the country to exchange invalid/(D) currency notes and getting cash to/(E) meet their daily needs.

7. (A) Olympics silver medallist PV Sindhu and Ajay Jayaram/(B) advanced to the quarterfinals after registered thrilling/(C) three-game wins over their respective opponents/(D) in the second round of/(E) the China Super Series Premier.

8. (A) The Akali Dal, which had subsumed itself in the Indian/(B) National Congress during the 1957 polls,/(C) was now a contestant and/(D) was fighting on the plank/(E) of a Punjabi Suba.

9. (A) At a time when the country is going through a major monetary/(B) upheaval with the demonetization of old Rs 500 & 1000 notes/(C), it is pertinent to look after our financial services/(D) and the opportunities that a moment in history/(E), even like this, can throw up for us.

10. (A) Bharmour Vikas Manch, a local organisation/(B), has urged the state government to undertake/(C) construction for Bharmour-

Gaurikund/(D) road for making the famous/(E) Manimahesh pilgrimage easy.

Practice Set 11

1. (A) Climate change is causing Himalayan/ (B) glaciers to melt at an alarming rate, /(C) creating huge glacial lakes which/(D) could burst its banks./(E) No error

2. (A) Conservation efforts appear/(B) to be having scant impact as the/(C) index is showing a steep plunge/(D) than two years ago./(E) No error

3. (A) Police have arrested officials/(B) in charge of environmental protection in central/(C) China after they were accused of/(D) tempering with air quality monitoring data./(E) No error

4. (A) Environment Minister Anil Dave has said/(B) India will no longer permit the release of HFC-23,/ (C) a family of potent greenhouse gas,/(D) released when local companies produce the refrigerant HCFC-22./(E) No error

5. (A) Procedural delays/ (B) and laxity in administration is/(C) the main reasons for/(D) the dip in ranking./(E) No error

6. (A) Sobha Limited will be leaving no stone unturn/(B) to deliver their best with the apartments/(C) at Sobha City, incidentally their first /(D) apartment project in North India./(E) No error

7. (A) Reply to the allegations he Chief Minister's/(B) Office said that the rates quoted/(C) by Patanjali were not below than what the/(D) committee of four secretaries had decided./(E) No error

8. (A) Rangers and rescue teams have arrived/(B) at the site and injured were being shifted/(C) to nearby hospitals for/(D) immediate treatment./(E) No error

9. (A) It is not a coincident that we get/(B) to repeatedly hear about/(C) "the last 30 years" in political rhetoric/(D) in many parts of the world./(E) No error

10. (A) It is this very ordinariness of our words/(B) that count because they are/ (C) society's shorthand for/(D) its subliminal feelings/(E) No error

Practice Set 12

1. (A) Langar said the work/(B) showed that endothelial cells/ (C) could line veins, arteries and lymph tissues/.(D) No Error

2. (A) Technical innovations and experiments/(B) with alternative ways of providing infrastructure/ (C) indicates the different principals./(D) No Error

3. (A) The aim of Baconian/(B) philosophy was to provide/ man with what he required / (C) while he continued to be a man./(D) No Error

4. (A) Bacon fixed his eye/(B) on a mark which was placed/(C) on the earth and hits it in the white./(D) No Error

5. (A) The martyrs who laid down their life/(B) for the freedom of our country/,(C) had a lofty vision of the future/.(D) No Error

6. (A) The phenomenon of terrorism signifies/(B) violence by disgruntled groups of people determined/(C) to achieve certain political goals/(D) whom they find are not attainable lawfully./(E) No Error

7. (A) Under the constitution which takes over/(B) three years to write, South Africa's mutiracial /(C)'government of national unity'/ (D) has a term of five years./(E) No Error

8. (A) Love of reading books is/(B) a great source to happiness/(C) to beat boredom,/(D) to defeat loneliness and to resume daily work with new vigour./(E) No error

9. (A) Love is ever waiting for/ something to turn up;/(B) labour with keen eyes and/(C) strong will always turn up something./(D) No Error

10. (A) The danger of poetry's becoming a kind/(B) of after-dinner amusement is far greatest/(C) than the

danger of its reverting to/(D) a method of moral instructions/(E) No Error

Practice Set 13

1. (A) To evolve a shared vision of national development/(B) priorities,sectors and strategy with the active/(C) involvement of States in the light of national objective./(D) No error

2. (A) The ninth plan launched in/(B) the fifth year of India's independence aimed at/(C) achieved a targeted GDP growth rate of seven percent./(D) no error

3. (A) The involvement of the community in planning,/(B) execution and monitoring of the developmental/(C) programmes are imperative for planning and implementation./(D) No error

4. (A) Rural development imply/(B) both the economic/(C) development and social transformation./(D) No error

5. (A) The Resource blocks initiated during/(B) the year 2012-13 have shown impressing/(C) results in terms of quality of community institutions./(D) No error

6. (A) The ministry has been actively/(B) encouraging use of local available /(C) construction material as well as new technologies./(D) No error

7. (A) Mutually beneficial working relationship/(B) and formal platforms for consultations/(C) among PRIs and institutions of the poor need to be facilitated./(D) No error

8. (A) The policy envisages integrating/(B) land use and transport planning,/(C) significant improvements in public transport./(D) No error

9. (A) The needs of the specific users/(B) are take care by the National Atlas/(C) and Thematic Mapping organisation./(D) No error

10. (A) The programme relating to/(B) nuclear power and nuclear fuel/(C) cycles have been built on the

multidisciplinary R&F infrastructure of the department./(D) No error

Practice Set 14

1. (A) They were/ (B) waiting for/(C) the train arrival. /(D) No error

2. (A) He is/(B) a student of three/(C) year's degree course. /(D) No error

3. (A) The two friends pointed out/ (B) each other merits and demerits/ (C) before the teacher./(D) No error

4. (A) None of the/(B) two sisters has/(C) paid her tuition fees. /(D) No error

5. (A) She was more/(B) beautiful than/(C) either of her three sisters. /(D) No error

6. (A) The hotels of/(B) Kolkata are cheaper/(C) than Patna./(D) No error

7. (A) The principal as well as/(B) the teachers /(C) absented themselves from the office./(D) No error

8. (A) I am sure that all my monthly/(B) expenses would exceed the income/(C) if I do not economise./ (D) No error

9. (A) When it comes to comparison between the two/(B) quality is most/(C) important than quantity./(D) No error

10. (A)Your over-dependent on others/(B) even for trivial matters/(C) may prove disadvantageous./(D) No error

11. (A) When I reminded of the mistake/(B) I had made/(C) I was struck with remorse. /(D) No error

12. (A) Mr. Mishra had/(B) to be operate on/(C) to cure him of the disease./(D) No error

13. (A) He overcame with sorrow/(B) when he heard the sad news/(C) of his failure./(D) No error

14. (A) The book on Political science brought/(B) in the market recently is really an asset/(C) for all college students./(D) No error

15. (A) You must not held in high esteem/(B) those who

are dangerous/(C) to our society./(D) No error
16. (A) He read the message/(B) but he cannot/(C) understand it./(D) No error
17. (A) His mother thinks that/(B) somebody must have dared/(C) him steal the bicycle. /(D) No error
18. (A) Hard had he thrown the ball/(B) when it fell/(C) on the ground./(D) No error
19. (A) He ran so fastly that/(B) he reached the destination/(C) in just two minutes./(D) No error
20. (A) The old man continued live a hard life/(B) but he never asked for/(C) any help from neighbours./(D) No error

Practice Set 15
1. (1) He fell from the running train/ (2) and would have died/ (3) if the villagers did not get / (4) him admitted in the nearby hospital immediately./ (5) No error
2. (1) Wearing extremely fashionable / (2) and surrounded by photographers/ (3) and pressmen/ (4) she swept up the microphone. / (5) No error
3. (1) Although we are free/ (2) for the last forty five years/ (3) or so, yet we continue to/ (4) be economically backward. / (5) No error
4. (1) Having deprived from their homes/ (2) in the recent earthquake/ (3) they had no other option/ (4) but to take shelter in a school. / (5) No error
5. (1) In spite of working/ (2) very neat and careful/ (3) he could not win/ (4) even the third prize. / (5) No error
6. (1) Meerabai was sent away from home/ (2) because she spend most of / (3) the time / (4) in the company of holy men./ (5) No error
7. (1) The Hindi and Marathi are/ (2) different forms of the Sanskrit language/ (3) which were once spoken/ (4) in almost every part of India. / (5) No error

8. (1) As much as I admire him/ (2) for his sterling qualities/ (3) I cannot excuse him/ (4) for being unfair to his friends./ (5) No error

9. (1) Several prominent figures/ (2) involved in the scandal / (3) are required to appear/ (4) to the investigation committee./ (5) No error

10. (1) The town is not well known / (2) and there isn't / (3) much to see/ (4) so a few tourists come here. / (5) No error

Practice Set 16

1. (1) At no circumstances/ (2) should you/ (3) lend him/ (4) any money. / (5) No error

2. (1) I deny the/ (2) allegation that/ (3) less people/ (4) are buying our books./ (5) No error

3. (1) I think/ (2) she sang/ (3) very well./ (4) Isn't it? / (5) No error.

4. (1) She reads all/ (2) the time/; (3) she prefers/ (4) to read than to write./ (5) No error

5. (1) I shall not go into all the depressing details/; (2) suffice it to/ (3) say the whole affair/ (4) was an utter disaster. / (5) No error.

6. (1) He had been writing/ (2) the article for/ (3) two hours, (4) but he still/ had not finished./ (5) No error

7. (1) Hardly did I sit/ (2) on the chair/ (3) when there was an/ (4)explosion outside the house./ (5) No error

8. (1) A little/ (2) did I realise how/ (3) cleverly/ (4) I had been derived./ (5) No error

9. (1) I would have/ (2) come sooner if/ (3) I knew/ (4) they were here./ (5) No error

10. (1) India is/ (2) one of the/ (3) leading rice producing/ (4) country in the world./ (5) No error

Practice Set 17

1. sooner than he had arrived (a) / his friends arranged a reception (b) / in his honour in (c) / the best hotal in town (d) / No error (e).

2. The managing director well as the Board members (a) / was the favor to taking strict action (b) / against the workers on strike (c) / No error (d)

3. No sooner did the jeep arrive (a) / at the station (b) / than a young police officer (c)/ jumped out of it (d) / No error (e).

4. Neither the famine (A) / or the subsequent fire (b) / was able to destroy the spirit of the people (c)/ No error (d).

5. hardly had arrived (a)/ when the house caught fire (b) / and everything was reduced to ashes (c) / No error (d).

6. No sooner did (a)/ the Chairman begin speaking, some(b) / participaints started (c) / shouting slogans (d) / no error (e).

7 Though she was sick (a) / but (b) / she went to work (c) / No error (d).

8. Mohan could not (a) / go to picnic (b) / for his mother (c)/ was not will (d)/ No error (e).

9. Even though the shirt is rather expensive (a) / but i wish to (b) / purchase it with my own money (c) / no error (d).

10.The reason for (a) / his failure is because (b) / he did not work hard (c) / No error (d).

11. No sooner did the sun rise (a) / when we took a hasty breakfast (b) / and resumed the journey (c) / No error (d).

12. The manager of the bank was busy ; (a)/ so he asked them to come and (b) / see him between two to three in the afternoon (c) / No error (d).

13. The old woman has had the best medical facilities available(a)/ but she will not be cured (b) / unless she does not have a strong desire to live (c) / No error (d).

14. The downfall of this kind (a) / is to be attributed to (b) / nothing else than pride (c) / No error (d).

15. No sooner did I open the door (a) / when the rain, heavy and stormy, rushed in (b) / making us shiver form head to toe (c) / No error (d) .

Practice Set 18

1. For a poor man (A)/ even five rupees (B)/ are (C)/ a big sum. (D)/ No error. (E)

2. Science comprises (A)/ of many (B)/ branches of (C)/ learning.(D)/ No error. (E)

3. I shall avail (A)/ of this opportunity (B)/ to meet (C)/ you there. (D)/ No error. (E)

4. I asked him (A)/ whether (B)/ he has got (C)/ admission in the college. (D)/ No error. (E)

5. Walk slowly (A)/ lest (B)/ you may fall (C)/ in the ditch. (D)/ No error. (E)

6. Until he (A)/ does not confess his fault (B)/ he will not be (C)/ included in the team. (D)/ No error. (E)

7. By this time (A)/ next year (B)/ I had completed (C)/ my university degree. (D)/ No error . (E)

8. He is serving (A)/ under me (B)/ for the last (C)/ several years. (D)/ No error. (E)

9. No man (A)/ on the earth (B)/ is (C)/ immortal. (D)/ No error. (E)

10. Hardly (A)/ we had reached (B)/ the platform (C)/ when the train started. (D)/ No error. (E)

11. Everyone (A)/ of you (B)/ are required to do the (C)/ writing work in the classroom. (D)/ No error. (E)

12. John totally (A)/ disapproved with (B)/ his friend's behaviour (C)/ in the party. (D)/ No error. (E)

13. He walked (A)/ so fast (B)/ as he (C)/ fainted. (D)/ No error. (E)

14. Having complete his work (A)/ he (B)/ went home (C)/ to take rest. (D)/ No error. (E)

15. These kind of shoes (A)/ seem to be expensive (B)/ but they are relatively (C)/ easy to care for. (D)/ No error. (E)

16. Although these houses (A)/ are in need of repair (B)/ there have been much improvement (C)/ in their appearance. (D)/ No error. (E)

17. No sooner (A)/ did he ran (B)/ than he was chased (C)/ by everyone. (D)/ No error. (E)

18. Any help (A)/ that you can (B)/ give me (C)/ will be appreciate. (D)/ No error. (E)

19. If he will not work hard (A)/ he will not (B)/ be able to (C)/ score good marks. (D)/ No error. (E)

20. When I reached home (A)/ my father (B)/ already came (C)/ from office. (D)/ No error. (E)

Practice Set 19

1. Because of the emergency help (a) / that the patient received ()b) / he would have died (c) / No error (d) .

2. Arun's parents died when he was young and (a) /he looked after his aunt (b) / who had no children (c) / No error (d) .

3. All the boys (a) / returned back home (b) / well in time for lunch (c) / No error (d).

4. The article (a) / should not exceed (b) / more than five hundred words (c) / no error (d).

5. Atul's habit of (a) / delaying his work (b) / put his colleagues (c) / to a lot of trouble (d)/ No error (e).

6. On entering the room (a) / she was found hanging b(b) / from the ceiling (c)/ No error (d) .

7. Emphasis on quality of life ensures(a)/ for the health and happiness (b) / of every individual (c) / No error (d).

8. In the meeting (a)/ mr. mehta's suggestions with regard for (b) / certain administrative reforms (c) / were hailed by all the members (d) / No error (e).

9. He (a) / came across (b) / with a beggar (c) / No error (d).

10. You will be tired of writing (a) / at the time you (b) / finish your research (c) / No error (d).

11. I offered him part-time job (a) / but he turned it over

(b) / saying that he would (c)/ rather wait for a fulltime job (d) / No error (e).

12. We never buy any jam in the shops , (a) /because my wife makes all our jam with fruits of our garden, (b) / and these taste much better than the jam from the shops, we think (c)/ No error (d).

Practice Set 20

1. The Hindi and the Marathi are (a) / different forms of the sanskrit language ,(b) / which were once spoken (c) / in almost every part of India (d)/ No error (e).

2. The Committee Chief Warned the party members (a) / that if persist (b) / in their obstructionist attitude (c)/ they would be suspended (d) / No error (e)

3. More widely popular (a) / than the hunting of deer or fox (b) / were the pursuit of the here (c) / No error (e).

4. If i know (a) / that my friend had planned to visit the know today. (b) / I would have made his stay comfortable (c) / No error (d).

5. The future is (a) / yet to come (b) / but you have a (c) / right to shape it (d)/ No error (e).

6. He won't return the money (a) / that he borrowed (b) / will he ? (c) / No error (d).

7. The foremost criterion of selection we adopted (a)/ were the number of years of training (b) / a dancer had received (c) / under a particular guru (d) / No error (e).

8. The chief idea of (a)/ a very common type of traveller (b) / is to see as many (c) / objects of interest as he possibly could (d)/ No error (e).

9. When the dentist came in (a)/ my tooth was stopped aching (b) / out of fear that I might lose my tooth (C) / No error (d).

10. Rohan was leading (a) / a happy and leisurely (b) / life after his retirement (c) / from service (d)/ No error

(e).
11. One of the drawbacks (a) / of modern education
are (b) / that it does not encourage original thinking (c)
/ No error (d).
12. The child (a) / picked up a burned paper (b) /
from the street (c) / no error (d).
13. Many a student (a)/ are frustrated (b) / because of
unemployment (c)/ No error (d).
14. Since it was his first election campaign , the
candidate was confused ; (a)/ none could clearly
understand (b) / either the principles he stood for o the
benefits he promised (c) / No error (d).
15. As much as I admire him for his sterling qualities
(a)/ I cannot excuse him (b) / for being unfair to his
friends (c) / No error (e).
Practice Set 21
1. The famous Dr. Chandra (a)/ is only dentist (b)/ in
our village.(c) / No error (d).
2. The majority of the (a) / Computer professionals
recommends (b) / that effective measures (c)/ should be
taken against software piracy (d)/ No error (e).
3. The accelerating pace of life in our metropolitan city
(a) / has had the tremendous effect (b) / on the culture
and life-style of the people (c) / No error (d).
4. This town isn't very well known (a) / and there isn't
much to see, (b) / so a few tourists come here (c) / No
error (d).
5.On my request (a) / Lalit introduced me (b) / to his
friend (c) / who is singer and scientist (d) / No error (e).
6. My father is (a) / in bad mood (b) / today (c)/ No
error (d).
7. Sunita opened a almirah (a) / full of books (b) / and
took out one of them (c) / for reading (d) / No error (e).
8. according to the Bible (a) / it is meek and humble (b)
/ who shall inherit the earth (c) / No error(d).

9. These display (a) / the (b) /remarkable variety (c) / No error (d).

10. Now that she is living in her own flat ,(a)/ she cleans the windows, (b) / twice a week in the summer and once a week in the winter .(c) / No error (d).

11. The road (a) / to famous monument (b) / passes through a forest (c) / No error (d).

12. I will discuss the matter with him (a) / when I will see him (b) / in the next few days (c) / No error (d).

Practice Set 22

1. The car flew off the road (a) / and fell into the valley (b) / because Ashish (c) / was driving faster (d) / No error (e).

2. Watch how careful (a) / the sparrow knits the (b) / straws into one another (c) / No error (d).

3. Of all the friends (a) / i have had , he is the most helpful (b) / and less arrogant (c) / No error (d).

4. Geometry and Drawing (a) / are more easier than (b) / Geography and Social Studies (c) No error (d).

5. He is (a) / too intelligent (b) / to make a mistake (c) / No error (d).

6. My observation is that (a)/ between vivek and Shashi, (b) / Vivek is the most intelligent (c)/ No error (d).

7. The technician reminded (a) / them to have a (b) / thoroughly cleaning of the (c) / machine after each use (d) / No error (e).

8. Firstly you should (a)/ think over the meaning of the words (b)/ and then use them (c)/ No error (d).

9. I have had to work (a) /. at the fountain for almost (b)/ ten hours before it could (c)/ start functioning well (d) / No error (e).

10. I courteously asked him (a)/ where was he going (b) / but he did not reply (c) No error (d).

Practice Set 23

1. The statement made by the writer (a) / appears to be incorrect (b) / as Gandhiji was never born in Ahemdabad (c). / No error (d).

2. The crew were on board (a) / and they soon busied themselves (b) / in preparing to meet the storm (c) /No error (d).

3. The manager called the clerk and said whether (a) / he was in the habit of (b)/ sleeping at home as well (c) / No error (d).

4. A lot of travel delay is caused (a) / due to the inefficiency and lack of good management (b) / oh behalf of the railways (c) / No error (d).

5. The signpost at the rate (a)/ of the garden read : (b) / 'Trespassers will be persecuted'. (c) / No error (d).

6. Everyone felt that (a) / the big glittering diamond (b) / was most unique (c) / No error (d).

7. I advised my son (a) / to engage two coolies instead of one (b)/ because the luggage was too much heavy for a single coolie (c) / No error (d).

8. After toiling very hardly(a) / over a long period of time (b) / he found that people recognised him as a successful person (c) / No error (d).

9. The angry man walked hurriedly (a) / into the crowded room (b) / and shouted loud at the guest (c) / No error (d).

10. The tried both the dresses (a) / and finally decided (b) / to buy expensive one (c) / No error (d).

11. He ultimately decided (a) /to willingly and cheerfully accept (b) / the responsibility entrusted to him (c) / No error (d).

12. Being the only people there (a) / their presence was (b) / most important (c) / No error (d).

13. It is the duty of every citizen to do his utmost

(a)/ to defend the hardly-won (b)/ freedom of
the country (c) / No error (d).
14. Even though it was (a) raining bad (b)/ I went
out (c) / to get some medicines (d) / No error (e).
15. In spite of working (a) / very neat and careful (b) /
he could not win (c) / even the third prize (d) / No error
(e)

Practice Set 24

1. We did the job (a) / as good as we could (b) /
however it did not turn out to be satisfactory (c) / No
error (d).
2. One of the members (a) / expressed doubt if (b) / the
minister was an atheist (c) / No error (d).
3. Can I lend (a) / your pencil (b) / for a minute please ?
(c) / No error (d).
4. You are the man (a) / who is held (b) / in high esteem
by by everybody (c) / No error (d).
5. Experience has taught me (a) / not to ignore any
man, high or low (b) / not to ignore anything great or
small (c)/ No error. (d).
6. Even many people (a) / carry an infection (b)
/ without showing its symptoms (c)./ No error (d).
7. The higher we climb (a)/ up the mountain peak, (b)/
the cooler (c) / we feel (d) / No error (d).
8. While luminaries of the dance world (a) / have
dearth of opportunities to display their art ,
(b)/ upcoming dancers sufferfrom (c)/ an
unfortunate lack of exposure (d) / No error (d).\
9. I will spend (a) / my remaining life (b) / in the village
(c) / No error (d).
10. Each cigarette which (a) / a person smokes (b)
/ does some (c) / harm to him (d). / No error (e).
11. students should work (a) / hard in order to (b) /
build their carrier (c)/ No error (d).
12. Like the Commission (a) / has recommended in its

report, (b) / the rules need to be (c) / enforced more strictly (d). / No error (e).
13. The book is making (a) / waves and the sale (b)/ is quite brisk in (c) / all major cities (d). /No error (e).
14. My brother has been (a) / living in America (b) /with his family (c) / for the past ten years (d). /No error (e).
15. With the advancement of winter (a) / The days grow shorter (b) / while the nights grow longer (c) / No error (d).

Practice Set 25
1. In the course of time (a) / the winged reptiles growing bigger and bigger (b) / and better and better at flying (c) / No error (d)
2. Although er reached his house on time (a) / he was left (b) / for the airport (c) / No error (d).\
3. We wanted to purchase (a)/ something but all the three stores (b) / in that area (c) / were closed on that day (d) / No error (e).
4. Children who have had (a) / good preschool education (b) / are most likely to out do (c) / other children at school (d) / No error (e).
5. Sunita was popular (a) / with her classmate that (b) / she always had someone or (c) / the other coming to her house (d) / No error .(e).
6. People should decide (a) / to not give (b) / or take dowry (c) / No error (d).
7. Being a well known physicist (a) / he was invited (b) / to deliver (c)/ a lecture on Laser technology (d) No error (e).
8. The lawyer told his client (a) / that he would represent him (b) / only if he pays up his fee (c) / No error (d).
 24
9. Never I have listened to such beautiful music (a)/ as

the piece we heard (b) / on the radio last night (c) / No error (d).

10. The serial which appeared quite interesting initially (a) / turned out to be boring (b) / in its latter parts (c). No error (d).

11. what sort of a drug this is (a) / that no one seems to be able to predict its long-term effects (b) / with any certainly ? (c) / No error (d).

12. You will come (a) / to my party tomorrow, (b) / isn't it ? (c) / No error (d) .

13. I can't (a)/ afford to pay (b) / that much for it (c) / No error (d).

14 .He was not only involved (a) / in her kidnapping (b) / but also in her murder (c) / No error (d) .

15. Women are now working (a) / in every fields (b) / like teaching , medicine , law, business, etc. (c) / no error (d) .

Practice Set 26

1. The Trust plans (a) / to set on (b) / a special school for (c) the dumb and deaf children (d) / No error (e).

2. The student (a) / answered to (b) / the question (c) / asked by the inspector of the school (d) / No error (e).

3. There are several (a) / of investing money prudently (b) / and making substantial profit (c)/ From the investment (d) / No error (e).

4. when you have (a) / read these books , (b) / please return them to me (c) No error (d).

5. The director prefers (a) / your plan than (b) / that give by (c) / the other members of the committee (d) / No error(e).

6. Considering about these facts (a) / the principal has offered (b) / him a seat (c) / No error (d).

7. it is easy to see that (a) / a lawyer's demeanour in court (b) / may be prejudicial against the interests of his client (c) / No error (d).

8. To transport goods (a) / via sea is cheaper (b) / than land (c) / No error.

9. I am pleased to sanction (a) / one spacial increment (b) / to all the employees (c) / with this month(d) / No error (e).

10. He was honourably (a) / acquitted from (b) / the charge (c) / No error (d).

11. Several prominent figures (a) / involved in the scandal (b)/ are required to appear (c)/ to the investigation committee (d)/ No error (e).

12.Mr. Smith was aacused for murder (a) / but the court found him not guilty (b) / and acquitted him (c) / No error (d).

13. It is not possible for me (a)/ to exchange the goods (b) / once the sale has been completed (c) / No error (d).

14. On his attitude (a) / is seems that what he wants (b) / is that the decision making power (c)/ should rest with him (d) / No error (e).

15. A large scale exchange of nuclear weapons (a) / will produce unprecedented amount of radiation (b) / that can penetrate into the biological tissues (c) / No error (d).

Practice Set 27

1. If I had known (a) / this yesterday (b) / I will have helped him (c) / No error (d).

2. If I will have enough (a) / time tomorrow (v) / I'll come and see you (c) / No error (d).

3. 'The Arabian Nights' (a) / Have lots of interesting stories (b) / for young readers (c) / No error (d).

4. I was standing (a) / at the bus stop (b) / waiting for him (c) / since eight O'clock (d) /No error (e).

5. I was there (a) / many times (c) / in the past (c) / No error (d).

6. He is working in (a) / a bank in New Delhi (b) / for the

past several months (c) / No error (d).

7. He has been (a) / the picture (b) / yesterday(c) / No error (d).

8. I am trying to finish (a) / this letter for the last one hour (b). / I wish you would (c) / go away or stop disturbing me (d). / No error (e).

9. The Ahujas (a) / are living in this colony (b) / for the last eight years (c) / No error (d).

10. He couldn't but help (a) / shedding tears at the plight of the villagers (b) / rendered homeless by a devastating cyclone (c) / No error (d).

11. When learning to swim (a) / one of the most important things (b) / s to relax (c)/ No error (d),

12. She sang (a) very well (b) / isn't it ? (c) / No error (d).

13. The reason why (a) / he was rejected (b) / was because he was too young (c) / No error (d).

14. When Anil was not (a) / able to show his ticket (b) / the conductor made him (c)/ Buying ticket (d) / No error (e).

15. He speaks (a) / not only Tamil (b) / but Telugu as well (c) / No error (d).

16. If I were (a) / in his shoes (b) / I would die with shame (c) / No error (d).

Practice Set 28

1. Involving of terrorists (A)/ in the blast (B)/ has been ruled out (C)/ by the police. (D)/ No error. (E)

2. The doctor has (A)/ prescribed two (B)/ spoonsful of medicine (C)/ thrice daily. (D) No error. (E)

3. The police could not (A)/ ascertain the (B)/ reason of the (C) girl's death. (D)/ No error. (E)

4. The government (A)/ has been incurring (B)/ loss at the rate of (C)/ fifty thousand annually. (D)/ No error. (E)

5. The mother rushed (A)/ to catch the child (B)/ who was leaning (C)/ over the wall. (D)/ No error. (E)

6. It is unfortunate (A)/ that she could not (B)/ avail of

the opportunity (C)/ that presented itself. (D)/ No error. (E)

7. She was not allowed (A)/ to enter into the examination hall (B)/ as he had (C)/ lost her admit card. (D)/ No error. (E)

8. When I will write (A)/ to my brother (B)/ I will convey (C)/ your message. (D)/ No error. (E)

9. Neither of the two books (A)/ could be (B)/ traced (C)/ anywhere. (D)/ No error. (E)

27

10. You would not have (A)/ failed in the test (B)/ if you would have (C)/ worked hard. (D)/ No error. (E)

11. These customs are (A)/ prevalent between the (B)/ inhabitants of (C)/ the lower regions. (D) No error. (E)

12. The police has been (A)/ accused of (B)/ connivance along the thieves (C)/ in his case. (D)/ No error. (E)

13. The essays (A)/ given on page ten (B)/ are relevant (C)/ to your topic. (D)/ No error. (E)

14. What to speak (A)/ of India (B)/ even developed countries (C)/ are faced with this problem. (D)/ No error. (E)

15. Persons engaged (A)/ in teaching line (B)/ lead a (c) comfortable life. (D)/ No error. (E)

Practice Set 29

1. In management , as you rise higher,(a) / the problems you face become more and more unstructured and you can't just fall back on (b)/ the tools you had been (c)/ taught (d)/ No error(e).

2. The whole thing moves (a)/ around the concept of building a small dynamic (b)/ organisation into a larger one (c)/ No error (d).

3. Remember that you are part of (a)/ the team and your success depends on the support (b)/ you are able to give and get from your other team member(c)/ No error (d).

4. Another reason for pharmaceutical companies beefing up their (a)/ OTC (over the Counter) divisions is that prescription drugs with proven safety records which have been reached (b)/ the end of their patent protection period are (c) / allowed to be sold without a prescription (d) / No error (e).

5." Meatless Days" (a)? have been made (b)/ into a film (c) / No error (d).

6. The difficult situation in which I found myself (a)/ is not made easy (b)/ by her constant nagging and grumbling (c)/ No error (d).

7. Swift's Gulliver's Travels (a) / Have been read by me (b) / several times (c) / No error (d).

8. A high level meeting (a) / of officials is reporting (b) / to have discussed (c) / the issue in great detail (d) / No error(e).

9. This room would look much better (a)/ if you put a furniture (b)/ in that corner (c) / No error (d).

10. The little boy knows (a) / how to start the engine (b) / but does not know to stop it (c)/ No error (d).

11. My friend is the kind of person (a) / who will face up (b)/ to the most demanding tasks (c) / No error(d).

12. Tell me the name of (a)/ a country where every citizen is law-abiding (b)/ and no trouble is there (c) / No error (d).

13. As poor as they are (a) / They never refuse to donate, (b) / for any noble cause (c) / No error (d).

14. The cause of earth quakes (a) / is the heat in the (b) / earth interior (c) / No error (d).

15. Sheela has scored a first class (a) / in her final exams (b) / isn't it ? (c) / No error (d).

Practice Set 30

1. The nation (A)/ heave a sigh (B)/ of relief (C)/ when monsoon arrives. (D)/ No error. (E)

2. Of the two men (A)/ in the office (B)/ the fat one is

elder (C)/ to the thin one. (D)/ No error.(E)

3. The girl (A)/ advised her brother (B)/ to work hard lest (C)/ he may fail. (D) No error. (E)

4. Scarcely had (A). we reached the station (B)/ when the train (C)/ arrived. (D)/ No error. (E)

5. The teacher told (A)/ the students (B) that the earth went (C)/ round the sun. (D)/ No error. (E)

6. He behaves (A)/ as if (B)/ he was the chief (C)/ of the organisation. (D)/ No error. (E)

7. You will not (A)/ be successful (B)/ until you will not (C)/ give up this bad habit. (D)/ No error.(E)

8. Both India (A)/ as well as Russia (B) are participating (C)/ In the games. (D)/ No error. (E)

9. The child (A)/ as well as his parents (B)/ were killed in (C)/ the accident , (D) No error. (E)

10. No sooner (A)/ did the dog (B)/ see the lion (C)/ when it jumped. (D)/ No error. (E)

11. Students as well as (A)/ the teacher (B)/ were present (C)/ for the show . (D)/ No error. (E)

12. India broke (A)/ all previous records (B)/ during this year's (C)/ cricket match. (D)/ No error. (E)

13. It s known fact (A)/ that the English (B) is an (C)/ international language. (D) No error.(E)

14. These facilities (A)/ are meant for (B)/ a M.P or a minister (C)/ o this country. (D)/ No error . (E)

15. Summer of last year (A)/ was very hot (B)/ compared with (C)/ this year's . (D) No error. (E)

Answers- Practice Set 1

1. C; Train's arrival will be used.

2. B; Years' should be used instead of year's.

3. B; Each other's merits should be used.

4. A; Neither will be used in place of none.

5. C; Either should be replaced by any. (Either is used for two persons.)

6. C; Than those of should be used before Patna.

7. C; Themselves should be replaced by himself. (Subject-Verb-Agreement)

8. A; All will not be used before monthly expenses because expenses include all expenditures.

9. B; Most should be replaced by more.

10. A; Over- dependent should be replaced by overdependence.

11. A; When I was reminded will be used.

12. B; Operate should be replaced by operated.

13. A; He was overcome will be used in the place of he overcame.

14. A; Brought should be replaced by introduced because a new thing is introduced.

15. A; Held should be replaced by held.

16. B; Cannot should be replaced with could not.

17. C; To should be used before use.

18. A; Hard should be replaced by hardly.

19. A; Fastly should be replaced by fast because fastly is no word in English language.

20. A; Live should be replaced by living.

Answers- Practice Set 2

1. B; have will be used instead of has because here have will be used for those great sons which is in plural, not for Raman.

2. B; The will not be used before happiness because it is a singular uncountable noun

3. C; advertisements should be used instead of announcements because an announcement is something spoken and advertisement is related to a printed notice or news.

4. D; Sales representative is the correct word. Sale representative is an incorrect word.

5. B; A rich heiress will be used to refer to a lady.

6. E; No error

7. C; His or her will be used instead of one's to refer to the person we are talking about

8. D; It should be used instead of this. Because it
personal pronoun is more suitable with the book.
9. D; Their names is the correct answer because
possessive pronoun of they is their.
10. C; Answers. Revolutionaries will be used instead of
revolutionary because plural noun is used after most
other/some other/ many other.
Answers- Practice Set 3
1. 3; Replace 'under' with 'into'
2. 2; 'department' instead of 'departments' (With the
use of 'entire' noun will be considered singular.)
3. 1; Replace 'father' with 'far'
4. 3; Replace 'contact' with 'contracted'
5. 2; Replace 'depended on' with 'dependable'
6. 3; replace 'in' with 'under'
7. 3; Replace 'its' with 'their'
8. 1; Omit 'a'
9. 2; Replace 'anomaly' with 'anomalies
10. 3; Replace 'extended' with 'extend'
Answers- Practice Set 4
1. 4; Replace 'to' with 'of;.
2. 1; Add 'the' before 'youngest'.
3. 5; No error
4. 3; Replace 'lay' with 'laid'.
5. 3; Replace 'hold' with 'holding'.
6. 2; Replace 'are' with 'is'
7. 1; Replace 'Recycle' with 'Recycling'
8. 2; Replace 'found' with 'fond'
9. 5; No error
10. 4; Replace 'towards' with 'towards'
Answers- Practice Set 5
1. B; fell into is the right phrase.
2. A; of should be used instead of for.
3. C; provide should be used.
4. B; but also should be used.

5. A; lengthened should be used.

6. A; influence should be used.

7. B; contributes should be used.

8. A; She told me should be used.

9. B; indoor pool should be used.

10. B; fairly interesting should be used. Rather is used for bad qualities.

Answers- Practice Set 6

1. 2; Replace 'over' with 'via'

2. 4; omit 'the' before 'U.P'

3. 5; No error

4. 4; Replace 'on' with 'in'

5. 2; Replace 'allow' with 'allows'

6. 4; Replace 'to' with 'on'

7. 1; add 'the' before 'increasing'

8. 3; replace 'evoke' with 'evoked'

9. 5; No error

10. 1; Replace 'with' with 'on'

Answers- Practice Set 7

1. D; On a certain day should be used.

2. D; by scooter is correct. a should be removed.

3. B; this type of man is correct. a should be removed.

4. A; now a days is the correct answer.

5. A; the knowledge should be used.

6. D; for a long time is correct.

7. D; than the latter is correct.

8. B; the last one year is correct.

9. A; sent to prison is correct.

10. D; a singer and scientist is correct.

Answers- Practice Set 8

1. C; She had should be used.

2. B; electrical should be used.

3. D; produces should be used.

4. C; Hatred of is the correct phrase.

5. A; In the wake of is the correct phrase.

6. B; between should be used instead of among.

7. A; has should be used instead of have.

8. D; information is the correct word to be used.

9. C; themselves should be used instead of itself.

10. A; One of the groups is the correct answer.

Answers- Practice Set 9

1. E; No error

2. C; which was should be used.

3. A; a pair of goggles

4. C; if he had not should be used

5. C; had been should be used

6. A; No other fruit should be used.

7. C; their should be used instead of there.

8. D; vivid should be used.

9. A; economic should be used instead of economy.

10. D; much less should be used.

Answers- Practice Set 10

1. C; by should be used after cards.

2. B; thumping his nose at is the correct idiom.

3. B; to should be used instead of for.

4. E; besides should be used.

5. C; for should be used instead of to.

6. D; get cash will be used.

7. B; registering will be used.

8. A; under should be used instead of in.

9. C; look at is the correct phrase.

10. C; construction of is the correct answer.

Answers- Practice Set 11

1. D; their will be used instead of its.

2. C; steeper will be used.

3. D; tampering will be used.

4. C; gases will be used.

5. B; are will be used.

6. A; unturned will be used.

7. A; Replying will be used.

8. B; are will be used.

9. A; coincidence will be used.

10. B; counts will be used.

Answers- Practice Set 12

1. D; no error

2. C; indicate will be used

3. D; no error

4. C; hit will be used.

5. A; lives will be used

6. D; which will be used

7. A; took over

8. B; source of happiness

9. C; turns up will be used

10. B; greater will be used.

Answers- Practice Set 13

1. B; strategies should be used in place of strategy.

2. C; achieving should be used in place of achieved.

3. C; is should be used instead of are.

4. A; implies should be used.

5. B; impressive should be used instead of impressing.

6. B; locally should be used.

7. C; between should be used instead of among.

8. A; integrated should be used instead of integrating.

9. B; Taken care of is the correct form.

10. C; has been will be used instead of have been.

Answers- Practice Set 14

1. C; Train's arrival will be used.

2. B; Years' should be used instead of year's.

3. B; Each other's merits should be used.

4. A; Neither will be used in place of none.

5. C; Either should be replaced by any. (Either is used for two persons.)

6. C; Than those of should be used before Patna.

7. C; Themselves should be replaced by himself. (Subject-Verb-Agreement)

8. A; All will not be used before monthly expenses because expenses include all expenditures.

9. B; Most should be replaced by more.

10. A; Over- dependent should be replaced by overdependence.
11. A; When I was reminded will be used.
12. B; Operate should be replaced by operated.
13. A; He was overcome will be used in the place of he overcame.
14. A; Brought should be replaced by introduced because a new thing is introduced.
15. A; Held should be replaced by held.
16. B; Cannot should be replaced with could not.
17. C; To should be used before use.
18. A; Hard should be replaced by hardly.
19. A; Fastly should be replaced by fast because fastly is no word in English language.
20. A; Live should be replaced by living.

Answers- Practice Set 15

1. (3); had not got	2. (5); No error
3. (1); we have been	4. (1); Having been
5. (2); neatly and carefully	6. (2); spent
7. (3); which was	8. (1); howsoever I admire him

9. (4); before the investigation committee
10. (4); Few tourists come here

Answers- Practice Set 16
1. (1); under no circumstances
2. (3); less number of people
3. (4); Didn't she?
4. (4); reading to writing
5. (3); say that the whole affair
6. (1); he has been writing
7. (1); hardly had I sat
8. (1); Little
9. (3); I had known
10. (4); countries in the world

Answers- Practice Set 17

1. The correct form is 'As soon as he arrived'   2. Add 'as' before 'well'
3. No error   4. Replace 'or' by 'nor'
5. No error'   6. Add 'than' before 'some'
7. Replace 'but' by 'yet'   8. No error
9. Remove 'but'   10. Replace 'because ; by 'that'
11. Replace ' when' by 'than'   12. Replace ' to' by 'and'
13. Replace 'does not have' by 'has'   14. Replace'than' by 'but'
15. Replace 'when' by 'than'

Answers- Practice Set 18
1. (C) The subject sum should take a singular auxiliary verb. Hence, are should be replaced by is.
2. (B) The verb comprise is not followed by any preposition. The preposition of should be deleted.
3. (A) Write I shall avail myself instead of I shall avail in section (A).
4. (C) The principal clause is in the past tense. Therefore, the subordinate clause he has got should be placed in the past tense. The correct usage is he had got.
5. (C) Lest is always followed by should. You should fall is the correct usage.
6. (B) Until conveys the negative sense and hence, the second negative does not should be deleted. The correct usage is confesses his fault.
7. (C) The sentences denotes the completion of a future action and hence, future perfect tense i shall have completed should be used in place of I had completed.
8. (A) The sentence denotes a present perfect continuous action. Therefore, He has been serving is the correct answer.
9. (B) Man on earth is a phrase. Therefore, article the should be deleted.
10. (B) Hardly is followed by the auxiliary had and third form (past participle) of the verb. The correct usage is

had we reached.
11. (C) Everyone always takes the singular helping verb. Hence, the correct usage is is required to do the .
12. (B) Wrong preposition with has been used. Disapprove is followed by of. Hence, the correct usage is disapproved of.
13. (C) Use that instead of as. So in the principal clause is followed by that in the subordinate clause. Hence, the correct usage is that he.
14. (A) The present perfect participle having is followed by third form of the verb. The correct usage is having completed his work.
15. (A) Here, kind refers to type and therefore, it should be used in plural. These kinds of shoes is the correct usage.
16. (C) Improvement being singular should take the singular helping verb has. The correct usage is there has been much improvement.
17. (B) Did is followed by first (present) form of the verb; did he run is the correct usage.
18. (D) Be is followed by third form of the verb. Hence, the correct usage is will be appreciated.
19. (A) Whenever there are two future actions in one sentence, the principal clause is placed in present simple tense. Hence, the correct usage is if he does not work hard.
20. (C) The sentence denotes a past perfect action and hence, past simple already came should be replaced by had already come.

Answers- Practice Set 19
1. Replace 'because of' by 'but for'
2. The correct form is 'he was looked after by his aunt'
3. Remove 'back'
4. Remove 'more than'
5. Replace 'to' by 'into'   6. No error

7. Remove 'for'

8. Replace 'for' by 'to'

9. Remove 'with'

10. Replace 'at' by 'by'

11. Replace 'over' by 'down'

12. Replace 'in' by 'from'

Answers- Practice Set 20

1. Replace 'were' by 'was'

2. Replace 'persist' by 'persisted'

3. Replace 'were' by 'was'

4. No error

5. Replace 'is' by 'has'

6. Replace 'will' by would'

7. Replace 'were' by 'was'

8. Replace 'could' by 'can'

9. Remove 'was'

10. Replace 'was' by 'is'

11. Replace 'are' by 'is'

12. Replace 'burned' by 'burnt'

13. Replace 'are' by 'is' Many a takes singular subject and singular verb

14. No error

15. Replace 'as much as' by ' howsoever much'

Answers- Practice Set 21

1. Add 'the' before 'only'

2. The correct form is 'A majority of the ......'

3. Replace 'the' by 'a'

4. Remove 'a'

5. Add 'a' before 'singer'

6. Add 'a' before 'bad mood '

7. Replace 'a' by 'an'

8. Add 'the' before 'meek'

9. Replace 'the' by 'a'

10. Remove 'the' before 'winter' and 'summer'

11. Add 'the' before 'famous'. 'The' is used before particular objects.

12. Remove 'will'.

Answers- Practice Set 22

1. Replace 'faster' by 'fast' . No comparison has been made here and so positive degree should be used.

2. Replace 'careful' by carefully'

3. Replace 'less' by 'least'

4.Remove 'more' Double comparatives are not used

5. No error

6. Replace 'the most' by 'more'

7. Replace ' thoroughly' by 'thorough'

8. Replace 'firstly' by 'first'

9. No error

10. The correct from is 'where he was going'

Answers- Practice Set 23

1. Replace 'never' by 'not'

2. Replace 'meet' by 'face'

3. Replace 'said' by 'asked' Whether' is not preceded by 'said'

4. Replace 'on behalf' by 'on the part of Behalf' means
'in place of someone'

5. Replace 'persecuted ' by 'prosecuted'

6. Remove ' most'

7. Remove 'much'

8. Replace 'hardly' by 'hard'

9. Replace 'loud' by 'loudly'

10. Add 'more' before 'expensive'

11. No error

12. Remove 'most'

13. Replace ' hardly' by 'hard'

14. Replace ' bad' by 'badly'

15. The correct form is 'very neatly and carefully'

Answers- Practice Set 24

1. Replace ' good' by 'well'

2. Replace ' if ' by 'that'

3. Replace 'lend' by 'borrow' .Borrow means
'taking something from someone' and lend means
'giving something to someone '.

4. Replace ' everybody ' by 'all'

5. Replace 'great' by 'big'

6. Replace 'even' by 'often'

7. Remove 'peak'. 'peak' is the highest point of a
mountain .So it correct to say that we climbed up the
mountain , not mountain peak.

8. Add 'no' before 'dearth'

9. Replace 'my remaining life' by 'the rest of my life'

10. Replace ' each' by 'every'

11.Replace ' carrier' by 'career'. 'Carrier' is something that carries

12. Replace ' like' by 'as'

13. Replace ' quite' by 'very'

14. Replace 'past' by 'last'

15. Replace ' advancement' by 'advent'

Answers- Practice Set 25

1. Replace ' growing' by 'grew'

2. Replace ' was' by 'had'

3. Replace 'That' by 'the'

4. No error

5. add 'so' before 'popular'

6. The correct from is ' ..... not to give ....'

7. No error

8. Remove ' up'

9. The correct from is '. ..... I would have died of shame

10. The correct from is '...... towards the end '

11. Replace 'this is' by 'is this'

12. Replace 'isn't it ' by 'won 't you ' ?

13. No error

14. The correct from is 'He was involved not only in ......'

15. Replace ' every ' by 'all'

Answers- Practice Set 26

1. Replace 'on' by 'up'

2. Remove 'to'

3. No error

4. Replace 'when' by 'after'

5. Replace 'than' by 'to'

6. Remove 'about'

7. No error

8. Add 'transporting by' after 'than'

9. Replace 'with ' by 'from'

10. Replace 'from' by 'of' The verb 'acquitted takes

preposition 'of '

11. Replace 'to' by before'

12. The correct from is 'accused of .....'

13. Replace 'once' by 'after'

14. Replace 'on' by 'form'

15.Remove 'into' the verb 'penetrate ' doesn't take any preposition.

Answers- Practice Set 27

1. (c) : Replace ' will' by 'would'

2. (a) : Remove 'will'

3. (b) : Replace 'Have' by 'has'

4. (a) : Replace ' was ' by ' had been'

5. (a) : Replace 'was' by 'have been'

6. (a) : Replace ' is ' by ' has been '

7. (a) : Replace ' has been ' by 'saw'

8. (a) : Replace ' am' by ' have been '

9. (b) : Replace ' are' by ' have been'

10. (a): Remove 'But'

11. (b) : Add 'to remember' after 'things'

12. (c) : The correct from is didn't she ?

13. (c) : Replace ' because' by 'that'

14. (d) : Replace " buying ticket' by 'buy one'

15. (c) : Replace ' as well as' by 'also'

16. (c) : The correct form is ' .....I would have died of shame '.

Answers- Practice Set 28

1. (A) Write Involvement instead of Involving in part (A). Here, the noun form of the word involving is required which is involvement and not involving.

2. (C) Write spoonfuls instead of spoonsful in part (C). Spoonful is a compound word, the plural of which is formed by adding s to full and not to spoon.

3. Replace reason with cause in part (C). Reason refers to the explanation or justification of sone happening whereas cause refers to something that brings about a

certain happening.

4. (D) Write rupee instead of rupees in part (D).

5. (D) Change over to against in part (D). To lean means to stand with the support of something. So, in this situation the prepositions against will be used.

6. (C) Write avail herself of in part (C). With avail we always use reflexive pronouns. The reflexive pronouns are myself, herself, himself, yourself, etc. Here, we have she as the subject, so, the proper reflexive pronoun will be herself.

7. (B) Delete into from part (B). The word enter is sufficient to convey the sense that one is going inside a certain place. Therefore, the prepositions into is not required.

8. (A) Remove will from part (A). According to the rules of grammar, if a sentence conveys two actions both of the future tense, the principal actions will be in simple future and the subordinate action will be in simple present

9. (E) No error.

10. (C) Write if you had in part (C). When an action of the party conveying a condition is referred to. the verb used is in past perfect.

11. (B) Write among in place of between in part (B). Be tween is used while talking of two persons only. But when the persons are more than two, as in the case of inhabitants in this sentence, among is used.

12. (C) Change along to with in part (C). Connivance always takes the prepositions with.

13. (B) Change on to at in part (B). Page used in this context always gets the prepositions at.

14. (A) Remove What and write Not in its place in part (A). The right usage is Not to speak.

15. (B) Write teaching profession instead of teaching line in part (B). The expression teaching line is a slang

word and is not used in standard English.

Answers- Practice Set 29

Ans 1. Fall back upon

Ans 2. Large dynamic one

Ans 3. 'a' part 'of'

Ans 4. Remove 'been'

Ans 5. Replace 'have' by 'has'

Ans 6. Replace 'is' by 'was'

Ans 7. Replace 'have' by 'has'

Ans 8. Replace 'reporting ' by 'reported'

Ans 9. Remove 'a'

Ans 10. Add 'how' after 'know'

Ans 11. No error

Ans 12. No error

Ans 13. The correct form is ' Poor as they are .....'

Ans 14. Replace 'earth' by 'earthquakes'.

Ans 15. Replace 'isn't it? by 'hasn't she ?'

Answers- Practice Set 30

1. (B) Write heaves instead of heave in part (B). Nation is a singular noun, so, the verb used will also be singular. In the simple present tense, the singular of a verb is obtained by adding s to it. So, have becomes heaves.

2. (C) Change elder into older in part (C). Elder is used while talking of two persons related blood. But in this sentence, the persons are not related, but working in the same office. So, older will used.

3. (D) Write should instead of may in part (D). Lest is always followed by should.

4. (E) No error.

5. (C) Write goes instead of went in part (C). According to the rules of grammar, if hte reporting verb is in the past tense, the reported speech will also be in the past tense. But if the reported speech contains some

geographical, historical or universal fact, etc... it will be in present tense. The reported speech of the given sentence has a geographical truth i.e., the earth goes round the sun. So it will be in present tense.

6. (C) Change was into were in part (C). Although the subject here is singular, the verb will be plural When a sentence conveys a condition in the past tense through the phrase as if, hte verb is in hte tense form irrespective of the nature of the subject.

7. (C) remove will not from part (C). Until is negative in nature. As such, will not cannot be used with it.

8. (B) Remove as well as from part (B) and write and in its place, Both and as well as cannot be used together in a sentence as they both convey the same meaning.

9. (C) Write was in place of were in part (C). According to the rules of grammar, the verb in Sentence, having two subjects joined by as well as should agree with the first subject.

10. (D) Write than in place of when in part (D). No sooner is always followed by than and not when.

11. (E) No error.

12. (B) Remove previous from part (B). Records in itself conveys the sense of past achievements here. So previous is not required.

13. (B) Delete the from part (B). English being the name. of a language, the definite article the will not be used before it.

14. (C) Write an M.P. instead of a M.P. in part (C). if a word begins with a consonant but its used before it.

15. (A) Add The before Summer in part (A). Here, we are talking of a particular summer and not of summers in general, so, the will be used before it.

Let Us Start

We will point out some of the basic pre-requisite of using good English while speaking and writing.

Some of the divisions of grammar, as prominently pointed out by different thinkers, are as follows:

There are four great divisions of Grammar, viz.:

a) Orthography, Etymology, Syntax, and Prosody.

b) Orthography treats of letters and the mode of combining them into sets of words.

c) Etymology treats nature of the various classes of words as grouped in the grammar work and the changes they undergo.

d) Syntax treats the connection and arrangement of words to be made perfectly in formation of sentences.

e) The manner of speaking and reading and accommodation of different kinds of verse (Prosody).

f) The three first mentioned concern us most.

g) A distinct sound produced by a single effort of shall, pig, dog [A syllable]. In every set of such distinct sound there must be at least one vowel.

h) A word, having adequate capability of expressing things, works or ideas meaningfully, consists of one syllable or a combination of syllables.

i) The best way to divide words into syllables is to follow, as closely as possible, the divisions made by the organs of speech in properly pronouncing them.

j) There are two distinct types of articles: a or an and the. A or an is called the indefinite article because it does not point put any particular person or thing but indicates the noun in its widest or generalised sense. The points out any particular person, thing or place distinctly.

k) Inflection by which we signify whether the noun is the name of a male, a female, of an inanimate object or something which has no distinction of sex [Gender].

Grammar refers to the way words are used, classified, and structured together to form coherent written or spoken communication. This guide takes a traditional approach to teaching English grammar, breaking the topic into three fundamental elements: Parts of Speech, Inflection, and Syntax. Each of these is a discrete, individual part, but they are all intrinsically linked together in meaning.

The parts of speech are the categories to which different words are assigned, based on their meaning, structure, and function in a definite format of a sentence. We'll look in basic patterns and use of the seven main parts of speech—nouns, pronouns, verbs, adjectives, adverbs, prepositions, and conjunctions—as well as other categories of words that don't easily fit in with the rest, such as particles, determiners, and gerunds.

Inflection: Although the parts of speech provide the building blocks for writing and speaking pattern of English, another very important element in this regard is inflection; the process by which words are changed in form to create new and specific meanings. There are two main categories of inflection: conjugation and declension.

Conjugation refers to the inflection of verbs, while declension refers particularly to the inflection of nouns, pronouns, adjectives, and adverbs. Whenever we change a verb from the present tense to the past tense, for an example, we use conjugation. For making a noun plural to show that there is more than one of it, we use declension.

There are four simple moods,—the Infinitive, the Indicative, the Imperative and the Subjunctive.

The Mood of a verb basically denotes the mode or manner in which it is used in a sentence. Thus if it is used in its widest sense without reference to person or number, time or place, it is in the Infinitive Mood; as "To run."

A verb is used to indicate or declare or ask a simple question or make any direct statement [Indicative Mood]. "The boy likes his book most." Here a direct statement is made concerning the boy. When the verb is used to express a command or entreaty it is in the Imperative Mood as, "Go away." "Give me a penny."

There are different aspects of the Grammar of English language which we come across during the interaction through this workbook. Most prominent ones will be from the daily use of English language to ensure effective communication. Noun, Verbs, Adjectives and Adverbs form open class of Parts of Speech as they readily accept new members in a sentence.[11] Words belonging to similar Parts of Speech exhibit similar syntactical behaviour. Determiners are traditionally classified with adjectives, and have no special place as Parts of Speech in the set of rules. Words having derivational suffixes can be identified as a member of Parts of Speech but general words attain such status only after placing it in a sentence. For an example, run can serve as either a verb or a noun (these cases are regarded as two different lexemes[12]). The lexeme run has some of the common forms runs, ran, runny, runner, and running.

We consider all naming words as Nouns. It is evident from our daily use that many common suffixes form nouns from other nouns or from other types of words, such as -age (as in shrinkage), -hood (as in sisterhood), and so on, although some other nouns are base forms not containing any such suffix (such as cat, grass, eagle, India, France). Pronouns replace a Noun in a sentence and take the role of possessives also (for example: This is his pen.)

English determiners constitute a relatively small class of words and are principally grouped under the head Adjectives. They include the articles "the" and "a[n]"; certain demonstrative and interrogative words such as this, that, and which; possessives such as my and whose (the role of determiner can also be played by noun possessive forms such as John's and the girl's); various quantifying words like all, some, none, scanty, many, various; numerals of ordinal type (first, second, fifth etc.) and numerals of cardinal type (one, two,

---

[11] *Carter, Ronald; McCarthy, Michael (2006), Cambridge Grammar of English: A Comprehensive Guide, Cambridge University Press, p. 984, ISBN 0-521-67439-5*
[12] *In general consideration a lexeme is a unit of lexical meaning that underlies a set of words that are related through inflection. It is a basic abstract unit of meaning, a unit of morphological analysis in linguistics related to English Language that roughly corresponds to a set of forms taken by a single root word.*

etc.). There are also many phrases being used in day to day communication (such as a couple of) that can play the role of determiners.

To go through this concept of using determiners in a sentence we rely upon availability of some group of words as determiner. In many contexts, as evident from our daily use, it is required for a noun phrase to be completed with an article or some other determiner. It is not grammatically appropriate to say or write "Cat sat on table."; one must say: " [Our/My/His/A black] cat sat on the table". There exists some common situations in which a complete noun phrase can be formed without a determiner when it refers generally to a whole class or concept (Example: Lions are violent. Dogs are dangerous. Beauty is subjective) and when we speak about a name (Jane, Spain, etc.).

.

Common Errors

Common Errors

Mr. Bhatia is my English teacher	Mr . Bhatia is my Teacher of English.
I Frogive him for his faults.	I forgave him his faults.
Chiranjiv Is my cousin Brother.	Chiranjiv is my cousin.
Credit this sum to my name.	Credit this sum to my account.
He is very miser	He is very miserly.
My all friends are very helpful	All my friends are very helpful.
She does not know swimming.	She does not know how to swim.
My uncle lives at Janpath Road.	My uncle lives at Janpath.
He is family man.	He is a man with a family.
This is more batter	This is better.
One must do his duty	One must do one's duty.
He made a blunder mistake.	He made a blunder.
It is a female compartment.	It is a ladies' compartment.
Open your book on page ten.	Open your book at page ten.
He has gone to foreign	He has gone abroad
He married his daughter	He got his daughter married.
Madhu is very proudy.	Madhu is very proud.
He live in the boarding	He lives in the boarding house.
Sachin and myself helped you.	Sachin and I helped you.
Please write with ink.	Please write in ink.
He died from cancer	He died of cancer.
He died of overwork	He died from overwork.
He has no lust of money.	He has no lust for money.

My younger brother goes to the collage daily.	My younger brother goes to college daily.
What a fun!	What fun !
She was crying the glasses in a tray.	She was carrying the glasses on a tray.
He sat in a tree.	He sat on a tree.
He is taller then me.	He is taller than I (am).
He is not as tall as his brother.	He is not so tall as his brother.
I have lost my patience.	I have lost patience.
He likes cutting jokes.	He likes cracking jockes.
You have a chance to win.	You have a chance of winning.
Don't mention.	Mention not.
Are you living in Delhi?	Do you live in Delhi?
It is a true fact.	Is is a fact.
As you like.	As you like it.
Radha resembles to her mother.	Radha resembles her mother.
Please pay for your bill.	Please pay your bill.
The police is looking for the culprit.	The police are looking for the culprit.
He said a lot to lies.	He told a lot of lies.
I believe you are better now.	I hope that you are better now.
He shirks from his studies.	He shirks his studies.
I need a house to live.	I need a house to live in.
I want a pen to write.	I want a pen to write with.
I have no influence on him	I have no influence over him.
I am too happy to see you.	I am very happy to see you.
He invited me on tea.	He invited me to tea.
We go to college by foot.	We go to college on foot.
You have no excuse to be late.	You have no excuse for being late.
Public does not like it.	Public do not like it.
This is somewhat true.	This is partially true.
I do not like the poetries of keats.	I do not like the poetry of Keats.
I prefer lassi than tea.	I prefer lassi to see.
Please give key to your watch.	Please wind up your watch.
There is no harm to do so.	There is no harm in doing so.
He gave a speech.	He made a speech.

I will return just now.	I will return presently.
I will wait here until you do not return.	I will wait here until you come.
He needs not worry.	He need not worry.
He hanged his head in shame.	He hung his head in shame.
The satellite has been sent to space.	The satellite has been launched.
Mohan insisted to go there.	Mohan insisted on going there.
He lives through honest labour.	He lives by honest labour.
Mohan and sohan are fast enemies.	Mohan and Sohan are sworn enemies.
His grandmother is died.	His grandmother is dead.
Send this letter on my address.	Send this letter to my address.
I have seen him today morning	I have been his this morning.
Are you a member in the committee?	Are you a member of the committee?
He is fail in Mathematics.	He failed in Mathematics.
We reached safely.	We reached safe.
Sachin is good in English.	Sachin is good at English.
My elder brother is in the teaching line.	My elder brother is in the teaching profession.
I have read four-fifth of this book.	I have read four-fifth of this book.
Our teacher will take your test tomorrow.	Our teacher will give us a test tomorrow.
All his family members are mad.	All members of his family are mad.
She does not know swimming.	She does not know how to swim.
Our examination starts from Monday next.	Our examination starts on Monday next.
I shall return this book after one week.	I shall return this book in one week.
Thousands were injured in the war.	Thousands were wounded in the war.
He has grown into a beautiful youth.	He has grown into a handsome youth.
There is no other alternative.	There is no alternative.
What is the cost of this pen?	What is the price of this pen?
Translate this passage from English to Hindi.	Translate this passage from English into Hindi.

I have learnt this lesson word by word.	I have learnt this lesson word for word.
I am going to cut my hair.	I am going to have my hair cut.
My watch is two minutes behind .	My watch is two minutes slow.
I asked him that why he was late.	I asked him why he was late.
He pays more attention to Hindi than English.	He pays more attention to Hindi than to English.
Close your door at once.	Shut the door at once
Verbal orders will not be obeyed.	Oral orders will not be obeyed.
Burn the lamp at once.	Light the lamp at once.
Sachin has made ten goals.	Sachin has scored ten goals.
He admitted that he had committed the murder.	He confessed that he had committed the murder.
A dictator generally misuses his political power.	A dictator generally abuses his political powers.
This is the house whose roof leaks.	This is the house, the roof of which leaks.
Being a cloudy day, we did not go out.	If being a cloudy day, we did not go out.
It is possible to score cent per cent marks in Mathematics.	It is possible to score hundred per cent marks in Mathematics.
Mohan has a thirst of knowledge.	Mohan has a thirst for knowledge.
My neighbor is five years elder to me.	My neighbor is five years older than me.
His service has been terminated.	His services have been terminated.
Please see the dictionary to find out the meaning of this word.	Please consult the dictionary to find out the meaning of this word.
Mohan asked his servant to bring water.	Mohan told his servant to bring water.
He got down from his bicycle.	He got off his bicycle.
I lived in that hotel for two days.	I stayed in that hotel for two days.
Please tell us everything in brief.	Please tell us everything in short.

I shall write him tomorrow.	I shall write to him tomorrow.
We have reached the final conclusions.	We have reached the conclusions.
To make dolls is his professions.	Making dolls is his profession.
Finishing his work, he went to see a movie.	Having finished his work, he went to see a movie.
I saw a bad dream last night.	I had a bad dream last night.
If you will abuse me, I will break tour head.	If you abuse me, I shall break you head.
If you will take tae, I shall also take.	If you take tea, I shall also rake.
You need not to tell me all this.	You need not tell me all this.
My elder brother is in the teaching line.	My elder brother is in the teaching profession.
I have read four-fifth of this book.	I have read four-fifth of this book.
Our teacher will take our test tomorrow.	Our teacher will give us a test tomorrow.
All his family members are mad.	All members of his family are mad.
Our examination starts from Monday next.	Our examination starts on Monday next.
I shall return this book after one week.	I shall return this book in one week.
Thousands were injured in the war.	Thousands were wounded in the war.
He has grown into a beautiful youth.	He has grown into a handsome youth.
There is no other alternative.	There is no alternative.
What is the cost of this pen?	What is the price of this pen?
Translate this passage from English to Hindi.	Translate this passage from English into Hindi.
I have learnt this lesson word by word.	I have learnt this lesson word for word.
I am going to cut my hair.	I am going to have my hair cut.
My watch is two minutes behind.	My watch is two minutes slow.
I asked him that why he was late.	I asked him why he was late.
He pays more attention to	He pays more attention to

Hindi than English.	Hindi than to English.
Close the door at once.	Shut the door at once.
Verbal orders will not be obeyed.	Oral orders will not be obeyed.
Burn the lamp at once.	Light the lamp at once.
Sachin has made ten goals.	Sachin has scored ten goals.
He admitted that he had committed the murder.	He confessed that he had committed the murder.
A dictator generally misuses his political powers.	A dictator generally abuses his political powers.
This is the house whose roof leaks.	This is the house, the roof of which leaks.
Being a cloudy day, we did not go out.	It Being a cloudy day, we did not go out.
It is possible to score cent per cent marks in mathematics.	It is possible to score hundred per cent marks in mathematics.
Mohan has a thirst knowledge.	Mohan has a thirst for knowledge.
My neighbour is five years elder to me.	My neighbour is five years older than me.
His service has been terminated.	His services have been terminated.
Please see the dictionary to find out the meaning of this word.	Please consult the dictionary to find out the meaning of this word.
Mohan asked his servant to bring water.	Mohan told his servant to bring water.
He got down from his bicycle.	He got down off his bicycle.
I lived in that hotel for two days.	I stayed in that hotel for two days.
Please tell us everything in brief.	Please tell us everything in short.
I shall write him tomorrow.	I shall write to him tomorrow.
We have reached the final conclusion.	We have reached the conclusion.
To make dolls is his profession.	Making dolls is his profession.
Finishing his work, he went to see a movie.	Having finished his work, he went to see a movie.
I saw a bad dream last night.	I had a bad dream last night.
His father has resigned from	His father has resigned his

his post.	post.
If you will abuse me, I will break your head.	If you abuse me, I shall break your head.
If you will take tea, I shall also take.	If you take tea, I shall also take.
You need not to tell me all this.	You need not tell me all this.
Let us pass away our time in the canteen.	Let us pass our time in the canteen.
I cannot pull on with this man.	I cannot get on with this man.
First, I told him about his mistakes.	At First, I told him about his mistakes.
Do not interfere in my work.	Do not interfere with my work.
I want a fresh basket of flowers.	I want a basket of fresh flowers.
The students will give their test tomorrow.	The students will take their test tomorrow.
The interview will be held between 10a.m to 12 noon.	The interview will be held between 10a.m and 12 noon.
There was a hell of a rush at the tickets window.	There was a hell of a rush at the ticket- window.
My hairs are black.	My hair is black.
Now, I shall go to my quarter.	Now I shall go to my quarters.
Law and order have to be maintained.	Law and order has to be maintained.
What is the cost of this shirt?	What is the price of this shirt?
Our examination is approaching near.	Our examination is approaching .
Good Night, sir, have a cup of tea.	Good Evening, sir, have a cup of tea.
The chairman is the wholly solely in our establishment.	The chairman is the all in all in our establishment.
We must fight-poverty with tooth and nail.	We must fight-poverty tooth and nail.
The English have left India with bag and baggage.	The English have left India bag and baggage.
We go to college by foot.	We go to college on foot.
I have many works to do on Sundays.	I have much works to do on Sundays.

He secured only passing marks in Mathematics.	He secured only pass marks in Mathematics.
Please give me a ten - rupees note.	Please give me a ten - rupee note.
This pen is superior than that.	This pen is superior to that.
I am not on talking terms with Mohan.	I am not on speaking terms with Mohan.
Sachin is our mutual friend.	Sachin is our common friend.
He picks up a quarrel over petty matters.	He picks a quarrel over petty matters.
Summon could not be issued.	Summons could not be issued.
When you say so, I must believe it.	Since you say so, I must believe it.
No less than fifty soldiers were injured in the blast.	No fewer than fifty soldiers were injured in the blast.
What is the fresh news of today?	What is the latest news of today?
I have something to ask from you.	I have something to ask you.
The train left at 3 o' clock.	The train departed at 3 o' clock.
You are requested to substitute the old picture for a new one.	You are requested to replace the old picture by a new one.
Due to illness. I could not go to college.	Owing to illness. I could not go to college.
This news was broadcasted from All India Radio only yesterday.	This news was broadcast from All India Radio only yesterday.
I will teach you reading and writing English.	I will teach you how to read and writing English.
It is the first time I have said so.	This is the first time I have said so.
Failed students cannot be promoted to the next higher class.	Students who have failed in the examination cannot be promoted to the next higher class.
Please do the needful and oblige.	Please do what is necessary and oblige.
Accompanied with my friends,	Accompanied by my friends,

I went there.	I went there.
What to speak of English, he cannot speak even Hindi.	Not to speak of English, he cannot speak even Hindi.
The plane circled the airport two times before landing.	The plane circled the airport twice before landing.
He became a rich man by and by.	He became a rich man in course of time.
My dear respected father, you are really great.	My dear father, you are really great.
Send your reply by return post.	Send your reply by return of post.
Please speak to the concerned authority.	Please speak to the authority concerned.
He is a noted dacoit.	He is a notorious dacoit.
It was very wonderful.	It was really wonderful.
I am quite sorry to hear of your failure.	I am very sorry to hear of your failure.

***.

1. Use of Clauses

CLAUSES AS PARTS OF SPEECH

A clause is a group of words that forms part of a sentence and that contains a subject and a predicate.

A clause used as a part of speech is called a subordinate clause.

A subordinate clause may be introduced by (1) a relative or an interrogative pronoun, (2) a relative or an interrogative adverb, (3) a subordinate conjunction.

The relative pronouns are: who, which, what, that (= who or which), as (after such or same), and the compound relatives whoever, whichever, whatever.

The chief relative adverbs are: where, whence, whither, wherever, when, whenever, while, before, after, till, until, since, as, how, why.

The interrogative pronouns are: who, which, what.

The interrogative adverbs are: where, when, whence, whither, how, why.

The most important subordinate conjunctions are: because, since (= because), though, although, if, unless, that (in order that, so that), lest, as, as if, as though, than, whether (whether … or).

According to their use as parts of speech, subordinate clauses are adjective, adverbial, or noun clauses.

I. ADJECTIVE CLAUSES

A subordinate clause that modifies a substantive is called an adjective clause.

- {Able men | Men of ability | Men who show ability} can always find employment.
- {Smart girls| Girls who are smart| Girls who are smart} always move forward.
- {Treeless spots | Spots without trees | Spots where no trees grew} were plainly visible.

In each of these groups, a noun (men, spots) is modified (1) by an adjective, (2) by an adjective phrase, (3) by an adjective clause. The sense remains unchanged.

Adjective clauses may be introduced (1) by relative pronouns, (2) by relative adverbs of place (where, whence, whither, etc.) or time (when, while, etc.).

II. ADVERBIAL CLAUSES

A subordinate clause that serves as an adverbial modifier is called an adverbial clause.

Jack spoke {thoughtlessly. | without thinking. | before he thought.}

The schoolhouse stands {there. | at the crossroads. | where the roads meet.}

We pay our rent {monthly. | on the first of every month. | when the first of the month comes.}

In each of these groups, the verb (spoke, stands, pay) is modified (1) by an adverb, (2) by an adverbial phrase, (3) by an adverbial clause.

Adverbial clauses may be introduced (1) by relative adverbs (when, where, before, etc.); (2) by subordinate conjunctions (if, though, because, etc.); (3) by relative or interrogative pronouns.

Adverbial clauses oftenest modify verbs, but they are also common as modifiers of adjectives and adverbs.

Angry because he had failed, he abandoned the undertaking. [The clause modifies angry.]

I am uncertain which road I should take. [The clause modifies uncertain.]

Farther than eye could see extended the waste of tossing waters. [The clause modifies farther.]

Here, where the cliff was steepest, a low wall protected the path. [The clause modifies here.]

An adverbial clause with that may be used to modify verbs and adjectives.

* He rejoiced that the victory was won.
* I am glad that you are coming.
* He was positive that no harm had been done.

-     They were unwilling that the case should be brought to trial.

NOTE. In this use that is equivalent either to "because" or to "as to the fact that." The clause may be explained as a noun clause in the adverbial objective construction.

For the classification of adverbial clauses according to their meaning (place, time, cause, concession, etc.),

III. NOUN (OR SUBSTANTIVE) CLAUSES

A subordinate clause that is used as a noun is called a noun (or substantive) clause.

-     {Agreement | To agree | That we should agree} seemed impossible.
-     {Victory | To win | That we should win} was out of the question.
-     The merchant feared {loss. | to lose. | that he might lose money.}
-     I expect {success. | to succeed. | that I shall succeed.}

In each of these groups a noun (agreement, victory, etc.) is replaced (1) by an infinitive, (2) by a noun clause. In the first two examples, the noun clause is the subject; in the last two, it is the object of a verb (feared, expect).

Noun clauses may be used in any of the more important constructions of nouns:—(1) as subject, (2) as direct object of a transitive verb, (3) in apposition with a substantive, (4) as a predicate nominative.

-     That Milton was spared has often caused surprise. [Subject.]
-     Brutus said that Cæsar was a tyrant. [Object of said.]
-     Cæsar commanded that the prisoners should be spared. [Object.]
-     I wish that you would work harder. [Object.]
-     The traveller inquired where he could find the inn. [Object.]
-     He asked me what my name was. [Second object of asked.]
-     My fear that the bridge might fall proved groundless. [Apposition with fear.]
-     One fact is undoubted,—that the state of America has been kept in continual agitation.—BURKE. [Apposition with fact.]
-     The old saying is that misery loves company. [Predicate nominative.]

Noun clauses may be introduced (1) by the subordinate conjunctions that, whether (whether ... or), and if (in the sense of whether); (2) by the interrogative pronouns who, which, what; (3) by the interrogative adverbs where, whence, whither, how, why, when.

Noun clauses are common as objects of verbs (1) of commanding, desiring, etc.; (2) of telling, thinking, etc.; (3) of asking, doubting, etc.

Object clauses frequently omit that .
•   Charles said [that] he was sorry.   Mohini says [that] she is feeling tired.
•   I hope you will come.   We expect the clouds move further north by this evening.
•   I wish he would help me.

For the infinitive clause replacing a that-clause as object,
389. A noun clause may be used as the retained object of a passive verb.

ACTIVE VOICE (CLAUSE AS OBJECT)	PASSIVE VOICE (RETAINED OBJECT)
They informed me that the train was late.	I was informed that the train was late.
Charles told us that the ice was thin.	We were told that the ice was thin.
They asked me whether (or if) I liked tennis.	I was asked whether I liked tennis.

A noun clause may be the object of a preposition.
•   I see no reason for a lawsuit except that both parties are stubborn. [Compare: except the stubbornness of both.]
•   She never studies, except when she can find nothing else to do.
•   I could say nothing but [=except] that I was sorry.
•   Justice was well administered in his time, save where the king was party.—BACON.
•   She could see me from where she stood.

- There is a dispute as to which of the miners first staked out the claim.

391. Noun clauses with that are common in the predicate when the expletive it is the grammatical subject.

- It was plain that war was at hand.
- It was clear that this administration would last but a very short time.
- It must be admitted that there were many extenuating circumstances.
- It was by slow degrees that Fox became a brilliant and powerful debater.
- It was under the command of a foreign general that the British had triumphed at Minden.

In such sentences the real subject of the thought is the clause. This, however, may be regarded as grammatically in apposition with it, as if one said "It (that war was at hand) was plain."

NOTE. This useful idiom enables us to adopt a kind of inverted order (§ 5), and thus to shift the emphasis. Contrast "That war was at hand was plain" with "It was plain that war was at hand." In the former sentence, the noun clause is made prominent; in the latter, the adjective plain.

392. The following sentences, taken from distinguished authors of different periods, illustrate the usefulness of the noun clause in its various constructions.

- 1. That the king would ever again have received Becket into favor is not to be believed.—SOUTHEY.
- 2. That in education we should proceed from the simple to the complex is a truth which has always been to some extent acted on.—SPENCER.
- 3. How great his reputation was, is proved by the embassies sent to him.—COLERIDGE.
- 4. It vexed old Hawkins that his counsel was not followed.—FULLER.
- 5. It became necessary, at last, that I should arouse both master and valet to the expediency of removing the treasure.—POE.

- 6. There is no doubt that breeds may be made as different as species in many physiological characteristics.—HUXLEY.
- 7. The main definition you could give of old Marquis Mirabeau is, that he was of the pedant species.—CARLYLE.
- 8. The fact seems to be that we have survived the tremendous explosion.—BROUGHAM.
- 9. The question is, whether the feigned image of poesy, or the regular instruction of philosophy, have the more force in teaching.—SIDNEY.
- 10. I feared that some serious disaster had befallen my friend.—POE.
- 11. I think with you that the most magnificent object under heaven is the great deep.—COWPER.
- 12. Aureolus soon discovered that the success of his artifices had only raised up a more determined adversary.—GIBBON.
- 13. Harold alleged that he was appointed by Edward.—TEMPLE.
- 14. That we shall die, we know.—SHAKSPERE.
- 15. Her Majesty has promised that the treaty shall be laid before her Parliament.—SWIFT.
- 16. Deerslayer proposed that they should circle the point in the canoe.—COOPER.
- 17. I remembered how soft was the hand of Sleep.—LANDOR.
- 18. I cannot see what objection can justly be made to the practice.—REYNOLDS.
- 19. No man knew what was to be expected from this strange tribunal.—MACAULAY.
- 20. We may imagine with what sensations the stupefied Spaniards must have gazed on this horrid spectacle.—PRESCOTT.
- 21. Observe how graciously Nature instructs her human children.—COLERIDGE.
- 22. My friend asked me if there would not be some danger in coming home late.—ADDISON.
- 23. A message came that the committee was sitting at Kensington Palace.—THACKERAY.

- 24. Jeffreys had obtained of the king a promise that he would not pardon her.—BURNET.
- 25. The present age seems pretty well agreed in an opinion that the utmost scope and end of reading is amusement only.—FIELDING.
- 26. He suddenly alarmed me by a startling question—whether I had seen the show of prize cattle that morning in Smithfield.—LAMB.
- 27. I am told that the Lancashire system is perfect.—KINGSLEY.

THE SUBORDINATE CLAUSES

Subordinate clauses may be classified not only according to their use as parts of speech, but also, in quite a different way, in accordance with their various meanings. These distinctions in idea are of capital importance for the accurate and forcible expression of thought.

394. The variety of meanings which subordinate clauses may express is great, but most of these meanings come under the following heads:—(1) place or time, (2) cause, (3) concession, (4) purpose, (5) result, (6) condition, (7) comparison,43 (8) indirect discourse, (9) indirect question. The general meaning of the clause is usually indicated by the word which introduces it.

I. CLAUSES OF PLACE AND TIME

395. An adjective or an adverbial clause may express place or time.

I. ADJECTIVE CLAUSES

- The house where the robbery occurred is No. 14.
- The bridge over which we rode is in ruins.
- There is a point beyond which you cannot go.
- The day when (or on which) I was to sail arrived at last.
- The day before you came was rainy.
- His terror while it thundered was pitiable.

II. ADVERBIAL CLAUSES

- Remain where I can see you.
- That belongs where you found it.
- Whithersoever I go, fear dogs my steps.
- Whenever the bell rings, you must take down the receiver.
- Esmond heard the chimes as he sat in his own chamber.
- I have lived in Cairo since my father died.

396. Adjective clauses of place and time may be introduced by relative pronouns (see examples above).

Adjective and adverbial clauses of place and time may be introduced by relative adverbs. Thus,—

•   PLACE: where, whence, whither, wherever, whithersoever, wherefrom, whereto, etc.

•   TIME: when, whenever, while, as, before, after, until, since.

Clauses of time are sometimes shortened by the omission of the copula and its subject.

•   When [he was] rescued, he was almost dead.

•   Tom was attacked by cramp while swimming across the river.

II. CAUSAL CLAUSES

An adverbial clause may express cause.

Causal clauses are introduced by the subordinate conjunctions because, since, as, inasmuch as, and sometimes that.

•   I came home because I was tired.

•   As the day was clear, we decided to climb the mountain.

•   Since you will not relent, you must take the consequences.

•   We were glad that the wreck was no worse.

•   Tom was delighted that his friend was safe.

Since is a preposition or an adverb when it denotes time; as is an adverb when it denotes time. Both since and as are conjunctions when they express cause.

III. CONCESSIVE CLAUSES

An adverbial clause may express concession.

A concessive clause is usually introduced by a subordinate conjunction, though, although, or even if. It admits (or concedes) some fact or supposition in spite of which the assertion in the main clause is made.

•   Although I do not like his manners, I respect his character.

•   We won the game, though we expected to lose.

•   Even if you fail, you will have gained experience.

•   Even if you were a king, you would find somebody or something more powerful than yourself.

•   Though he should read books forever, he would not grow wise.

NOTE. While is often used as a weaker or more courteous synonym for although.

The main clause, when it follows the concessive clause, may be emphasized by means of yet, still, nevertheless.

- Although the task was heavy, yet his courage never failed.
- Though his reputation was great at home, yet it was greater abroad.

Concessive clauses sometimes omit the copula and its subject.

- Though [he was] tired, he was not disheartened.
- This punishment, though perhaps necessary, seems rather severe.

A concessive clause may be introduced by the conjunction as, or by a relative pronoun or a relative adverb.

- {Whatever you say, | Whichever argument you present, | However much you object,} he will carry his point.
- Weak as I am, I will make the effort.
- Gay as the scene was, 'twas but a dreary place for Mr. Esmond.

Concession is sometimes expressed by a subjunctive clause without a conjunction to introduce it.

- Be it ever so humble, there's no place like home.
- I will help you, cost what it may!

IV–V. CLAUSES OF PURPOSE AND OF RESULT

403. A subordinate clause may express purpose or result.

I. CLAUSES OF PURPOSE

- These men died that we might live.
- I will take care that you are not harmed.
- John worked day and night that the plans might be ready in time.
- We threw our ballast overboard, so that the airship might clear the treetops.
- All our arrangements have been made with the utmost precision, in order that the ship may be launched promptly and without accident.

II. CLAUSES OF RESULT

- He has recovered his strength, so that he can now work.

- The town stood at the foot of the volcano, so that every building was destroyed.
- Quentin started so suddenly that he almost dropped his weapon.
- His rancor against the duke was so apparent that one saw it in the first half-hour's conversation.
- Their minds were so much embittered that they imputed to each other nothing less than deliberate villany.
- You make such a noise that I cannot hear the music.

404. Clauses of purpose may be introduced by the subordinate conjunction that or by a phrase containing it (so that, in order that, to the end that, etc.).

Negative clauses of purpose may be introduced by that ... not or by lest. For lest with the subjunctive, see § 284.

- Take heed lest thou fall.
- I feared lest I might anger thee.—SHAKSPERE.

Clauses of result may be introduced by the phrase so that, consisting of the adverb so and the subordinate conjunction that; or by that alone, especially when so, such, or some similar word stands in the main clause.

A clause of purpose or of result may be either an adverbial clause or a substantive clause.

- I intend that you shall be elected. [Object.]
- My intention is that you shall be appointed. [Predicate nominative.]
- The result is that he is bankrupt. [Predicate nominative.]
- His exertions had this effect, that the vote was unanimous. [Appositive.]

A substantive clause of purpose is often used as the object of a verb of commanding, desiring, or the like.

- The general ordered that the fort should be blown up.
- The prisoner begged that his fetters might be struck off.

For subordinate clauses with shall or should, implying purpose or expectation,

Purpose may be expressed by the infinitive with to or in order to, and result by the infinitive with to or as to.

•	He abandoned his profession to [or in order to] become a missionary. [Purpose.]

•	He was kind enough to help me. [Result. Compare: He was so kind that he helped me.]

•	He was so kind as to help me. [Result.]

Negative result is often expressed by the adverb too and the infinitive.

Iron is too heavy to float. [Compare: Iron is so heavy that it does not float.]

Purpose may be expressed by an infinitive clause.

•	The teacher intended us to finish the book. [Compare: The teacher intended that we should finish the book.]

•	The foreman ordered the engine to be stopped. [Compare: The foreman ordered that the engine should be stopped.]

VI. CONDITIONAL SENTENCES

A clause that expresses a condition introduced by if, or by some equivalent word or phrase, is called a conditional clause.

A sentence that contains a conditional clause is called a conditional sentence.

•	If it rains, we shall remain at home.

•	I shall attend the convention if I am in town.

•	I will take this book, if you please.

A conditional sentence in its simplest form consists of two parts:—

(1) A subordinate (adverbial) clause, commonly introduced by if, and expressing the condition.

(2) A main clause expressing the conclusion, that is, the statement which is true in case the condition expressed in the if-clause is true.

Thus in the first example, the condition is if it rains; the conclusion is we shall remain at home.

Either the condition or the conclusion may come first.

The conditional clause is often called the protasis, and the conclusion is often called the apodosis.

The conclusion of a conditional sentence may be declarative, interrogative, imperative, or exclamatory.

- If you go to Philadelphia, where shall you stay? [Interrogative.]
- Sit here, if you wish. [Imperative.]
- If you win the prize, how glad I shall be! [Exclamatory.]

A conditional clause may be introduced by provided (or provided that), granted that, supposing (or suppose), on condition that.

- I will permit you to go, on condition that you come home early.
- You may have the money, provided you will put it in the bank.
- Supposing (or suppose) it rains, what shall we do?

Suppose is really an imperative and supposing a participle, the clause being the object.

A negative condition is commonly introduced by if ... not or unless.

- I will wait for him, if you do not object.
- Unless you overcome that habit, you will be ruined.

Double (or alternative) conditions may be introduced by whether ... or.

- Whether he goes or stays, he must pay a week's board. [Compare: If he goes or if he stays, etc.]
- He is determined to buy that car, whether you approve or not. [That is: if you approve or if you do not approve.]

A conditional clause may be introduced by whoever, whenever, or some similar compound.

- Whoever offends, is punished. [Compare: If anybody offends, he is punished.]
- Whoever shall offend, shall be punished.
- Whomever you ask, you will be disappointed. [Compare: If you shall ask anybody.]
- He will come whenever [= if ever] he is called.

In older English and in poetry, who is common in this construction: as,— "Who [= whoever] steals my purse, steals trash" (SHAKSPERE).

A conditional clause sometimes omits the copula and its subject.

- I will go if [it is] necessary.
- If [it is] possible, come to-morrow.

The if-clause is sometimes used as an exclamation, with the conclusion omitted.

If I only had a rifle!

A condition may be expressed by means of an assertion, a question, an imperative, or the absolute construction.

- We take the receiver from the hook, and the operator answers. We replace it, and the connection is broken. [Compare: If we take the receiver from the hook, the operator answers, etc.]
- Press that button, and the bell will ring.
- Do you refuse? Then you must take the consequences.
- We shall sail on Monday, weather permitting.

In such cases, there is no subordinate conditional clause. Thus, in the first example, we have two independent coördinate clauses, making a compound sentence.

FORMS OF CONDITIONS

Conditional sentences show great variety of form, but it is easy to classify them according to the time of the supposed case and the degree of doubt that the speaker expresses.

Conditions may be present, past, or future.

PRESENT AND PAST CONDITIONS

Present and past conditions may be either (1) non-committal or (2) contrary to fact.

1. A condition is non-committal when it implies nothing as to the truth or falsity of the case supposed.

If James is angry, I am sorry. [Perhaps James is angry, perhaps not.]

2. A condition is contrary to fact when it implies that the supposed case is not or was not true.

If James were angry, I should be sorry. [James is not angry.]

In a non-committal present condition, the if-clause44 takes the present indicative; in a non-committal past condition, the past, the perfect, or the pluperfect.

The conclusion may be in any form that the sense allows.

I. PRESENT CONDITION, NON-COMMITTAL

- If this pebble is a diamond, {it is valuable. | guard it carefully. | you have made a great discovery. | you will get a large sum for it. | why are you so careless of it? | what a prize it is!}
- If it is raining, shut the window.

- If Jack lives in this house, {he is a lucky boy. | ring the bell. | he has moved since last May.}

II. PAST CONDITION, NON-COMMITTAL

- If that pebble was a diamond, {it was valuable. | why did you throw it away? | go back and look for it.}
- If Tom has apologized, {he has done his duty. | you ought to excuse him. | forgive him.}

If John had reached home before we started, he must have made a quick journey.

In each of these examples, the speaker declines to commit himself as to the truth of the supposed case. Perhaps the pebble was a diamond, perhaps not; Tom may or may not have apologized; whether or not John had reached home, we cannot tell.

423. In a condition contrary to fact, the if-clause takes the past subjunctive when the condition refers to present time, the pluperfect subjunctive when it refers to past time.

The conclusion regularly takes should or would (§ 286, 3).

- If John were here, I should recognize him. [Present condition, present conclusion.]
- If John were here, I should have recognized him before this. [Present condition, past conclusion.]
- If I had offended him, I should have regretted it. [Past condition, past conclusion.]
- If I had then offended him, I should regret it now. [Past condition, present conclusion.]

In each of these sentences, the speaker distinctly implies that the supposed case (or condition) is (or was) not a fact. It follows, of course, that the conclusion is not a fact:—John is not here; therefore I do not recognize him.

In conditions contrary to fact, the subjunctive without if is common. In this use, the subject follows the verb.

- Were he my friend, I should expect his help. [= If he were my friend. Present condition, contrary to fact.]
- Had he been my friend, I should have expected his help. [= If he had been my friend. Past condition, contrary to fact.]

NOTE. In older English, the subjunctive may be used in both clauses: as,—"He were no lion, were not Romans hinds" (SHAKSPERE).

FUTURE CONDITIONS

Future conditions always imply doubt, for no one can tell what may or may not happen to-morrow.

In all future conditions, some verb-form denoting future time is used in both clauses.

1. In a future condition which suggests nothing as to the probability or improbability of the case supposed, the present indicative is regularly used in the if-clause, and the future indicative in the conclusion.

If it rains to-morrow, I shall not go.

In very formal or exact language a verb-phrase with shall may be used in the if-clause: as,—"If it shall rain to-morrow, I shall not go."

2. The present subjunctive is sometimes used in the if-clause. This form commonly suggests more doubt than the present indicative.

If it rain to-morrow, I shall not go.

3. In a future condition which puts the supposed case rather vaguely, often with a considerable suggestion of doubt, a verb-phrase with should or would is used in both clauses.

If it should rain to-morrow, I should not go.

For the use of should or would in such clauses, see § 305.

A phrase with were to may replace the should-phrase in the if-clause. This form often emphasizes the suggestion of doubt.

If it were to rain to-morrow, I should not go.

The past subjunctive may stand in the if-clause instead of the should-phrase.

If it rained to-morrow, I should not go.

NOTE. The comparative amount of doubt implied in the different kinds of future conditions cannot be defined with precision; for it varies with the circumstances or the context, and often depends on emphasis or the tone of the voice. Thus, in "if it should rain to-morrow," should may be so emphasized as to make the supposed case seem highly improbable, whereas an emphasis on to-morrow would have a very different effect. As to the subjunctive, its use is often due rather to the writer's liking for that mood than to any special doubt in his mind.

VII. CLAUSES OF COMPARISON

An adverbial clause introduced by as if may express comparison.45

- You speak as if you were angry.46
- He breathes as if he were exhausted.
- She cared for me as if I had been her son.

As though is also used, but as if is now preferred by most writers.

The subjunctive were, not the indicative was, is used after as if (§ 282).

As and than, as subordinate conjunctions, introduce clauses of comparison or degree.

- You are as old as he [is].
- I am younger than you [are].
- He weighs as much as I [weigh].
- I pity you more than [I pity] her.

When the verb is omitted, the substantive that follows as or than is in the same case in which it would stand if the verb were expressed. Thus,—

- You are stronger than he. [NOT: than him.]
- I see you oftener than him. [NOT: than he.]
- He plays a better game than I. [NOT: than me.]
- They will miss John more than me. [That is: more than they miss me.]

VIII. INDIRECT DISCOURSE

A quotation may be direct or indirect.

A direct quotation repeats a speech or thought in its original form.

- I replied: "I am sorry to hear it."
- "Henceforth," he explained, "I shall call on Tuesdays."
- "You must see California," she insisted.
- "Elizabeth no longer lives here," he said.
- "I know nothing about it," was the witness's reply.
- "Where," thought I, "are the crew?"

An indirect quotation repeats a speech or thought in substance, but usually with some change in its form.

An indirect quotation, when a statement, is a subordinate clause dependent on some word of saying or thinking, and introduced by the conjunction that.

- I replied that I was sorry to hear it. [Direct: I am sorry.]
- He explained that henceforth he should call on Tuesdays.
- She insisted that I must see California.

A direct quotation begins with a capital letter, unless it is a fragment of a sentence. It is enclosed in quotation marks.

An indirect quotation begins with a small letter. It usually has no quotation marks.

A substantive clause introduced by that may be used with verbs and other expressions of telling, thinking, knowing, and perceiving, to report the words or thought of a person in substance, but usually with some change of form.

Such clauses are said to be in the indirect discourse.

For distinction, a remark or a thought in its original form (as in a direct quotation) is said to be in the direct discourse.

Statements in indirect discourse, being substantive clauses, may be used in various noun constructions: (1) as object of some verb of telling, thinking, or the like, (2) as subject, (3) as predicate nominative, (4) as appositive.

- He said that the box was empty. [Object.]
- That the box was empty was all he could say. [Subject.]
- My remark was that the bill is a menace. [Predicate nominative.]
- Your remark, that the bill is a menace, has aroused vigorous protest. [Apposition.]

The conjunction that is often omitted.

- Jack said [that] he was sorry.
- I hope [that] you can come.
- I know he is too busy a man to have leisure for me.—COWPER.

In indirect discourse, after the past or the pluperfect tense, the present tense of the direct discourse becomes past, and the perfect becomes pluperfect.

- 1.DIRECT: I am tired.

INDIRECT: John {said | had said} that he was tired.

2.DIRECT: I have won. INDIRECT: John {said | had said} that he had won.

But a general or universal truth always remains in the present tense.

DIRECT: Air is a gas.   INDIRECT: I told him that air is a gas.

INDIRECT: I had told him a hundred times that air is a gas.

The clause with that in indirect discourse is sometimes replaced by an infinitive clause.

The jury declared him to be innocent. [Compare: The jury declared that he was innocent.]

•   Morton admitted them to be counterfeit. [Compare: Morton admitted that they were counterfeit.]

In these sentences, him and them are, of course, the subjects of the infinitives, not the objects of declared and admitted.

436. When the verb of telling or thinking is in the passive voice, three constructions occur:—

1. A clause with that is used as the subject of the passive verb.

That Rogers desires the office is commonly reported.

2. The expletive it is used as the grammatical subject, and a that-clause follows the passive verb.

It is commonly reported that Rogers desires the office.

3. The subject of the that-clause becomes the subject of the passive verb, and the verb of the clause is replaced by an infinitive.

Rogers is commonly reported to desire the office.

The choice among these three idioms is largely a matter of emphasis or euphony. The first may easily become heavy or awkward, and it is therefore less common than either of the others.

NOTE. The third of these idioms is often called the personal construction, to distinguish it from the second, in which the grammatical subject is the impersonal it. The infinitive in this third idiom may be regarded as a peculiar adverbial modifier of the passive verb.

Further examples of the three constructions with passive verbs of telling, thinking, etc., are the following:—

•   That in vivacity, humor, and eloquence, the Irish stand high among the nations of the world is now universally acknowledged.— MACAULAY.

- It is admitted that the exercise of the imagination is most delightful.—SHELLEY.
- It must be owned that Charles's life has points of some originality.—STEVENSON.
- Porto Bello is still said to be impregnable, and it is reported the Dutch have declared war against us.—GRAY.
- He was generally believed to have been a pirate.—LYTTON.
- Pope may be said to write always with his reputation in his head.—JOHNSON.
- She was observed to flutter her fan with such vehement rapidity that the elaborate delicacy of its workmanship gave way.—HAWTHORNE.
- This is said to be the only château in France in which the ancient furniture of its original age is preserved.—LONGFELLOW.

437. A substantive clause with that is common after it seems, it is true, it is evident, and similar expressions.

- It seems that Robert has lost all his money.
- It is true that genius does not always bring happiness with it.
- It is evident that Andrews tells the truth.

The uses of shall and will, should and would, in indirect discourse are the same as in the direct,48 with the following exception:—

When the first person with shall or should in direct discourse becomes the second or third person in the indirect, shall or should is retained.

- DIRECT: You say, "I shall die."
- INDIRECT: You say that you shall die.
- DIRECT: You said, "I shall die."
- INDIRECT: You said that you should die.
- DIRECT: He says, "I shall die."
- INDIRECT: He says that he shall die.
- DIRECT: He said, "I shall die."
- INDIRECT: He said that he should die.

The reason for the retention of shall or should is that, in such cases, the second or third person of the indirect discourse represents the first person of the direct.

The change from shall (after says) to should (after said) is a mere change of tense.

NOTE. The general principle is, to retain in the indirect discourse the auxiliary of the direct, simply changing the tense if necessary. This principle of course covers the use of you or he shall or should to represent I shall or should. There is, however, one important exception to the general principle: when its application would result in the use of I will or I would to express mere futurity, I shall or I should is employed. Thus, John says to Charles, "If you fall overboard, you will drown"; but Charles, reporting this, must say, "John tells me that, if I fall overboard, I shall [NOT will] drown." The general rule, then, may be stated as follows: The indirect discourse retains the auxiliary of the direct (with a change in tense, if necessary), unless such retention makes will or would express simple futurity in the first person,—in that case, shall or should is used.

The following sentences illustrate the correct use of shall and will, should and would, in the indirect discourse:—

- 1. He writes me that he believes he shall be at Eton till the middle of November.—GRAY. [Direct: I shall be at Eton.]
- 2. He that would pass the latter part of his life with honor and decency, must, while he is young, consider that he shall one day be old.—JOHNSON. [Direct: I shall one day be old.]
- 3. Could he but reduce the Aztec capital, he felt that he should be safe.—PRESCOTT. [Direct: I shall be safe.]
- 4. Plantagenet took it into his head that he should like to learn to play at bowls.—DISRAELI. [Direct: I should like.]
- 5. He answered that he should be very proud of hoisting his flag under Sir John's command.—SOUTHEY. [Direct: I shall (or should) be, etc.]
- 6. He knew that if he applied himself in earnest to the work of reformation, he should raise every bad passion in arms against him.—MACAULAY. [Direct: If I apply myself ..., I shall raise, etc.]
- 7. He was pleased to say that he should like to have the author in his service.—CARLYLE. [Direct: I should like.]

- 8. Mr. Tristram at last declared that he was overcome with fatigue, and should be happy to sit down.—HENRY JAMES. [Direct: I should be happy.]
- 9. She vowed that unless he made a great match, she should never die easy.—THACKERAY. [Direct: Unless you make a great match, I shall never die easy.]
- 10. You think now I shall get into a scrape at home. You think I shall scream and plunge and spoil everything.—GEORGE ELIOT. [Direct: She will get into a scrape, etc.]
- 11. You in a manner impose upon them the necessity of being silent, by declaring that you will be so yourself.—COWPER. [Determination: I will be silent.]
- 12. He [Swift] tells them that he will run away and leave them, if they do not instantly make a provision for him.—JEFFREY. [Threat: I will run away.]
- 13. The king declared that he would not reprieve her for one day.—MACKINTOSH. [Direct: I will not.]
- 14. Horace declares that he would not for all the world get into a boat with a man who had divulged the Eleusinian mysteries.—COWPER. [Direct: I would not.]
- 15. I called up Sirboko, and told him, if he would liberate this one man to please me, he should be no loser.—SPEKE. [Direct: If you will liberate, etc., you shall be no loser.]
- 16. We concluded that, if we did not come at some water in ten days' time, we would return.—DE FOE. [Direct: If we do not, etc., we will return.]
- 17. With a theatrical gesture and the remark that I should see, he opened some cages and released half a dozen cats.—W. J. LOCKE. [Direct: You shall see.]

IX. INDIRECT QUESTIONS

A question expressed in the form actually used in asking it is called a direct question.

- What is your name?
- "What is your name?" he asked.

The direct form may be retained when the question is quoted or reported, as in the second example above. Often, however, a question is quoted or reported, not in the direct form, but in the form of a subordinate clause: as,— He asked what my name was.

Such a clause is called an indirect question.

An indirect question expresses the substance of a direct question in the form of a subordinate clause.

Indirect questions depend on verbs or other expressions of asking, doubting, thinking, perceiving, and the like.

•   Franklin asked where the difficulty lay. [Direct question: "Where does the difficulty lie?"]

•   The sergeant wondered how he should escape. [Direct question: "How shall I escape?"]

•   I have not decided which train I shall take. [Direct question: "Which train shall I take?"]

Both direct and indirect questions may be introduced (1) by the interrogative pronouns who, which, what; (2) by the interrogative adverbs when, where, whence, whither, how, why.

Indirect questions may be introduced by the subordinate conjunctions whether (whether ... or) and if.

The use of tenses in indirect questions is the same as in the indirect discourse.

•   The constable inquired whether (or if) I lived in Casterbridge. [His question was: Do you live in Casterbridge?]

•   Your father wishes to know if you have been playing truant. [Direct question: Have you been playing truant?]

•   I considered whether I should apply to Kent or to Arnold. [Direct question: Shall I apply to Kent or to Arnold?]

Indirect questions are usually noun clauses. They may be used in various noun constructions: (1) as object of some verb of asking or the like, (2) as subject, (3) as predicate nominative, (4) as appositive, (5) as object of a preposition.

•   The skipper asked what had become of the cook. [Object.]

•   He was asked what his profession was. [Retained object after the passive.

- How we could escape was a difficult question. [Subject.]
- The problem was how they should find food. [Predicate nominative.]
- The question who was to blame has never been settled. [Apposition with question.]
- They all felt great perplexity as to what they should do. [Object of a preposition.]

An indirect question may be an adverbial clause.

- They were uncertain what course they should take. [The clause modifies uncertain.]
- Edmund was in doubt where he should spend the night. [The clause modifies the adjective phrase in doubt.]

Since the pronouns who, which, and what may be either interrogative or relative, an indirect question may closely resemble a relative clause. These two constructions, however, are sharply distinguished. A relative clause always asserts something. An indirect question, on the contrary, has an interrogative sense which may be seen by turning the question into the direct form.

The sailor who saved the child is a Portuguese. [The clause who saved the child is a relative clause, for it makes a distinct assertion about the sailor,—namely, that he saved the child. Who is a relative pronoun and sailor is its antecedent.]

{I asked | I do not know | It is still a question | It is doubtful} who saved the child. [Here the clause who saved the child makes no assertion. On the contrary, it expresses a question which may easily be put in a direct form with an interrogation point: "Who saved the child?" Who is an interrogative pronoun. It has no antecedent.]

The following examples further illustrate the difference between these two constructions:—

- 1.I foresee the course which he will take. [Relative clause.]
- I foresee which course he will take. [Indirect question.]
- 2.I heard what he said. [Relative clause. What = "that which."]
- I wondered what he said. [Indirect question. What is an interrogative pronoun.]
- 3.This is the man who brought the news. [Relative clause.]

-       The king asked who brought the news. [Indirect question.]
-       4.Here is a paper which you must sign. [Relative clause.]
-       The clerk will tell you which paper you must sign. [Indirect question.]

NOTE. In such a sentence as "Tom knows who saved the child," the indirect question may at first appear to be a relative clause with an omitted antecedent (the man, or the person). If, however, we insert such an antecedent ("Tom knows the man who saved the child"), the meaning is completely changed. In the original sentence, it is stated that Tom knows the answer to the question, "Who saved the child?" In the new form of the sentence, it is stated that Tom is acquainted with a certain person, and to this is added an assertion about this person in the form of a relative clause.

An indirect question is sometimes expressed by means of an interrogative pronoun or adverb followed by an infinitive.

-       Whom to choose is a serious question. [Direct question: Whom shall we choose?]
-       John asked what to do. [John's question was: What shall I do?]
-       I know where to go. [Direct question: Where shall I go?]
-       Tell me when to strike the bell.
-       I was at a loss how to reply.
-       I am in doubt how to begin this essay.

In the first four examples the italicized phrase is used as a noun (either as subject or object). In the fifth, the phrase how to reply is adverbial, modifying the adjective phrase at a loss.

The subjunctive was formerly common in indirect questions, and is still occasionally used after if or whether.

-       I doubt if it be true.
-       Elton questioned whether the project were wise.

The rule for shall (should) and will (would) in indirect questions is, to retain the auxiliary used in the direct question, merely changing the tense (shall to should; will to would) when necessary.

1.   DIRECT: What shall I do?

      INDIRECT: •   I wonder what I shall do.

-       You ask me what you shall do.

- He asks me what he shall do.
- I wondered what I should do.
- You asked me what you should do.
- He asked me what he should do.

2.   DIRECT: Shall you lose your position?

INDIRECT: •   {I ask | He asks} you if you shall lose your position.

- {I asked | He asked} you if you should lose your position.

3.   DIRECT: Will Charles lose his position?

INDIRECT: •   I ask if Charles will lose his position.

- {I | You | Tom} asked if Charles would lose his position.

I. MERE FUTURITY

4.   DIRECT: Will you help me?

INDIRECT: •   You ask if I will help you.

- He asks if I will help him.
- You asked if I would help you.
- He asked if I would help him.
- {I asked him | You asked him | Tom asked him} if he would {help me. | help you. | help him.}

***.

2. Error Correction Rules

Language reflects personality of a person. It also ensures perfect character building.

-    *Chandan Sengupta*

Some Examples of Error Spotting

I: The condolence messages (a) / received on the (b) / death of Mrs. Gandhi (c)/ speaks highly of her greatness (d) / no error (e).

Explanation

Answer: d. In the above statement the subject is condolence messages which is in plural form. So, the verb should also be in plural form. But the verb here is speaks, which is singular. So we have to use speak instead of speaks. **Thus, answer is (d).**

Eg: They write – plural, he writes – singular.

Sentence should contain Singular subject + singular verb

Plural subject + plural verb

II: He took me to restaurant (a) / and ordered for two cups (b) / of cold coffee (c) / which the waiter brought in an hour (d) / no error (e).

Explanation

In this sentence, after ordered, for cannot be used.

Preposition like for, on, to, etc., should not follow transition verbs like moved, ordered, etc., So, remove for from the sentence. **Thus the answer is (b).**

Eg: I moved the chair. (no preposition after moved).

III: I would rather (a) / pay for my education (b) / than financial aid (c)/ no error (d).

Explanation

In the sentence, the part b has noun – education and verb – pay but in part c there is only a noun - aid and no verb. The word rather defines that he can do any one of the above mentioned activities. So both the sentence should have same pattern. **Thus, answer is (c).**

IV: If I would have realised (a) / what a bad driver, you were (b) / I would not have (c) / come with you (d) / no error (e).

Explanation

If + past perfect and I + would have – If conditional. So, I had realised should come in the place of would have realised. **Thus, the answer is (a).**

V: All the woman teachers (a) / are agitated (b) / because of the haughty attitude (c) / of the Principle (d)/ no error (e).

Answer: a

Explanation

In the sentence, "all" is plural form and then "teachers" is also a plural form so instead of woman we should women. **Thus, answer is (a)**

VI: The Chairman had not taken (a) / any decision until (b) / he had studied (c) / the case thoroughly (d) / no error (e).

Answer: a

Explanation

In this sentence, had comes in both the places. But the correct tense is did not take. The past perfect (had not) should follow a simple past tense to maintain its past perfect tense. **Thus, answer is (a)**

VII: Building biogas plant will (a) / help to reduce (b) / the consuming of conventional fuel (c) / such as firewood and kerosene (d) / no error (e).

Explanation

Here the sentence answers for the question what like what will be reduced? The answer is consumption of conventional fuel. So, replace the word consuming with consumption. **Thus, answer is (c).**

VIII: Both the rich (a) / along with the poor (b) / are responsible for a great many vices (c) / with which our country is inflicted (d) / no error (e).

Answer: b

Explanation

This sentence is an example for co relative sentence.

- And follows both
- Than follows no sooner
- When follows hardly
- But also follows not only.

So, in this sentence **and** should replace **along. Thus, answer is (b).**

IX: The six partners (a) / are at daggers drawn (b) / so they do not talk (c) / to each other (d) / no error (e).

Explanation

In this sentence, there are more than 2 persons. So ,use the word one another instead of each other. **Thus, (d) is the correct answer.**

Example 10.

He is almost quite competent (a) / for the post of Manager(b) / so if given a chance (c) / he can show the results (d) / no error (e).

Explanation

It is a superfluous word, that is both contain same meaning.

Eg:

- most unique
- More better
- Almost quite

These words cannot be used together.

So, in this sentence almost is not necessary. **Thus, (a) is the correct answer.**

Rules based on Tenses

Present Tense:-

Simple Present Tense

Simple Present Tense sentences include happening of work in present time.

Subject + 1 st form of Verb

1. Subject (Singular form /third person) + 1st Form of Verb + s/es
Noun Subject is also a third person.

2. Subject(Plural) + 1st Form of Verb

3. For I and You , we will not use 's' and 'es' with Verb.

Example :I study on daily basis.

Present continuous tense

Expresses an action continued at present time.

1. Subject (Singular /third person/He,She,It) + is + (1st Form of Verb + ing) + Object

2. Subject (Plural /You,We,They) + are + (1st Form of Verb + ing) + Object

3. I + am + (1st Form of Verb + ing)

Example:I am reading a novel.
Ram is going office.
We are getting late.

Present perfect tense

An action which happened or completed in the present time

1. Subject (Singular /third person/He,She,It) + has + 3rd Form of Verb + Object

2. Subject (Plural /I,You,We,They) + have + 1st Form of Verb + Object

Example:Divya has gone to school.
He has filled a case.

Past Tense :-

Simple Past Tense

1. Subject (Singular/third person/Plural) + 2nd Form of Verb

2. Different number of subject can not change verb.

Example:I worked on the project last night.

Past continuous tense
1. Subject (Singular /third person/He,She,It) + was + (1st Form of Verb + ing) + Object
2. Subject (Plural /You,We,They) + were + (1st Form of Verb + ing) + Object

Example :
I was reading harry potter last night

Past perfect tense
An action which happened or completed in the past time or usually the two actions which happened or completed one by one in the past time.
1. Subject (Singular /third person/Plural) + had + 3rd Form of Verb + Object

Example:Ramya went to school after she had completed her homework.
I had already heard this news.

Future Tense
Simple future tense
1. Subject (Singular/third person/Plural) + will + 1st Form of Verb
2. I or We + shall + 1st Form of Verb

Example:
We shall go to school tomorrow.
You will read a book.

Future continuous tense
1. I,We + Shall be + (1st Form of Verb + ing) + Object
2. Subject(Other than I,We) + will be + (1st Form of Verb + ing) + Object

Example:We shall be coming to your house.
We will be playing football in evening.

Future perfect tense
1. Subject + will have/shall have + 3rd Form of Verb + Object

2. Wherever you'll see the use of the two sentences in this tense, the action which would be completed first would be in 'Future Perfect Tense' and the action completed after would be in 'Present Simple Tense'.

Example:They will have played the match before the sun sets.
I shall have read my book before you come.

Rule 1.
In Present Indefinite sentences the number and the person of the subject play very important role. If the subject is Singular number third person, affix 's' or 'es' to the verb. If the verb ends in any of the following : ss, o , x, z, sh,ch , add, 'es' instead of 's' with the verb.
Eg: Pass-passes, miss-misses, do – does, mix – mixes, fix – fixes etc.

Rule 2.
When the main verb is in Future Tense, use Present Simple in clauses with if, till, as soon as, when, unless, before, until, even if, in case and as.
Eg:
We shall wait till she arrives.
I shall not go there even if it rains.
Rule 3.
Present Simple Tense must be used instead of Present Continuous Tense with verbs of perception (feel, hear, smell etc.), verbs of cognition (believe, know, think etc.), verbs of emotion (hope, love, hate etc.) which cannot be used normally in continuous form.
Eg:
Incorrect – We are seeing with our eyes. Correct – We see with our eyes.
Incorrect – The water is feeling cold. Correct – The water feels cold.
But these words can be used in progressive form in the following cases.
The Session Judge is hearing our case.
We are thinking of going to London next year.
I am seeing my lawyer today.
I am having some difficulties with this puzzle.
Rule 4.
One must not use adverbs of past time like yesterday, last year, last month, ago, short while ago etc. with Present Perfect Tense.
Eg:

Incorrect – He has completed his book yesterday. Correct – He completed his book yesterday.

Incorrect – We have met 3 days ago. Correct – We met 3 days ago.

Rule 5.

If two or more actions took place in sequence, we use Simple Past to denote the actions. (Otherwise Past Perfect is used to denote the earlier action). This is usually used with conjunction Before.

Eg:

He switched on the light before he opened the door.

The train started just before I reached the station.

When Rahul reached home, Tina had had her lunch.

Rule 6.

The use of Simple Past Tense with , 'wish' and 'If only' shows unreal Past and present state of things.

Eg:

I wish I were a millionaire! (I am not a millionaire)

I wish I were a queen! (I am not a queen)

If I only knew her! (I don't know her.)

Rule 7.

In the following structure the use of Simple Past denotes unreal past and present time situation.

Eg:

It is time we went home. (It is time for us to go home.)

It is time you finished. (It is time for you to finish.)

Rule 8.

Use of Past Continuous with 'When' and 'While'

When is usually used when one action was completed and another action was going on.

When gives the meaning 'at the time that'.

Eg:

When he arrived, his wife was washing her clothes.

When she went to Banaras, she bought a sari.

While is used to denote a period.

Eg:

While I was teaching, I put through my best.

While I was in Opera, I could enjoy very much.

Rule 9.

Past Perfect is used when we look back on earlier action from a certain point in the past.

Eg:

She had completed her work, before I reached there.

I had started teaching before Manu came to my class.

Rule 10.

The Past Perfect is also used for an action which began before the time of speaking in the Past and which stopped sometime before the time of speaking.

Eg:

He had served in a bank for twenty years; then he retired and established his business. His children were now well settled.

Rule 11.

Past Perfect Continuous is used when the action began before the time of speaking in the past, and continued up to that time.

Eg:

It is now eight and she was tired because she had been cleaning the house since dawn.

This city has been prosperous since a very long time.

Rule 12.

When two actions are to be taken place on some future time, we use Future Perfect for the action completed first and Present Simple for the action to be completed afterwards.

Eg:

The student will have left the class before the teacher comes.

The Principal will have started before I reach there.

Rule 13.

Future Perfect is also used for such incidents/actions about which we presume that another person had the knowledge of that incident or the action is already completed.

Eg:

You will have heard about Mother Teresa.

He will have read the newspaper so far.

Exercise

1. Adarsh hopes to become(a)/an officer after he complete(b)/his higher education(c)/No error(d)

2. The police have found (a) / who they believe to be (b) / the prime suspect in a murder case (c) / no error (d).

3. Now-a-days he teaches English (a)/ because the teacher of English. (b)/ has gone for a month's leave. (c)/ No Error (d).

4. I will let you know (a)/ as soon as I will get (b)/ any news in this regard. (c)/ No Error (d)

Answers
1. (B) complete should be replaced with completes ,because 1 verb is in future tense

2. (B) believe should be replaced with believed, as 1st part is in past tense.

3. (A)Replace 'he teaches' by 'he is teaching'.

4. (B) replace i will get with i get.

Rules of Noun
Rule 1
The nouns such as – Jury, choir, committee, council, crowd, herd, orchestra, team, government, mob, community, union, club, opposition, firm, flock etc. are used as collective nouns to denote a group. They are considered to be singular and a singular verb is used with them.
Example
The committee has submitted its report.

Rule 2
The unit of measurement (such as - hour, pound, kilo, mile…etc.) is always used in the singular form in the structure –'Half + a/an + unit of measurement'; as, 'Half a kilo', 'Half an hour'.
Note: The unit of measurement (such as – hour, pound, kilo, mile…etc.) is also used in the singular form in the structure – 'A + half + unit of measurement'; as, 'A half kilo', 'A half hour'.
Example

Only Half an hour left to finish this work.

Rule 3
A plural noun is used after 'one and a half'; as 'One and a half kilos'
While 'A/An + singular noun + and + a half' is used in English
Language; as,
'A kilo and a half kilos',
'An hour and a half'.

Rule 4
The structure – 'Numeral Adjectives + plural noun + and + a half' or
Numeral Adjectives + and + a half + plural noun is used in the English
Language. Numeral Adjectives: One, two, three, four…..etc. some, all,
many, few…..etc. are called Numeral Adjectives; as,
'Two kilos and a half' 'Five hours and a half' 'Two and a half kilos'.

Rule 5
A plural noun is used after 'Cardinal Adjectives except one'. Cardinal
Adjectives: One, two, three, four, five, six….etc. are called Cardinal
Adjectives; as 'Five kilometres'
Example
I have fifty rupees.

Rule 6
Generally, the plural of a proper noun is not possible. But the plural of a
proper noun can be formed (=made) by adding 's' according to need.
Example
There are two Mohans in my class.

Rule 7
These nouns such as – barracks, corps, crossroads, Innings, headquarters,
précis, series, species, Issue, offspring, aircraft, craft, swine are used in
the same form both in singular and plural.
Example
All the police barrack of Gorakhpur are old.

Rule 8

The structure – 'Noun + preposition + same noun' is always used in the singular. A singular noun is always used before preposition and after a preposition; as'
Example
Village after village has been swept away.

Rule 9
A plural noun or a plural pronoun is used after these phrases – one of, each of, either of, neither of, any one of, a few of, very few of, half of, a lot of, a large number of etc.
Example
One of the boys was innocent.

Rule 10
If we add 's' or 'es' to some Adjectives, they become plural nouns; as'
Example
We have to taste the sweets and bitters of our lives.

Rule 11
Some nouns always remain in plural form. They take plural verb. These nouns have no singular form. These are -
Assets, alms, amends, annals, archives, ashes ,arrears, athletics, auspices, species, scissors , trousers, pants. clippers, bellows, gallows, fangs, measles, eyeglasses, goggles, belongings, breeches. Bowels , braces ,binoculars, dregs, earnings, entrails, embers ,fetters, fireworks, longings, lees, odds ,outskirts, particulars, proceeds, proceedings ,riches, remains, shambles, shears, spectacles , surroundings ,tidings ,tactics ,tongs ,vegetables, valuables, wages etc.
Means' — In the sense of income'. Means always takes a plural verb. In the sense way to achieve some end, Means takes a singular verb. When 'a' or 'every' is used before Means', it is singular.
Examples
(a) My means were reduced substantially.
(b) Every means is good if the end is good.

Rule 12

If two adjectives are joined by 'and' and 'The' is used before the first adjectives, A plural noun is used after the second Adjective.
Example
Dr. S.S. Prasad was an examiner of the Patna and Bihar universities.
Incorrect: Dr. S.S. Prasad was an examiner of the Patna and Bihar university.

Rule 13

If two adjectives are joined by 'and' and 'The' used before both Adjectives or each Adjective, A singular noun is used after the second Adjectives.
Example
The first and the second chapter of this book are interesting.
Incorrect: The first and the second chapters of this book are interesting.

Rule 14

Some nouns look plural in form but have singular meaning. Such nouns take singular verb. These are: news, innings, politics, summons, physics, economics, ethics. mechanics, mathematics, measles, mumps, rickets, billiards, draughts, etc.

Rule 15

Some nouns look singular but have plural meaning. Such nouns take plural verbs. These are: cattle, clergy, cavalry, infantry, poultry,peasantry, children, gentry, police etc.

Rule 16

Some nouns are always used in singular . These are uncountable nouns. We should not use article A/An with such nouns. These are -
Scenery, poetry, furniture, advice, information, hair, language. business, mischief, bread, stationery, crockery, luggage, baggage, postage, knowledge, wastage, money, jewellery, breakage etc,
We can not pluralise such nouns by adding `S' or 'es'.
Example It is incorrect to write sceneries, informations, furnitures, hairs.
If hair is used as countable it can be pluralised : e.g., one hair, two hairs.
Example I need three hairs of a black horse.

Rule 17

Some nouns have plural meaning. If a definite numeral adjective is used before them they are not pluralised. e.g., pair, score. Gross , stone ,hundred, dozen, thousand. million. billion. etc.

Otherwise these nouns can well be pluralised:

Dozens of women, Hundreds of people, Millions of dollars, Scores of shops. Many pairs of shoes, thousands millions etc.

Rule 18

If a numeral adjective and a fraction are used with a noun, the noun is used with the numeral and the noun will be in singular.

Examples

(a) He gave me one rupee and a half.

(b) She gave me two rupees and a quarter.

Avoid the following structure

Examples

(a) He gave me one and a half rupees. (Incorrect).

(b) She gave rite two and a quarter rupees. (Incorrect)

If the numeral adjective and the fraction refer the multiplication, the noun be placed in the end (after the fraction) and it must be plural.

Examples

(a) Your deposits has grown two and a half times within two years.

(b) My salary has increased three and a quarter times within three years.

Rule 19

Some nouns are known as common gender nouns. They can be used for either sex; Male or Female. These are called dual gender nouns. Such nouns are : teacher, student, child, clerk, candidate. advocate, worker, writer, author, leader, musician, politician, enemy, client, president, person, neighbour etc. When these are used in singular, use third person singular masculine (his) pronoun with them.

Examples

(a) Every candidate should write his (not her) name.

(b) Every person should perform his (not her) duty.

Each. either, everyone. everybody, no one, nobody, neither, anybody are also common gender pronouns.

Rule 20

Some nouns are used for specifically for feminine gender only. i.e., blonde, maid, mid wife, coquette, virgin etc.

Now a days nouns 'bachelor' and 'virgin' are being used for masculine and feminine gender as well .

Use of Apostrophe with 's'

(A) You can form the possessive case of a singular noun that does not end in 's' by adding an apostrophe and `s' We should use apostrophe in following situations only

(1) Living things -> Mohan's book

(2) Thing personified; as —> week's holiday

(3) Space time or weight ; as —> a day's leave

(4) Certain dignified objects; as

The court's orders

At duty's call

(5) Familiar phrases; as —

At his wit's end

At a stone's throw

It there are hissing sounds (sounds of sh or s) ending a word, use apostrophe without 's' with such words. e.g., For Jesus' sake, For conscience' sake, The roses' fragrance etc. (It can be noted that if we use apostrophe with s with such words it couldn't be pronounced well)

(B) You can form the possessive case of a plural noun that does not end in 's' by adding an apostrophe and a 's,' as in the following example.

Example The men's cricket team will play as soon as the women's team is finished.

(C) You can form the possessive case of a plural noun that does end in 's' by adding an apostrophe.

Example The concert was interrupted by the 'dogs' barking, the 'ducks' quacking, and the 'babies' squalling.

(D) Do not use apostrophe with possessive pronouns

i.e., his, hers, yours, mine, ours, its, theirs etc.

Yours faithfully, yours truly, ours garden , his pen, hers purse, theirs room.

(E) Use apostrophe with the last word in following titles.

Examples

(a) Governor-general's instructions.

(b) Commander-in-chiefs orders.

(c) My son-in-law's sister.

(d) Ram and Sons's shop.

(F) Do not use 'Double apostrophe'. Avoid double apostrophe in a sentence.

Example

(a) My wife's secretary's mother has expired. (Incorrect)

The mother of my wife's secretary has expired. (Correct)

(G) Apostrophe with 's' is used with; Anybody/ Nobody / Everybody / Somebody / Anyone / Someone / No one / Everyone.

Example Everyone's concern is no one's concern.

If else is used after these words, use apostrophe with else as per following:

Example I can rely on your words, not somebody else's.

Rules of Adjectives

Much / Many :

Many: It refers large quantity of plural countable noun.

Example: There are much cows in the field.(incorrect)

There are many cows in the field.(correct)

Much: It refers large quantity of uncountable material noun.

Example: There are many water in the river.(incorrect)

There are much water in the river.(correct)

Elder / Older:

Elder: It is used for family members only.

" To" is used after elder

Example: Shyam is elder than Sohan. (incorrect)

Shyam is elder to Sohan. (correct)

Older: It is for persons out of family or non-living things.

"Than" is used with older.

Example: I am older to you.(incorrect)

I am older than you.(correct)

Few / a Few / The Few:

Few: It means hardly any or nothing. It is used in negative sense.

Example: There were few members in meeting so the meeting was cancelled.(correct)

There are few rupees in my wallet, I cannot go home.(correct)

A few: It means some or small amount. It is used in positive sense.

Example: A few politician are hard working.(correct)

There are a few students present in the school.(correct)

The few: It means all the amount which is present or remained on said time.

Example: I have read the few books present in library.(correct)

The professor taught the few student that had come.(correct)

Little/A little/the little:

These are used to express quantity of Uncountable Material noun.

Little: This implies "hardly any" or "nothing". It is used in negative sense.

Example: There is little ink in my pen so I cannot write. (correct)

There is little water left in tank, so we cannot bath.(correct)

A little: It means "very small amount ". It is used in positive sense.

Example: There is a little water left in tank, so you can bath.(correct)

The little : It means all the amount , which is available.

Example: I drank the little milk present in the bottle.(correct)

less / fewer:

These are used to express quantity of material

Less: It is used to express the quantity of uncountable material noun.

Example: Not fewer than five litres of oil Is present in tanker.(incorrect)

Not less than five litres of oil is present in the tankers.(correct)

Not fewer than five hundred kilograms of rice present in stock.(incorrect) .

Not less than five hundred kilograms of rice is present in the stock.(correct)

Fewer: It is used to express the quantity of plural countable noun.

Example: Not less than hundrerd students were present last monday.(incorrect)

Not fewer than hundred students were present last Monday.(correct)

Next/ Nearest:

Next: It is used to express order. Example: left, Right etc.
Example: Sita is sitting next to geeta. (correct)
Ram is my next bench classmate. (correct)
Nearest: It is used to express distance.
Example: Sent Paul school is nearest school to my home.(correct)
Ram-lila ground is nearest playground to my school.(correct)

later/ latter:
Later: It is used to express time (in the after).
Example: He came later than me. (correct)
He came latter than me.(incorrect)
Latter: It is used to express order.
Example: Ajay and Amit are brothers but the former is more handsome
than later.(incorrect)
Ajay and Amit are brothers but the former is more handsome than latter.
(correct)

Kinds of Adjective:

Proper Adjective:
This type of Adjective qualifies proper Noun.
Example: Indian, American, etc.
Virat kohli is an Indian player.
Donald Trump is an American president.

Quantitative Adjective:
This type of Adjective qualifies quantity of material noun.
Example: A great deal of, enough, all, no, some, much etc.
He is kind enough.
All the student are safe.
There is much water in swimming pool.
The baby has drunk much milk.

Demonstrative Adjective:
It qualifies the degree of distance for Noun / Pronoun.
Example: This, That, These, Such, Any etc.
This pen is Blue.

This bike is heavier than car.
Those politicians are good.

Descriptive Adjective:
This kind of Adjective explains the size, characteristic, colour, type of Noun / Pronoun.
Example: Tall, Large, Tiny, Rectangular, Square, Blue, Black, Ugly, Heavy, Dry etc.
I am a tall boy.
He is heavy wrestler.
My playground is triangular.

Distributive Adjective:
It qualifies one object or person between two or more than two person.
Example: Each, Every, either, neither etc.
Neither pen writes well.
Every child goes school.
Either of the Laptop works.

Possessive Adjective:
This kind of Adjective qualifies the possession or relation of noun / pronoun.
Example: Your, My, Our, His, Her etc.
My jacket is red but yours is blue.
That is your car.
This is my college.

Emphasizing Adjective:
This kind of Adjective is used to make special pressure on noun / Pronoun.
Example: Own, Very, Such, Same, Very etc.
I saw her at the Railway station with my own eyes.
This is my own pen.
This is the very thief who has stolen my smart phone.
(very means same to that person who is already known)

Interrogative Adjective:

This kind of adjective is used to make sense of question.

Example: What, How, Where, When etc.

Whose bike is this?

Which book is the best?

What type of laptop do you want to buy?

Numerical adjective:

It qualifies the number of countable noun.

Example: All, Some, No, Many, A good many, A number of etc.

There are many books in the library.

A cow has four legs.

All the students are present in the class.

Note: Enough, All, No, A lot of, Some etc are quantitative and numerical adjective

both, but their uses are different. (Will be discussed in rules of adjective topic)

Kinds of Numerical Adjective:

Definite numerical adjective:

Cardinal: One, Two, Three etc.

Ordinal: First, Second, Third etc.

Multiplicative: Single, Double, Triple etc.

Indefinite Numerical Adjective:

Much, many, some, enough, a lot of, several etc.

Exclamatory Adjective:

This kind of adjective is used to express emotion of heart.

Example: What! , How! etc.

What a beautiful day!

What nonsense this is !

What a kind of man he is!

What a nice story is! etc.

Relative Adjective:

This kind of adjective is used to make sense of relation for Noun or Pronoun.

Example: Who, Which, That etc.

This is the laptop that is used for best gaming experience.
This the singer who sings spiritual songs.

Present / Past participle Adjective:
This kind of Adjective is used where past or present Participle is needed.
Example: Burning train, flying kite, Singing baby, Tiring journey,
Moving car etc.
I like a flying kite.
Old woman slipped down from the moving train.
I am fond of a tiring journey.

.

3. Tenses : Exercise

Exercise 1

Simple Present / Present Continuous
1. Every Monday, Sally (drive) .... her kids to football practice.
2. Usually, I (work) .... as a secretary at ABT, but this summer I (study)
.... French at a language school in Paris. That is why I am in Paris.
3. Shhhhh! Be quiet! John (sleep) .... 4. Don't forget to take your umbrella. It (rain)
....
5. I hate living in Seattle because it (rain, always) .... 6. I'm sorry I can't hear what
you (say) .... because everybody (talk) .... so loudly.
7. Justin (write, currently) .... a book about his adventures in Tibet. I hope he can
find a good publisher when he is finished.
8. Do you want to come over for dinner tonight. Oh, I'm sorry, I can't. I (go) .... to a
movie tonight with some friends.
9. The business cards (be, normally)................ printed by a company in New York.
Their prices (be)................. inexpensive, yet the quality of their work is quite good.
10. This delicious chocolate (be) .... made by a small chocolatier in Zurich,
Switzerland.

Exercise 2

Simple Present / Present Continuous

Today (be) .... the second day of my trek around Mount Annapurna. I am exhausted

and my legs (shake) ....; I just hope I am able to complete the trek. My feet

(kill, really)............. me and my toes (bleed) ...., but I (want, still).......... to continue.

Nepal is a fascinating country, but I have a great deal to learn. Everything (be) ....

so different, and I (try)........... to adapt to the new way of life here. I (learn).......... a little

bit of the language to make communication easier; unfortunately, I (learn,

not)............... foreign languages quickly. Although I (understand, not) .... much

yet, I believe that I (improve, gradually) ....

I (travel, currently) .... with Liam, a student from Leeds University in England.

He (be) .... a nice guy, but impatient. He (walk, always) .... ahead of me

and (complain)............ that I am too slow. I (do) .... my best to keep up with

him, but he is younger and stronger than I am. Maybe, I am just feeling sorry for myself because I am getting old.

Right now, Liam (sit)................ with the owner of the inn. They (discuss)................ the differences between life in England and life in Nepal. I (know, not) .... the real name of the owner, but everybody (call, just)................ him Tam. Tam (speak)

.... English very well and he (try) .... to teach Liam some words in Nepali. Every time Tam (say).............. a new word, Liam (try).............. to repeat it.

Unfortunately, Liam (seem, also)............. to have difficulty learning foreign languages. I just hope we don't get lost and have to ask for directions.

Exercise 3

Simple Past / Past Continuous

1. A: What (you, do) .... when the accident occurred?
B: I (try) .... to change a light bulb that had burnt out.
2. After I (find) .... the wallet full of money, I (go, immediately) .... to the police and (turn)
.... it in.
3. The doctor (say) .... that Tom (be) .... too sick to go to work and that he (need)
.... to stay at home for a couple of days.
4. Sebastian (arrive) .... at Susan's house a little before 9:00 pm, but she (be, not)
.... there. She (study, at the library) .... for her final examination in French.
5. Sandy is in the living room watching television. At this time yesterday, she (watch, also)
.... television. That's all she ever does!
6. A: I (call) .... you last night after dinner, but you (be, not) .... there. Where were you?
B: I (work) .... out at the fitness center.
7. When I (walk) .... into the busy office, the secretary (talk)
.... on the phone with a
customer, several clerks (work, busily) .... at their desks, and two managers (discuss, quietly)
.... methods to improve customer service.
8. I (watch) .... a mystery movie on T.V. when the electricity went out. Now I am never going to
find out how the movie ends.
9. Sharon (be) .... in the room when John (tell).......... me what had happened, but she didn't
hear anything because she (listen, not) ....
10. It's strange that you (call) .... because I (think, just)
.............................about you.
11. The Titanic (cross) .... the Atlantic when it (strike)
.........................an iceberg.
12. When I entered the bazaar, a couple of merchants (bargain, busily)
.... and (try) .... to
sell their goods to naive tourists who (hunt) .... for souvenirs. Some young boys (lead)

.... their donkeys through the narrow streets on their way home. A couple of men (argue)
..................over the price of a leather belt. I (walk) .... over to a man who (sell) ....

fruit and (buy) .... a banana.

13. The firemen (rescue) .... the old woman who (be) ....trapped on the third floor of the burning
building.

14. She was so annoying! She (leave, always) .... her dirty dishes in the sink. I think she
(expect, actually) .... me to do them for her.

15. Samantha (live) .... in Berlin for more than two years. In fact, she (live) .... there when the Berlin wall came down.

Exercise 4

Simple Past / Past Continuous

Last night, while I was doing my homework, Angela (call) .... She said she (call)......... me on her

cell phone from her biology classroom at UCLA. I asked her if she (wait) .... for class, but she said that the professor was at the front of the hall lecturing while she (talk) .... to me. I couldn't believe

she (make) .... a phone call during the lecture. I asked what was going on. She said her biology professor was so boring that several of the students (sleep, actually) .... in

class. Some of the students (talk) .... about their plans for the weekend and the student next to

her (draw) .... a picture of a horse. When Angela (tell) ....me she was not satisfied

with the class, I (mention) .... that my biology professor was quite good and (sugest)..............

that she switch to my class. While we were talking, I (hear).............. her professor yell, "Miss, are

you making a phone call?" Suddenly, the line went dead. I (hang).............. up the phone and went to

the kitchen to make dinner. As I (cut) .... vegetables for a salad, the phone rang once again. It (be)
.... Angela, but this time she (not sit)........in class.

Exercise 5

Simple Past / Present Perfect
1.A: Did you like the movie "Star Wars"?
B: I don't know. I (see, never) .... that movie.
2. Sam (arrive) .... in San Diego a week ago.
3. My best friend and I (know) ..... each other for over fifteen years. We still get together once a week.
4. Stinson is a fantastic writer. He (write) .... ten very creative short stories in the last year.
One day, he'll be as famous as Hemingway.
5. I (have, not) .... this much fun since I (be) ....
a kid.
6. Things (change) .... a great deal at Coltech, Inc. When we first (start) .... working here
three years ago, the company (have, only) .... six employees. Since then, we (expand).......... to
include more than 2000 full-time workers.
7. I (tell) .... him to stay on the path while he was hiking, but he (wander) .... off
into the forest and (be) .... bitten by a snake.
8. Listen Donna, I don't care if you (miss) .... the bus this morning. You (be) .... late to
work too many times. You are fired!
9. Sam is from Colorado, which is hundreds of miles from the coast, so he (see, never) .... the
ocean. He should come with us to Miami.
10. How sad! George (dream) .... of going to California before died, but he didn't make it. He
(see, never) .... the ocean.
11. In the last hundred years, traveling (become) .... much easier and very comfortable. In the
19th century, it (take) .... two or three months to cross North America by covered wagon. The trip
(be) ....very rough and often dangerous. Things (change)............ a great deal in the last hundred and
fifty years. Now you can fly from New York to Los Angeles in a matter of hours.
12. Jonny, I can't believe how much you (change)......... since the last time I (see).............. you. You

(grow) .... at least a foot!

13. This tree (be)....... planted by the settlers who (found)........... our city over four hundred years ago.

14. This mountain (be, never) .... climbed by anyone. Several mountaineers (try)

.... to reach the top, but nobody (succeed, ever) .... The climb is extremely

difficult and many people (die) .... trying to reach the summit.

15. I (visit, never) .... Africa, but I (travel) .... to South America several times. The

last time I (go)............... to South America, I (visit) .... Brazil and Peru. I (spend)............ two

weeks in the Amazon, (hike) .... for a week near Machu Picchu, and (fly) ..... over the Nazca Lines.

Exercise 6

Simple Past / Present Perfect

1. Since computers were first introduced to the public in the early 1980's, technology (change)

.... a great deal. The first computers (be) .... simple machines designed

for basic tasks. They (have, not) .... much memory and they (be, not)

.... very powerful. Early computers were often quite expensive and customers often

(pay) .... thousands of dollars for machines which actually (do) ....

very little. Most computers (be) .... separate, individual machines used mostly as

expensive typewriters or for playing games.

2. Times (change) .... Computers (become) .... powerful machines

with very practical applications. Programmers (create) .... a large selection of

useful programs which do everything from teaching foreign languages to bookkeeping. We are still

playing video games, but today's games (become) .... faster, more exciting interactive

adventures. Many computer users (get, also) .... on the Internet and (begin)
.... communicating with other computer users around the world. We (start)
.... to create international communities online. In short, the simple, individual machines
of the past (evolve) .... into an international World Wide Web of knowledge.

Exercise 7

Present Perfect / Present Perfect Continuous
1.Robin: I think the waiter (forget) .... us. We (wait)....... here for over half an hour and nobody
(take) .... our order yet.
Michele: I think you're right. He (walk) ..... by us at least twenty times. He probably thinks we (order,
already) ....
Robin: Look at that couple over there, they (be, only) ..... here for five or ten minutes and they already
have their food.
Michele: He must realize we (order, not) .... yet! We (sit) .... here for over half an hour staring at him.
Robin: I don't know if he (notice, even) .... He (run)............. from table to table taking
orders and serving food.
Michele: That's true, and he (look, not) .... in our direction once.

Exercise 8

Present Perfect / Present Perfect Continuous
1. A: How long (be) .... in Canada?
B: I (study) .... here for more than three years.
2. I (have) .... the same car for more than ten years. I'm thinking about buying a new one.
3. I (love) ....chocolate since I was a child. You might even call me a "chocoholic".
4. Matt and Sarah (have) .... some difficulties in their relationship lately, so they (go)

.... to a marriage counselor. I hope they work everything out.
5. John (work) .... for the government since he graduated from Harvard University. Until
recently, he (enjoy) .... his work, but now he is talking about retiring.
6. Lately, I (think) .... about changing my career because I (become) .... dissatisfied
with the conditions at my company.
7. I (see)............ Judy for more than five years and during that time I have (see) .... many
changes in her personality.

Exercise 9

Present Continuous / Present Perfect Continuous
1. It (rain) .... all week. I hope it stops by Saturday because I want to go to the
beach.
2. A: Where is Gary?
B: He (study, at the library) .... for his German test on Wednesday. In fact, he
(review) .... for the test every day for the last week.
3. You look really great! (You, exercise) .... at the fitness center ?
4. Frank, where have you been? We (wait) .... for you since 1 P.M..
5. A: What is that sound?
B: A car alarm (ring) .... somewhere down the street. It (drive)............. me crazy - I wish it
would stop! It (ring) .... for more than twenty minutes.
6. Joseph's English (improve, really) ...., isn't it? He (watch) .... American television
programs and (study) .... his grammar every day since he first arrived in San Diego. Soon he
will be totally fluent.
7. A: You look a little tired. (You, get) .... enough sleep lately?
B: Yes, I (sleep) .... relatively well. I just look tired because I (feel) .... a little sick for the
last week.

A: I hope you feel better soon.
B: Thanks. I (take, currently) .... some medicine, so I should feel better in a couple of days.

Exercise 10

Present Continuous / Present Perfect Continuous
Mr. Smith: So tell me a little bit about yourself, Mr. Harris. I would like to find out a little bit more
about your background.
Mr. Harris: I (work) .... in the insurance industry for over ten years. I worked for Met Life
for six years and World Insurance for four and a half. During that time, I heard many good things
about Hollings Life Insurance and that's why I (apply) ....for the new sales position.
Mr. Smith: Tell me a little about your hobbies and interests.
Mr. Harris: In my spare time, I hike in the mountains outside of town, volunteer at the Sierra Club and
play tennis. In fact, I (compete) .... in a tennis tournament this weekend.
Mr. Smith: Really, how long (you, play) .... tennis ?
Mr. Harris: I (play) .... since high school. I love the sport.
Mr. Smith: Great! We like dedication here at Hollings Life. You mentioned you volunteer at the Sierra
Club. I (work, currently) .... with them on the sea turtle project. We (try)
............to create a wildlife sanctuary near the bay.
Mr. Harris: Do you know Frank Harris? He's my brother. He (work, presently) ....
on the same project.
Mr. Smith: I know Frank quite well. Any brother of Frank's would be a welcome addition to Hollings
Life. Just one more thing, we (look) ....for somebody who is fluent in Spanish; many of our clients
are from Mexico.
Mr. Harris: No problem. I (study) .... Spanish since elementary school.
Mr. Smith: Sounds like you are the perfect candidate.

Exercise 11

Simple Past / Past Perfect
I can't believe I (get) ....that apartment. I (submit) .... my application last week, but I
didn't think I had a chance of actually getting it. When I (show) .... up to take a look around,
there were at least twenty other people who (arrive) .... before me. Most of them (fill, already)
.... out their applications and were already leaving. The landlord said I could still apply,
so I did. I (try) .... to fill out the form, but I couldn't answer half of the questions. They
(want) .... me to include references, but I didn't want to list my previous landlord because I
(have) .... some problems with him and I knew he wouldn't recommend me. I (end) .... up
listing my father as a reference. It was total luck that he (decide) .... to give me the apartment.
It turns out that the landlord and my father (go) .... to high school together. He decided that I
could have the apartment before he (look) ....at my credit report. I really lucked out!

Exercise 12

Simple Past / Present Perfect / Past Perfect
1. When I (arrive) .... home last night, I discovered that Jane (prepare) .... a
beautiful candle-lit dinner.
2. Since I began acting, I (perform) .... in two plays, a television commercial and a
TV drama. However, I (speak, never even) .... publicly before I came to Hollywood in 1985.
3. By the time I got to the office, the meeting (begin, already) .... without me. My
boss (be) .... furious with me and I (be) .... fired.

4. When I (turn) .... the radio on yesterday, I (hear) .... a song that
was popular when I was in high school. I (hear, not) ....he song in years, and it (bring)
.............back some great memories.
5. Last week, I (run) .... into an ex-girlfriend of mine. We (see, not) ....
each other in years, and both of us (change) .... a great deal. I (enjoy) ....
talking to her so much that I (ask) .... her out on a date. We are getting together tonight for dinner.
6. When Jack (enter) .... the room, I (recognize, not) .... him beКуприна
P. H. 6
cause he (lose) ....so much weight and (grow) .... a beard. He looked totally different!
7. The Maya established a very advanced civilization in the jungles of the Yucatan; however, their
culture (disappear, virtually) .... by the time Europeans first (arrive)
.... in the New World.
8. I (visit) .... so many beautiful places since I (come) .... to Utah. Before
moving here, I (hear, never) .... of Bryce Canyon, Zion, Arches or Canyonlands.

Exercise 13

Past Perfect / Past Perfect Continuous
I'm sorry I left without you last night, but I told you to meet me early because the show started at
8:00. I (try) .... to get tickets for that play for months, and I didn't want to miss it. By the
time I finally left the coffee shop where we were supposed to meet, I (have) .... five cups of coffee
and I (wait) .... over an hour. I had to leave because I (arrange) .... to meet Kathy in
front of the theater.

When I arrived at the theater, Kathy (pick, already) .... up the tickets and she was waiting

for us near the entrance. She was really angry because she (wait) .... for more than half an hour.

She said she (give, almost) .... up and (go) ....into the theater without us.

Kathy told me you (be) .... late several times in the past and that she would not make plans with

you again in the future. She mentioned that she (miss) .... several movies because of your late arrivals.

I think you owe her an apology. And in the future, I suggest you be on time! several movies

because of your late arrivals. I think you owe her an apology.

Exercise 14

Present Perfect / Past Perfect

Present Perfect Continuous / Past Perfect Continuous

1. It is already 9:30 pm and I (wait) ....here for over an hour. If John does not get here in the

next five minutes, I am going to leave.

2. I was really angry at John yesterday. By the time he finally arrived, I (wait) .... for over

an hour. I almost left without him.

3. Did you hear that Ben was fired last month? He (work) .... for that import company for

more than ten years and he (work) ....in almost every department. Nobody knew the company

like he did.

4. I (see) .... many pictures of the pyramids before I went to Egypt. Pictures of the monuments

are verymisleading. The pyramids are actually quite small.

5. Sarah (climb) .... the Matterhorn, (sail) ....around the world, and (go) .... on

safari in Kenya. She is such an adventurous person.

6. Sarah (climb) .... the Matterhorn, (sail) ....around the world and (go) .... on

safari in Kenya by the time she turned twenty-five. She (experience) .... more by that age than most people do in their entire lives.

7. When Melanie came into the office yesterday, her eyes were red and watery. I think she (cry)

.....

Exercise 15

Present Continuous / Simple Past

Present Perfect Continuous / Past Perfect Continuous

My English is really getting better. I (try) .... to learn the language since 1985, but only recently

have I been able to make some real progress. By the time I started high school in 1988, I (study)

.... the language for almost three years; however, I was only able to introduce myself and utter

a few memorized sentences. For a couple more years, I (struggle) ....through grammar and vocabulary

lessons, which made absolutely no difference. Nothing worked, so I decided to study abroad.

I found an exchange program in England that sounded like the perfect answer. I (stay) ....

with a host family for one month. It was a huge disappointment! I (sit) .... there the whole

time staring at the host mother and father hoping that there would be some breakthrough. Nothing.

When I returned, I mentioned to a friend that I (have) .... problems with the language for years.

He recommended that I spend a year in an English speaking country. I decided to go abroad again. I

(research) .... exchange programs for a couple of weeks and finally decided on a school in the

Куприна Р. Н. 7

United States.

Well, it worked. I (live) .... and (study) .... in the U.S. for more than two years. I (stay)

.... here for at least another year before I return home. By then, I should be completely fluent.

Exercise 16

Present and Past Tenses
and Non-Continuous Verbs
1.a. Look, I (have) .... two tickets for the circus.
1.b. Look, I (hold) .... two tickets for the circus.
2.a. We (be) .... there for more than half an hour by the time the show began.
2.b. We (wait) .... there for more than half an hour by the time the show began.
3.a. Sam (sit) .... in the seat next to me when the clown threw a bucket of water at me.
3.b. Sam (be) .... in the seat next to me when the clown threw a bucket of water at me.
4.a. One clown was juggling while he (balance) .... a glass of wine on his head.
4.b. One clown was juggling while he (have) .... a glass of wine on his head.
5.a. I (love) .... the circus ever since I was a child.
5.b. I (go) .... to the circus ever since I was a child.
6.a. Right now, I (see) .... two elephants doing tricks in the ring.
6.b. Right now, I (look) .... at two elephants doing tricks in the ring.

Exercise 17

Present and Past Tense Review
Lars: Excuse me, which movie are you waiting for?
Tony: We (wait) .... for the new Stars Wars Phantom Menace movie. In fact, we
(wait) .... here for more than five hours.
Lars: Five hours? When did you arrive?
Tony: We (get) got here at 6:00 o'clock this morning. More than forty people (stand,already)
.... here waiting for tickets when we arrived.
Lars: I can't believe that! Are you serious?
Tony: Yeah, people (take) .... Star Wars movies seriously. In fact, this particular

showing has been sold out for over a week. We (wait, just) .... in line to get a good
seat in the theater.
Lars: When did you buy your tickets?
Tony: I (buy) .... them last week by phone. I (know) .... tickets
would be hard to get because I (hear) .... on the news that a group of people in Los
Angeles (wait) .... in line for almost a month to buy some.
Lars: I don't believe that!
Tony: It's true. They (camp) .... out in front of Mann's Chinese Theater in Los Angeles
for about a month because they (want) .... to be the first people to see the
movie.

Exercise 18

Will / Be Going to
1. A: Why are you holding a piece of paper?
B: I (write) .... a letter to my friends back home in Texas.
2. A: I'm about to fall asleep. I need to wake up!
B: I (get) .... you a cup of coffee. That will wake you up.
3. A: I can't hear the television!
B: I (turn) .... it up so you can hear it.
4. We are so excited about our trip next month to France. We (visit) .... Paris, Nice and Grenoble.
5. Sarah (come) .... to the party. Oliver (be)........... there as well.
6. A: It is so hot in here!
B: I (turn) .... the air conditioning on.
7. I think he (be) .... the next President of the United States.
8. After I graduate, I (attend)....... medical school and become a doctor. I have wanted to be a doctor
all my life.
Куприна Р. Н. 8
9. A: Excuse me, I need to talk to someone about our hotel room. I am afraid it is simply too small for

four people.

B: That man at the service counter (help) .... you.

10. As soon as the weather clears up, we (walk) .... down to the beach and go swimming.

Exercise 19

Will / Be Going to

1.Mark: What are you doing with those scissors?

Beth: I (cut) .... that picture of the ocean out of the travel magazine.

Mark: What (you, do) .... with it?

Beth: I (paint) .... a water color of the ocean for my art class, and I thought I could use this

photograph as a model.

2. Mark: (You, do) .... me a favor Sam?

Sam: Sure, what do you want me to do?

Mark: I (change) .... the broken light bulb in the lamp above the dining room table. I need

someone to hold the ladder for me while I am up there.

Sam: No problem, I (hold) .... it for you.

3. Gina: Where are you going?

Ted: I (go) .... to the store to pick up some groceries.

Gina: What (you, get) ....?

Ted: I (buy) .... some milk, some bread, and some coffee.

4. John: Wow, it's freezing out there.

Jane: I (make) .... some coffee to warm us up. Do you want a piece of pie as well?

John: Coffee sounds great! But I (have) ...... dinner with some friends later, so I'd better skip the pie.

Jane: I (go) .... to dinner tonight too, but I'm having a piece of pie anyway.

5. Frank: I heard you're taking a Spanish class at the community college.

Tom: Yeah, I (go) .... to Guatemala next spring and I thought knowing a little Spanish would

make the trip easier.

Frank: I (visit) .... my brother in Marseilles next year. Maybe I should take a French class.

Tom: I have a course catalog in the other room. I (go) .... get it, and we can see whether or

not they're offering a French course next semester.

Exercise 20

Will / Be Going to

1. Michael: Do you think the Republicans or the Democrats (win) .... the next election?

Jane: I think the Republicans (win) .... the next election.

John: No way! The Democrats (win) ....

2. Susan: We (go) .... camping this weekend. Would you like to come along?

Sam: That sounds great, but I don't have a sleeping bag.

Susan: No problem. I (lend) .... you one. My family has tons of camping gear.

3. Barbara: I (buy) .... a new car this weekend, but I'm a little worried because I don't

really know much about cars. I'm afraid the salesman (try) .... to take advantage of me when he sees how little I know.

Dave: I used to work for a mechanic in high school and I know a lot about cars. I (go) .... with you to make sure you are not cheated.

4. Gina: Fred and I (visit) .... Santa Fe next summer. Have you ever been there?

Margaret: My family lives in Santa Fe! I (give) .... you my parents' phone number. When

you get to Santa Fe, just call them and they (give) .... you a little tour of the town. They can

show you some of the sights that most tourists never see.

5. Pam: Can you see my future in the crystal ball? What (happen) .... next year?

Fortune Teller: You (meet) .... a man from the East Coast, perhaps New York or maybe

Boston. You (marry) .... that mystery man.

Pam: Forget the man! I want to know if I (get) .... a new job.

Exercise 21

Simple Present / Simple Future

1. Today after I (get).... out of class, I (go) .... to a movie with some friends.

2. When you (arrive) .... in Stockholm, call my friend Gustav. He (show)......... you around the
city and help you get situated.

3. A: Do you know what you want to do after you (graduate) ....?
B: After I (receive) .... my Master's from Georgetown University, I (go) .... to graduate
school at UCSD in San Diego. I (plan).......... to complete a Ph.D. in cognitive science.

4. If it (snow) .... this weekend, we (go) .... skiing near Lake Tahoe.

5. Your father (plan) .... to pick you up after school today at 3:00 o'clock. He (meet).................
you across the street near the ice cream shop. If something happens and he cannot be there, I
(pick)............. you up instead.

6. If the people of the world (stop, not) .... cutting down huge stretches of rain forest, we (experience)...............
huge changes in the environment during the twenty-first century.

7. If Vera (keep) .... drinking, she (lose, eventually) .... her job.

8. I promise you that I (tell, not) .... your secret to anybody. Even if somebody
(ask)............. me about what happened that day, I (reveal, not)........ the truth to a single person.

9. She (make) .... some major changes in her life. She (quit)........................ her job and go
back to school. After she (finish) .... studying, she (get)............ a better paying job and buy a
house. She is going to improve her life!

10. Tom (call) .... when he (arrive) .... in Madrid. He (stay).......... with you for two or
three days until his new apartment (be) .... available.

Exercise 22

Simple Present / Simple Future

1. Michael: After you (leave) .... work, will you please drop by the grocery store and pick up some milk.

Marie: No problem, I (pick) .... up the groceries and be home by 6 o'clock.

Michael: Great. You will probably get home before I (do) ....

2. Ari: By the time we (get) .... to the movie theater, the tickets are going to be sold out.

Sarah: Don't worry. I told Jane we might be arriving just before the movie (start) .... She (buy)

.... our tickets and meet us in the lobby.

Ari: That place is huge! We (find, never) .... her in that crowded lobby.

Sarah: Calm down, we (meet) .... each other near the entrance.

3. Terry: If the weather (be) .... good tomorrow, we will go to the beach.

Jennifer: I have a better idea. If it (be) .... nice out, we'll go to the beach; and if it (rain)...........,

we'll see a movie.

Terry: I guess we will have to wait until we (get) .... up in the morning to find out what we are going

to do.

3. Max: What are you going to do tomorrow after work?

Sean: I (meet) .... some friends at the cafe across the street. Would you like to come along?

Max: No thanks! My brother is coming to town and I (pick) ....him up from the airport at 7

o'clock.

Sean: We (be, probably) .... at the cafe until 9 o'clock. Why don't you join us after you (pick)

.... him up.

Max: Sounds good. We (see) .... you around 8 o'clock.

5. Lucy: I (call) .... you as soon as I arrive in Dublin.

Dwain: If I am not there when you (call) ...., make sure to leave a message.

Lucy: I will. And please don't forget to water my plants and feed the cat.

Dwain: I promise I (take) .... care of everything while you are in Ireland.

Exercise 23

Simple Future / Future Continuous

1. Sandra: Where is Tim going to meet us?

Marcus: He (wait) .... for us when our train arrives. I am sure he (stand) .... on the platform when we pull into the station.

Sandra: And then what?

Marcus: We (pick) .... Michele up at work and go out to dinner.

2. Ted: When we get to the party, Jerry (watch) .... TV, Sam (make).......... ... drinks, Beth

(dance) ....by herself, and Thad (complain) .... about his day at work.

Robin: Maybe, this time they won't be doing the same things.

Ted: I am absolutely positive they (do) .... the same things; they always do the same things.

3. Florence: Oh, look at that mountain of dirty dishes! Who (wash) ....all of those?

Jack: I promise I (do) .... them when I get home from work.

Florence: Thanks.

Jack: When you get home this evening, that mountain will be gone and nice stacks of sparkling clean

dishes (sit) .... in the cabinets.

4 .Doug: If you need to contact me next week, I (stay) .... at the Hoffman Hotel.

Nancy: I (call) .... you if there are any problems.

Doug: This is the first time I have ever been away from the kids.

Nancy: Don't worry, they (be) .... fine.

5. Samantha: Just think, next week at this time, I (lie) .... on a tropical beach in Maui drinking

Mai Tai's and eating pineapple.

Darren: While you are luxuriating on the beach, I (stress) .... out over this marketing project.

How are you going to enjoy yourself knowing that I am working so hard.

Samantha: I 'll manage somehow.

Darren: You're terrible. Can't you take me with you?

Samantha: No. But I (send) .... you a postcard of a beautiful, white-sand beach.

Darren: Great, that (make) .... me feel much better.

Exercise 24

Simple Present / Simple Future
Present Continuous / Future Continuous
1. Right now I am watching T.V. Tomorrow at this time, I (watch) .... T.V. as well.
2. Tomorrow after school, I (go) .... to the beach.
3. I am going on a dream vacation to Tahiti. While you (do) .... paperwork and (talk) ....to
annoying customers on the phone, I (lie) .... on a sunny, tropical beach. Are you jealous?
4. We (hiding) .... when Tony (arrives) .... at his surprise party. As soon as he opens
the door, we (jump) .... out and (scream) ...."Surprise!"
5. We work out at the fitness center everyday after work. If you (come) ....over while we
(work) ....out, we will not be able to let you into the house. Just to be safe, we (leave) .... a
key under the welcome mat so you will not have to wait outside.
6. While you (study) .... at home, Magda (be) ....in class.
7. When I (get) ....to the party, Sally and Doug (dance) ....,
John (make) ....drinks,
Sue and Frank (discuss) .... something controversial, and Mary (complain) .... about
something unimportant. They are always doing the same things. They are so predictable.
8. When you (got) .... off the plane, I (wait) .... for you.
9. I am sick of rain and bad weather! Hopefully, when we (wake) .... up tomorrow morning,
the sun (shine) ....
10. If you (need) ..... to contact me sometime next week, I (stay) ...... at the Sheraton in San Francisco.

Exercise 25

Future Perfect / Future Perfect Continuous
1. Margaret: Do you think everything will be finished when I get back from the store?
Jerry: Don't worry. By the time you get back, I (pick) .... up the living room and (finish)

...........washing the dishes. Everything will be perfect when your parents arrive.

Margaret: I hope so. They (arrive) .... around 6 o'clock.

Jerry: Everything (be) .... spotless by the time they get here.

2. Nick: I just have two more courses before I graduate from university. By this time next year, I

(graduate) ....and I will already be looking for a job.

Stacey: Does that scare you? Are you worried about the future?

Куприна Р. Н. 11

Nick: Not really. I (go) .... to a career counselor and get some advice on how to find a good job.

Stacey: That's a good idea.

Nick: I am also going to do an internship so that when I leave school, I (complete, not, only) ....

over 13 business courses, but I (work, also) ....the real world.

3. Stan: Did you hear that Christine (take) .... a vacation in South America this winter?

Fred: I can't believe how often she goes abroad. Where exactly does she want to go?

Stan: She (visit) ....Peru, Bolivia and Ecuador.

Fred: At this rate, she (visit) .... every country in the world by the time she's 50.

4. Judy: How long have you been in Miami?

Elaine: I have only been here for a couple of weeks.

Judy: How long do you plan on staying?

Elaine: I love Miami, so I (stay) ....here for an extended period of time. When I go back home, I

(be) .... here for more than three months.

Judy: Wow, that's quite a vacation! You (see, definitely) .... just about everything there is to see

in Miami by then.

5. Jane: I can't believe how late we are! By the time we get to the dinner, everyone (finish) ...... eating.

Jack: It's your own fault. You took way too long in the bathroom.

Jane: I couldn't get my hair to look right.

Jack: Who cares? By the time we get there, everyone (left).........Nobody (see,ever)..... . your hair.

Exercise 26

Future Perfect / Future Perfect Continuous
1. By the time we get to Chicago this evening, we (drive) .... more than four hundred miles. We are
going to be exhausted.
2. When Sarah goes on vacation next month, she (study) .... German for over two years. She
should be able to communicate fairly well while she is in Austria.
3. I have not traveled much yet; however, I (visit)............. the Grand Canyon and San Francisco by the
time I leave the United States.
4. By the time you finish studying the verb tense tutorial, you (master)..... all twelve tenses including
their passive forms.
5. Drive faster! If you don't hurry up, she (have) .... the baby by the time we get to the hospital.
6. I came to England six months ago. I started my economics course three months ago. When I return
to Australia, I (study) .... for nine months and I (be) .... in England for exactly one year.
7. Margie just called and said she would be here at 8:00 o'clock. By the time she gets here, we
(wait)................. for her for two hours.
8. Frank just changed jobs again. If he keeps this up, he (change) .... jobs at least four or five
times by the end of the year.
9. Come over to my house around 9 o'clock. By then, I (complete) .... my history essay and we
can go see a movie.
10. In June, my grandmother and grandfather (be) .... married
for fifty years.

Exercise 27

Future Perfect / Future Perfect Continuous
1. Jack: Have you been watching the Eco-Challenge on TV?
Janet: Isn't that exciting? It has got to be the most unbelievably difficult sporting event in the world.

Jack: I know. By the time they finish the course, they (raft) .... more than 150 miles down a

raging river, (hike) .... through 80 miles of jungle, (climb) .... a volcano and (kayak)

.... through shark-infested waters.

Janet: And don't forget that they (move) .... for at least eight days straight.

2. Oliver: When are going to get your Bachelor degree, Anne?

Anne: I am going to finish my degree next June. By the time I graduate, I (go) .... to four different

colleges and universities, and I (study) .... for more than seven years.

Oliver: Wow, that's a long time!

Anne: And I plan to continue on to get a Ph.D.

Oliver: Really? How long is that going to take?

Anne: By the time I finally finish studying, I (be) .... a student for over 13 years.

3. Max: Sarah has been in the kitchen all day long.

Jake: It doesn't sound like she's having a very good Thanksgiving.

Max: She (cook) .... for over seven hours by the time everyone arrives for dinner this afternoon.

Hopefully, she (finish) .... everything by then.

Jake: Maybe we should help her out.

4. Mike: It's 6:00, and I have been working on my essay for over three hours.

Sid: Do you think you (finish) .... by 10:00. There's a party at Donna's tonight.

Mike: I (complete, probably) .... the essay by 10:00, but I (work) .... on it for more

than seven hours and I don't think I am going to feel like going to a party.

5. Fred: By the time they finish their trip across Yosemite National Park, they (hike) .... for more

than six days.

Ginger: And they (be, not) in a bed or (have) .... a shower in almost a week!

Fred: When we pick them up, they (eat) ....camping food for days, and I am sure they will be

starving.

Ginger: I think we had better plan on taking them directly to a restaurant.

Exercise 28

Future Continuous / Future Perfect Continuous

1.Simona: Margaret is really going to speak Spanish well when she gets back from that language school

in Mexico?

Isabelle: Hopefully! She (take) .... classes for more than six months.

Simona: She is going to be able to speak Spanish with some of our Latin American clients.

Isabelle: Good. Two clients from Peru (visit) .... us next month when Margaret returns. We

need someone to entertain them while they are here.

2. Jason: I am leaving!

Nurse: If you would please wait, the doctor will be with you in ten minutes. The doctor is having

some problems with a patient.

Jason: The doctor was having problems with that patient an hour ago. If I wait another ten minutes, I

am sure he (have, still) .... problems with her. By the time he's finally ready to see me, I

(wait) .... for more than two hours.

3. Frank: What are you going to be doing tomorrow at five?

Debbie: I (paint) .... painting my living room walls.

Frank: Still? How long have you been working on your living room.

Debbie: Forever. By the time I finish, I (redecorate) .... the living room for over a week.

Frank: Bad. I was going to ask go if you wanted to see a movie. What about the day after tomorrow?

Debbie: Sorry, I (move) .... furniture and (put) .... up drapes.

4. Mr. Jones: What are you going to be doing next year at this time?

Mr. McIntyre: I (work) .... for a big law firm in New Orleans.

Mr. Jones: I didn't know you were leaving Baton Rouge.

Mr. McIntyre: I got a great job offer which I just can't refuse. Besides, by the time I move, I (live)

...................in Baton Rouge for over twenty years. I think it's about time for a change.

Exercise 29

Cumulative Verb Tense Review

1. You look really great! (You, exercise) .... at the fitness center?
2. A: What (you, do) ....when the accident occurred?

B: I (try) ....to change a light bulb that had burnt out.

3. I (have) .... the same car for more than ten years. I'm thinking about buying a new one.
4. If it (snow) .... this weekend, we (go) .... skiing near Lake Tahoe.
5. A: What do you call people who work in libraries?

B: They (call) .... librarians.

6. I came to England six months ago. I started my economics course three months ago. When I return

Куприна Р. Н. 13

to Australia, I (study) .... for nine months and I (be) .... England for exactly one year.

7. Sam (arrive) .... in San Diego a week ago.
8. Samantha (live) .... in Berlin for more than two years. In fact, she (live) .... there

when the Berlin wall came down.

9. If Vera (keep) .... drinking, she (lose, eventually) .... her job.
10. The Maya established a very advanced civilization in the jungles of the Yucatan; however, their

culture (disappear, virtually) .... by the time Europeans first (arrive) .... in the New World.

11. Shhhhh! Be quiet! John (sleep) ....
12. It (rain) .... all week. I hope it stops by Saturday because I want to go to the beach.
13. Listen Donna, I don't care if you (miss) .... the bus this morning. You (be) .... late to

work too many times. You are fired!

14. I am sick of rain and bad weather! Hopefully, when we (wake) .... up tomorrow morning,

the sun (shine) ....

15. I have not traveled much yet; however, I (visit) .... the Grand Canyon and San Francisco
by the time I leave the United States.
16. I (see) .... many pictures of the pyramids before I went to Egypt. Pictures of the monuments
are very misleading. The pyramids are actually quite small.
17. In the last hundred years, traveling (become) .... much easier and very comfortable. In the
19th century, it (take) .... two or three months to cross North America by covered wagon. The
trip (be) ....very rough and often dangerous. Things (change) .... a great deal in the last
hundred and fifty years. Now you can fly from New York to Los Angeles in a matter of hours.
18. Joseph's English (improve, really) ...., isn't it? He (watch) ....American television programs
and (study) .... his grammar every day since he first arrived in San Diego. Soon he will
be totally fluent.
19. When I (arrive) .... home last night, I discovered that Jane (prepare) .... a beautiful candle-lit
dinner.
20. If you (need) ....contact me sometime next week, I (stay) ....at the Sheraton in San
Francisco.

Exercise 30

Cumulative Verb Tense Review
1. When Carol (call) .... last night, I (watch) ....my favorite show on television.
2. I (work) .... for this company for more than thirty years, and I intend to stay here until I retire!
3. Sharon (love) ....to travel. She (go) .... abroad almost every summer. Next year, she
plans to go to Peru.
4. Thomas is an author. He (write) .... mystery novels and travel memoirs. He (write) .... since

he was twenty-eight. Altogether, he (write) .... seven novels, three collections of short stories.

5. We were late because we had some car problems. By the time we (get) ....to the train station,

Susan (wait) ....for us for more than two hours.

6. Sam (try) .... to change a light bulb when he (slip) .... and (fell) ....

7. Everyday I (wake) .... up at 6 o'clock, (eat) .... breakfast at 7 o'clock and (leave)

.... for work at 8 o'clock. However, this morning I (get) .... up at 6:30, (skip) .... breakfast

and (leave) ....for work late because I (forget) .... to set my alarm.

8. Right now, Jim (read) .... the newspaper and Kathy (make) ....dinner. Last night at

this time, they (do) ....the same thing. She (cook) .... and he (read) .... the newspaper.

Tomorrow at this time, they (do, also) .... the same thing. She (prepare) .... dinner and he

(read) .... They are very predictable people!

9. By this time next summer, you (complete) ....your studies and (find) ....a job. I, on

the other hand, (accomplish, not) .....anything. I (study, still) ......and you (work) ......in some new job.

10. The students (be, usually) ....taught byMrs. Monty. However, this week they (be) ..... taught by

Mr. Tanzer.

11. Jane talks on the phone.

Bob has been talking on the phone for an hour.

Mary is talking on the phone.

Who is not necessarily on the phone now? ....

Куприна Р. Н. 14

12. I'm going to make dinner for Frank.

I'm making dinner for Judy.

I'll make dinner for Mary.

I make dinner for Ted.

I will be making dinner for Tony.

Who are you offering to make dinner for? ....

13. Jane left when Tim arrived.

Bob left when Tim had arrived.

Tim arrived when Mary was leaving.
John had left when Tim arrived.
After Tim arrived, Frank left.
Who did not run into Tim? ....
14. Jane is talking in class.
Bob always talks in class.
Mary is always talking in class.
Whose action bothers you? ....
15. Jane never left Jamestown.
Bob has never left Jamestown.
Who is still alive? ....

Overview

Simple Present Simple Past Simple Future
I study English everyday. Two years ago, I studied English
in England.
I am going to study English next year.
If you are having problems, I will
help you study English.
Present Continuous Past Continuous Future Continuous
I am studying English now.
I was studying English when you
called yesterday.
I will be studying English when you arrive tonight.
Present Perfect Past Perfect Future Perfect
I have studied English in several different countries.
I had studied a little English before
I moved to the U.S.
I will have studied every tense by the time I finish this course.
Present Perfect
Continuous Past Perfect Continuous Future Perfect Continuous
I have been studying English for five years.
I had been studying English for five years before I moved to the U.S.
I will have been studying English
for over two hours by the time you arrive.

.

4. Extended Activities

A. Tenses

Tenses: Present Simple vs. Present Continuous
1.	Put the verb into the correct tense form:
1.	Julia is very good at languages. She .... (speak) 4 languages fluently.
2.	Hurry up! Everybody .... (wait) for you.
3.	a. .... (you/listen) to the radio?
	b. No, you can turn it off.
4.	a. .... (you/listen) to the radio everyday?
	b. No, just occasionally.
5.	The River Nile .... (flow) into the Mediterranean.
6.	a. How's your English?
	b. Not bad. It .... (improve) slowly.
7.	a. Can you drive?
	b. I .... (learn). My father .... (teach) me.
8.	My parents .... (live) in Bristol. Where .... (your parents / live)?
9.	Sonia .... (look) for a place to live. She .... (stay) with her sister until she finds a flat.
10.	Usually I .... (enjoy) parties, but I .... (not/enjoy) this one very much.
11. I must go now. It .... (get) late.
12.	Can you hear those people? What .... (they/talk) about?

2.	Put the verb into the correct tense form:
	1.	Are you hungry? .... (you/want) something to eat?

2.   Jill is interested in politics but she .... (not/belong) to a political party.

3.   Don't put the dictionary away. I .... (use) it.

4.   Don't put the dictionary away. I .... (need) it

5.   Who's that man? What .... (he/want)?

6.   Who's that man? Why .... (he/look) at us?

7.   George says he is 45 years old but nobody .... (believe) him.

8.   She told me her name but I .... (not/remember) it now.

9.   I .... (think) of selling my car. .... (you/want) to buy it ?

10.   I think you should sell your car. You .... (not/use) it very often.

11. I used to drink a lot of coffee but these days I .... (prefer) tea.

12.   Air .... (consist) mainly of nitrogen and oxygen.

Tenses: Present Perfect vs. Simple Past

3.   Put the verb into the correct tense form:

1.   a. Where's your key?
        b. I don't know. I .... (lose) it.

2.   I did German at school but I .... (forget) most of it.

3.   I meant to phone Diane last night but I .... (forget) it.

4.   I .... (have) a headache earlier but I feel fine now.

5.   Look, there's an ambulance over there. There .... (be) an accident.

6.   The police .... (arrest) three people but later they let them go.

7.   Where's my bike? I .... (leave) it outside the house but now it .... (disappear)!

8.   Oh, I .... (cut) my finger! It's bleeding.

9.   My parents .... (get) married in London last spring.

10.   Mary is not at home. She .... (go) shopping.

11.   Your hair looks nice. .... (you/have) a haircut?

12.   a. When is your birthday?
        b. I .... (be) born on June the 30th, 1970.

Tenses: Present and Future

4.   Put the verb into the correct tense form:

1.   Don't call me between 7 and 8. I .... (have) dinner. Call me after 8 o'clock. We .... (finish) dinner by then.

2.   a. Can we meet tomorrow noon time?
        b. No, I .... (work).

3.   If he continues like this, he .... (spend) all his money by the end of his holiday.

4.   Do you think you .... (still/do) the same job in ten years' time?

5.   If you need to contact me, I .... (stay) at Knightsbridge Hotel till Friday.

6.   I .... (call) you when I .... (get) back from work.

7.   We must do something soon before it .... (be) too late.

8.   Brian looks very different now. When you .... (see) him again, you .... (not/recognize) him.

9.   I don't want to go out with you. I .... (stay) at home until you .... (be) back.

10.   I am going for lunch. If anybody .... (phone) while I .... (be) out, can you take a message?

11.   I am truly offended. I .... (not/speak) to her until she .... (apologise).

12.   James is travelling around Europe. By the end of his trip, he .... (cover) a distance of 3,000 miles.

Tenses: Simple, Continuous and Perfective Aspect

5.   Put the verb into the correct tense form:

1.   a. What .... (you/do) this time yesterday?

                       b. I was asleep.

2.   a. .... (you/go) out last night?

       b. No, I was too tired.

3.   a. Was Carol at the party last night?

       b. Yes, she .... (wear) a really nice dress.

4.   How fast .... (you/drive) when the accident .... (happen)?

5.   John .... (take) a picture of me when I .... (look) away.

6.   I .... (walk) along the street when suddenly I .... (hear) footsteps behind me. Somebody .... (follow) me. I was frightened and I .... (start) to run.

7.   When I was young, I .... (want) to be a bus driver.

8.   You look tired. .... (you/work) hard?

9.   I .... (lose) my address book. .... (you/see) it anywhere?

10. I .... (read) the book you lent me but I .... (not/finish) it yet.

11.   a. Sorry I'm late.

       b. That's alright. I .... (not/wait) long.

12. a. .... (you/ever/work) in a factory?

       b. No, never.

6.   Put the verb into the correct tense form:

          1.   a. Was Tom at the party when you arrived?

       b. No, he .... (go) home.

2.   I felt very tired when I got home, so I .... (go) straight to bed.

3.   The house was very quiet when I got home. Everyone .... (go) to bed.

4.   Sorry I'm late. The car .... (break) down on my way here.

5.   We were driving along the road when we
.... (see) a car which
.... (break) down, so we
.... (stop) to see if we could help.
6.   It was very noisy next door. Our neighbours
.... (have) a party.
7.   John and I went for a walk. I had difficulty keeping up with him because he .... (walk) so fast.
8.   When I arrived for dinner, their mouths were empty but their stomachs were full. They .... (already/eat).
9.   I was sad when I sold my car. I ....
(have) it for years.
10.   We were extremely tired at the end of the trip. We
.... (travel) for 24 hours.
11.   Mary was out of breath, sitting on the ground. She
.... (run).
            12.   Jim was on his hands and knees on the floor. He
.... (look) for his contact lens.

Tenses: Recap Drills
7.   Put the verb into the correct tense form:
1.   We can go out now. It .... (not/rain) any more.
2.   Ann .... (wait) for me when I
.... (arrive).
3.   I .... (get) hungry. Let's go and have something to eat.
4.   What .... (you/do) in your spare time? Have you got any hobbies?
5.   Mary usually .... (phone) me on Fridays but she .... (not phone) me last Friday.
6.   I'm looking for Paul. .... (you/see) him?
7.   a. When I last saw you, you .... (think) of moving to a new flat.
            b. That's right, but in the end I ....
(decide) to stay where I was.
8.   What is that noise? What .... (happen)?
9.   It's usually dry here at this time of the year. It
.... (not/rain) much.

10.   Yesterday evening, the phone .... (ring) three times while we .... (have) dinner.

11.   Linda was busy when we .... (go) to see her yesterday. She was .... (study) for an exam. We .... (not/want) to disturb her, so we .... (not stay) very long.

12.   When I first .... (tell) Tom the news, he .... (not/believe) me. He thought that I .... (joke).

8.   Put the verb into the correct tense form:
           1.   Everything is going well. We .... (not/have) any problems so far.

2.   Margaret .... (not/go) to work yesterday. She wasn't feeling well.

3.   Look! That man over there .... (wear) the same sweater as you.

4.   Your son is much taller than when I last saw him. He .... (grow) a lot.

5.   I still don't know what to do. I .... (not/decide) yet.

6.   I wonder why Jim .... (be) nice to me today. He isn't usually like that.

7.   Jane had a book open in front of her but she .... (not/read) it.

8.   When Sue heard the news, she .... (not/be) very pleased.

9.   This is a nice restaurant, isn't it? Is this the first time you .... (be) here?

10.   I need a new job. I .... (do) the same job for too long.

11. a. You look tired.
       b. Yes, I .... (play) basketball.

12.   Where .... (you/come) from? Are you British?

9.   Put the verb into the correct tense form:
1.   a. Where .... (you/go)?
        b. To the post office. I'll be back in a few minutes.

2.	a. Your house is very nice. How long ....
(you/live) here?
	b. Nearly ten years.
3.	a. .... (you/see) Julie recently?
	b. Yes, I met her a few days ago.
4.	a. Can you describe the woman you saw? What
.... (she/wear)?
	b. A red top and jeans.
5.	a. How long .... (it/take) you to get to
work in the morning?
	b. About 45 minutes.
6.	a. .... (you/finish) with the newspaper
yet?
	b. No, I'm still reading it.
7.	a. How well do you know Bill?
	b. Very well. We .... (know) each other
since we were kids.
8.	a. Did you enjoy your holiday?
	b. Yes, it's the best holiday I ....
(ever/have).
9.	a. Is Jack still here?
	b. No, he .... (leave) about ten minutes
ago.
10.	a. How did you cut your knee?
	b. I slipped and fell when I .... (play)
tennis.
11. a. How often do you go to the movies?
	b. Very rarely. It's nearly a year I ....
(not/be) to the cinema.
12. a. Do you like my new shoes?
	b. Yes, they're very nice. Where ....
(you/buy) them?

10.	Put the verb into the correct tense form:
1.	Who .... (invent) the bicycle?
2.	a. Do you still have a headache?
	b. No, it .... (go). I'm alright now.
3.	What .... (you/do) last weekend?
.... (you/go) away?

4.   We decided not to go because it .... (rain) quite hard.

5.   Jill is an experienced teacher. She .... (teach) for 15 years.

6.   I bought a new jacket last week but I .... (not/wear) it yet.

7.   A few days ago, I .... (see) a man at a party whose face .... (look) familiar. At first I couldn't think where I .... (see) him before. Then suddenly I remembered who he .... (be).

8.   .... (you/hear) of Agatha Christie? She was a writer who .... (die) in 1976. She .... (write) more than 70 novels. .... (read) any of them?

9.   a. What .... (this word / mean)?
        b. I've no idea. I .... (never/see) it before.

10.   I went to John's office and .... (knock) on the door but there .... (be) no answer. Either he .... (go) out or he .... (not/want) to see anyone.

11.   Angela asked me how to use the photocopier. She .... (never/use) it before, so she .... (not/know) what to do.

12.   Mary .... (go) for a swim after work yesterday. She .... (need) some exercise because she .... (sit) all day in front of her computer.

B. Conditionals / Passive Voice / Reported Speech

Conditionals

1.   Put the verb into the correct tense form:

1.   The accident was your fault. If you .... (drive) more carefully, it wouldn't have happened.

2.   a. Why do you read newspapers?
        b. Well, if I .... (not/read) newspapers, I wouldn't know what was happening in the world.

3.   If Liz .... (not/go) to bed so late, she wouldn't be tired all the time.
4.   I'd be surprised if Ann .... (come) to see us now.
5.   If I'd known you were busy, I .... (not/disturb) you.
6.   If you hadn't provoked the dog, it .... (not/attack) you.
7.   I wouldn't have got soaking wet, if I .... (have) an umbrella.
8.   If he hadn't been so nervous, he .... (not/fail) his driving test.
9.   I'd have gone out last night, if I .... (not/have) so much work to do.
10.   Cities would be nicer places, if they .... (be) cleaner.

2.   Put the verb into the correct tense form:
1.   Ken got to the airport in time for his flight. If he .... (miss) it, he .... (be) late for his interview.
2.   It's good that you reminded me about Ann's birthday. I .... (forget) it.
3.   I didn't have my address book in New York. Otherwise, I .... (send) you a postcard.
4.   a. Did you have a good time in Prague?
        b. We .... (enjoy) it more, if the weather .... (be) better.
5.   I'm not tired. If I .... (be) tired, I would go home now.
6.   I wasn't tired last night. If I .... (be) tired, I would have gone home earlier.
7.   If Jim .... (not/lend) me the money, I wouldn't have been able to buy the car.
8.   If Mary .... (not/wear) a seatbelt, she would have been severely injured in the car crash.
9.   If you had some breakfast, you .... (not/be) hungry now.

10.   If I .... (have) some money I
.... (get) a taxi, but unfortunately I've left my wallet at home.

3.   Put the verb into the correct tense form:
1.   If you .... (find) a wallet in the street, what would you do with it?
2.   I must hurry. My friend will be annoyed if I
.... (not/be) on time.
3.   I didn't realize that Gary was in hospital. If I
.... (know) that, I would have gone to visit him.
4.   If the phone .... (ring), can you answer it?
5.   I cannot decide what to do. What would you do if you
.... (be) in my position?
6.   a. What shall we do tomorrow?
        b. Well, if the weather .... (be) nice, we can go to the beach.
7.   a. Let's sit outside.
        b. No, it's too cold. If it .... (be) warmer, I wouldn't mind.
8.   a. Did you go for a picnic yesterday?
        b. No, it was too cold. If it .... (be) warmer, we might have gone.
9.   If you .... (have) enough money to go anywhere in the world, where would you go?
10.   I'm glad we had a map. I'm sure we would have got lost, if we
.... (not/have) one.

Passive Voice
4.   Put the verb into the correct passive form:
1.   There's somebody behind us. I think we
.... (follow).
2.   A mystery is something that ....
(can/not/explain).
3.   I've just called the airport. The flight ....
(cancel) due to adverse weather conditions.
4.   The television .... (fix) by magic! It's working again now.

5.   The painting .... (restore). The work is almost finished.
6.   If I didn't do my job properly, I .... (sack).
7.   After .... (arrest), I was taken to the police station.
8.   a. .... (you/ever/arrest)?
        b. No, never.
9.   Two people .... (report) to .... (injure) in explosion this morning.
10.   a. I cannot find the papers I left on my desk last night.
        b. Most probably, they .... (throw) away.

5.   Put the verb into the correct form, active or passive:
1.   This castle is quite old. It .... (build) over 400 years ago.
2.   My great-grandfather was a builder. He .... (build) this cottage over 80 years ago.
3.   a. Is your car still for sale?
        b. No, I .... (sell) it.
4.   a. Is this house still for sale?
        b. No, it .... (sell).
5.   Sometimes mistakes .... (make). It's inevitable.
6.   My bag has disappeared. It .... (must/steal).
7.   I cannot find my umbrella. Somebody .... (must/take) it by mistake.
8.   It's a serious problem. I don't know how it .... (can/solve).
9.   We didn't leave early enough. We .... (should/leave) earlier.
10.   A new bridge .... (build) across the river. Work started last year and the bridge .... (expect) to open next year.

6.   Put the verb into the correct form, active or passive:
1.   It's a big factory. Five hundred people .... (employ) there.

2.	Water .... (cover) most of Earth's surface.

3.	The park gates .... (lock) at 6:30 p.m. every evening.

4.	The boat .... (sink) quickly, but fortunately everyone .... (rescue).

5.	Ron's parents .... (die) when he was little. He .... (bring) up by his aunt and uncle.

6.	I was born in London, but I .... (grow) up in Manchester.

7.	My camera .... (disappear) from the hotel room while I was in the balcony.

8.	This company is a subsidiary. It .... (own) by a much larger company.

9.	I saw an accident last night. Somebody .... (call) an ambulance, but since no one .... (hurt) the ambulance .... (not/need).

10.	The e-mail .... (send) on Thursday, but for some weird reason it .... (arrive) only yesterday.

7.	Read the following announcements and put the verbs into the correct form, active or passive:

1.	Repair work started yesterday on the Birmingham-Leicester road. The road .... (resurface) and there will be long delays. Drivers .... (ask) to use an alternative route if possible. The work .... (expect) to last two weeks. Next Sunday, the road .... (close) and the traffic .... (divert).

2.	In Durham, yesterday, a salesgirl .... (force) to hand over 500 pounds after .... (threaten) by a man with a knife. The man escaped in a car which .... (steal) earlier in the day. A man .... (already/arrest) in connection with the robbery and two others .... (question) by the police.

Reported Speech
8.   Rewrite the sentences:
1.   a. It is expected that the strike will end soon.
        b. The strike

....

2.   a. It is expected that the weather will be good tomorrow.
        b. The weather

....

3.   a. It is believed that the thieves got in through the kitchen
window.
        b. The thieves

....

4.   a. It is thought that the prisoner escaped by climbing over the
wall.
        b. The prisoner

....

5.   a. It is alleged that the man was driving through the town at 90
miles an hour.
        b. The man

....

6.   a. It is reported that the building has been badly damaged by
the wildfire.
        b. The building

....

7.   a. It is said that the company is losing a lot of money.
        b. The company

....

8.   a. It is believed that the company lost a lot of money last year.
        b. The company

....

9.   Rewrite the sentences using reported speech:
1.   a. What does this word mean?
        b. I want to know

....

2.   a. What do you want?
        b. Tell me

....

3.   a. Where is the nearest bank?

b. Could you tell me

....

4.   a. What's the time?
        b. I wonder

....

5.   a. What time did your boss leave?
        b. Do you know

....

6.   a. Who's that woman?
        b. I have no idea

....

7.   a. How far is the airport?
        b. Can you tell me

....

8.   a. Do you have to pay to park here?
        b. Do you know

....

10.   Rewrite the sentences using reported speech:

1.   a. A beggar harassed me while I was having my coffee; I simply told him, "I don't have any money."

        b. A beggar harassed me while I was having my coffee, but I simply told him ....

2.   a. I was trying to plan today's meeting, all day yesterday, so I said to John, "Please let me know by some time tonight if   you are indeed coming. I need to fix the items on tomorrow's agenda."

        b. I was trying to plan today's meeting, all day yesterday, so I asked John ....
        because

....

3.   a. Mary is an awful driver. I asked her two months ago, "Why aren't you taking some lessons?". She answered back, "My schedule is very busy now. I promise to look for a driving school by the end of next week."

        b. Mary is an awful driver. I asked her two months ago
.... She

        answered .... but
promised ....

4.	a. I bumped into William last night. He told me, "I'm living in Bournemouth now. I'm enjoying my new flat very much. You can come and stay at my place whenever you fancy."

	b. I bumped into William last night. He told me
.... and
.... He also kindly told me ....

5.	a. William also told me, "I haven't seen Margaret for ages. Do you have any idea if she got married to the guy that she was dating at high school?"

	b. William also told me
.... and asked me
....

6.	a. I said to William, "Margaret has just had a baby. I saw her father the other day and he told me the good news."

	b. I said to William
.... I mentioned
....

7.	a. I also said to William, "I've heard Bob and Mary's car was stolen. They wanted to go on holiday but now they cannot afford it."

	b. I also said to William
.... I also noted
....

8.	a. William had recently visited New York. He told me, "New York is more lively than London. I said to him, "It is my dream to go to New York one day."

	b. William had recently visited New York. He told me
.... and I said to him
....

C. Modal Verbs / Gerund vs. Infinitive Forms / Relative Clauses

Modal Verbs (can / could / may / might / must / should / would / ought to)

1.	Complete the sentences using an appropriate modal verb together with the verb in brackets:

1.	a. I'm hungry.

b. But you've just had lunch. You .... (not/be) already hungry.

2.   Don't call Anne now. She .... (have) lunch.

3.   a. I haven't seen our neighbours for ages.

b. You're right. They .... (go) away.

4.   a. What's the weather like? Is it raining?

b. Not at the moment but it .... (rain) later.

5.   a. Where has Julia gone?

b. I'm not sure. She .... (go) to the bank.

6.   a. I didn't see you at John's party last week.

b. No, I had to work that evening, so I .... (not/go).

7.   a. I saw you at John's party last week.

b. It's impossible. You .... (not/see) me because I didn't go to that party.

8.   a. When did you post the letter to Mary?

b. This morning, so she .... (get) it by the end of the week.

2.   Complete the sentences using an appropriate modal verb together with the verb in brackets:

1.   I .... (not/eat) so much. Now I feel sick.

2.   a. I wonder why Tom didn't call me.

b. He was really busy. By all means, he .... (forget) it.

3.   You have signed the contract. It .... (not/change) now.

4.   He was in prison at the time the crime was committed, so he .... (not/do) it.

5.   You .... (arrive) at the office earlier. The meeting has already started.

6.   I'm surprised nobody told you that the road was dangerous. You .... (warn).

7.   a. We weren't sure which way to go. In the end, we turned right.

b. You went the wrong way. You .... (turn) left.
8. a. When was the last time you saw Bill?
b. Years ago. I .... (not/recognize) him if I saw him now.

Gerund vs. Infinitive
3. Put the verb into the correct form (gerund or infinitive - the preposition "to" must be supplied were needed):
1. How old were you when you learnt .... (drive)?
2. I don't mind .... (walk) home but I'd rather .... (get) a taxi.
3. I can't make a decision. I keep .... (change) my mind.
4. He had made his decision and refused .... (change) his mind.
5. I had a really nice time this summer. I enjoyed .... (be) by the sea again.
6. a. But you promised to come to the theatre with me!
b. I don't remember .... (say) that.
7. a. Remember .... (call) John tomorrow.
b. Okay, I won't forget.
8. The water here is a bit brackish. I'd avoid .... (drink) it if I were you.
9. I pretended .... (be) interested in the conversation, but really it was boring.
10. I got up and looked out of the window .... (see) what the weather was like.

4. Put the verb into the correct form (gerund or infinitive - the preposition "to" must be supplied were needed):
1. I can't find the tickets. I seem .... (lose) them.
2. You can walk to your hotel. It's not worth .... (take) a taxi.
3. I'm a bit tired. I don't fancy .... (go) out.
4. Tim isn't very reliable. He tends .... (forget) things.

5.   I've got a lot of luggage. Do you mind .... (help) me?

6.   I'm very tired after the guided tour. I'm not used .... (walk) so much.

7.   I have a friend who claims .... (be) able to speak five languages.

8.   I like .... (think) carefully about things before .... (make) a decision.

9.   Steve used .... (be) a great football player. He had to stop .... (play) because of an injury.

10.   a. How do you make this thing .... (work)?

        b. I'm not sure. Try .... (press) the button and see what happens.

5.   Put the verb into the correct form (gerund or infinitive - the preposition "to" must be supplied were needed):

1.   I wish that dog would stop .... (bark). It's driving me mad.

2.   Our neighbour threatened .... (call) the police if we didn't stop the noise.

3.   We were hungry, so I suggested .... (have) dinner early.

4.   Hurry up! I don't want to risk .... (miss) the train.

5.   I'm still looking for a job but I hope .... (find) something soon.

6.   I'm in a difficult position. What do you advise me .... (do)?

7.   She said the letter was personal and wouldn't let me .... (read) it.

8.   The film was very sad. It made me .... (cry).

9.   Carol's parents always encouraged her .... (study) hard at school.

10.   I wouldn't recommend .... (eat) at that restaurant. The food is awful.

6.   Put the verb into the correct form (gerund or infinitive - the preposition "to" must be supplied were needed):
1.   I cannot afford .... (go) out tonight. I don't have any money.
2.   Can you remind me .... (buy) some fruit on the way back home?
3.   Why do you keep .... (ask) me so many questions? I refuse .... (answer) any more of your questions!
4.   One of the boys admitted .... (break) the window. The boy's father promised .... (pay) for it.
5.   a. How did the thief break into the house?
             b. I forgot .... (shut) the windows.
6.   When I was a child, I hated .... (go) to bed early.
7.   I need a new job. I cannot stand .... (work) here any more.
8.   I'd love .... (come) to your wedding, but I'm afraid it isn't possible.
9.   I like .... (come) to work early, so I can make myself a cup of coffee first.
10.   I'm not quite ready yet. Do you mind .... (wait)?

Relative Clauses
7.   Merge the two sentences using a relative clause:
1.   a. A man answered the phone. He told me you were away.
             b. The man
....
2.   a. A waitress served us. She was very impolite and impatient.
             b. The waitress
....
3.   a. A building was destroyed in the fire. It has now been rebuilt.
             b. The building
....
4.   a. Some people were arrested. They have now been released.
             b. The people
....
5.   a. A bus goes to the airport. It runs every half hour.

　　　　　b. The bus

....

6.　　　a. The book is about a girl. She runs away from home.
　　　　　b. The book

....

7.　　　a. A dictionary is a book. It gives you the meaning of words.
　　　　　b. A dictionary

....

8.　　　a. Some people are never on time. I don't like these people.
　　　　　b. I don't like people

....

8.　　　　　　　Merge the two sentences using a relative clause:
1.　　　a. A black horse won the race. What was its name?
　　　　　b. What was the name of the black horse

....

2.　　　a. Two men stole my car. The police have caught them.
　　　　　b. The police have caught the two men

....

3.　　　a. I was born in a small town. I have recently gone back there.
　　　　　b. I have recently gone back to the small town

....

4.　　　a. Do you know a good restaurant? We want to have a nice
meal.
　　　　　b. Do you know a good restaurant

....

5.　　　a. Is there a shop near here? I want to buy some postcards.
　　　　　b. Is there a shop near here

....

6.　　　a. I had my car repaired at a garage. I cannot remember its
name.
　　　　　b. I cannot remember the name of the garage

....

7.　　　a. We have a new colleague at work. Her father works for the
European Commission.
　　　　　b. We have a new colleague at work

....

8.　　　a. I met a crazy guy last night. His ambition was to climb Mount
Everest.

b. I met a crazy guy last night

....

9.	Complete the sentences using the right relative pronoun:
1.	A cemetery is a place .... people are buried.
2.	A pacifist is a person .... believes in peace.
3.	An orphan is a child .... parents have died.
4.	I don't know the name of the woman to .... I spoke on the phone.
5.	It doesn't matter .... you work for but .... kind of tasks you carry out all day.
6.	I haven't decided for .... to vote yet. Democrats or Republicans?
7.	I couldn't decide .... to buy for my girlfriend's birthday.
8.	You cannot appreciate art outside the culture of .... it is a part.

10.	Complete the sentences using the right relative pronoun:
1.	What's the name of the man .... car you borrowed?
2.	My office, ... is on the 2nd floor, has an excellent view over town.
3.	The office .... I work is on the 2nd floor.
4.	The house .... we wanted to buy has now been sold.
5.	.... is your boss? .... orders are you supposed to follow?
6.	.... time do you go to bed? Before or after midnight?
7.	I haven't decided .... of these two shirts to buy. The blue one or the white one?
8.	I don't know .... to say. I'm speechless.

D. Conjunctions / Prepositions of Time / Prepositions of Place

Conjunctions

1. Use an appropriate conjunction to complete the sentences:

1. .... it rained a lot, we enjoyed our holiday.
2. .... our careful plans, a lot of things went wrong.
3. I'll try to be on time but don't worry .... I'm late.
4. Please report to the reception .... you arrive at the hotel.
5. She only accepted the job .... the salary, which was very high.
6. I managed to get to sleep .... there was a lot of noise.
7. Write down the name of the hotel you're staying at .... you forget it.
8. I regret that I left school .... I was 16.
9. I hope I'll be able to attend the meeting, but I'll let you know .... I cannot.
10. I have a lot of work, so please do not disturb .... it's something urgent.

2. Use an appropriate conjunction to complete the sentences:

1. I went home early .... I was feeling unwell.
2. I went to work the next day .... I was still feeling unwell.
3. We've arranged to play tennis, but we won't .... it's raining.
4. Jennifer is in her final year. She doesn't know what she is going to do .... she graduates.
5. She accepted the job .... the salary, which was rather low.
6. I couldn't get to sleep .... the noise.
7. We're not very close friends .... we've known each other for a long time.
8. It's not cold now but take your coat with you .... it gets colder.
9. Anne will be surprised .... she hears the news.
10. I like travelling by sea .... it's not rough.

Prepositions of Time

3.	Use the right preposition to complete the sentences:
1.	Jack is on a business trip. He'll be back .... a week.
2.	We're having a party .... Saturday. Are you coming?
3.	I've got an interview next Thursday .... 9:30.
4.	She isn't usually here .... weekends.
5.	We met a lot of people .... our holiday.
6.	We met a lot of people .... we were on holiday.
7.	I was very tired but .... the end I decided to go out for a drink.
8.	This area is very busy, even .... night.
9.	I was woken up by a loud voice .... the night.
10.	I haven't seen Helen .... last Friday.

4.	Use the right preposition to complete the sentences:
1.	Brian has been doing the same job .... five years.
2.	I'm busy .... the moment. Can you call back later?
3.	We've got some friends staying with us .... Friday.
4.	All applicants should submit their CVs .... the end of next week.
5.	The balance sheet reflects the financial position of the company as .... 31 December 2008.
6.	I was waiting for you .... half an hour. I thought you weren't coming.
7.	I finish work late, so I don't normally go out .... the week.
8.	The trains in Germany are always .... time.
9.	Give me a break! I cannot do five things .... the same time!
10.	Can you tidy up the room .... I'm doing the dishes?

5.	Use the right preposition to complete the sentences:
1.	I think I'll wait .... Thursday before making a decision.
2.	I have been offered a job and have to decide .... Thursday.
3.	Mozart was born in Salzburg .... 1756.

4.   The price of oil has gone up .... September.
5.   Hurry up! The check-in desk is closing .... ten minutes!
6.   Please excuse me. I'll be with you .... a moment.
7.   There's usually a lot of parties .... New Year's Eve.
8.   The course begins .... 7 January and ends sometime .... April.
9.   The book was short and pleasant. I read it .... a day.
10.   I normally take some friends out for a drink .... my birthday.

Prepositions of Place
6.   Use the right preposition to complete the sentences:
1.   Write your name .... the top of the page.
2.   There was an accident .... the crossroads this morning.
3.   I wasn't sure whether I had come .... the right office. There was no name .... the door.
4.   .... the end of the street, there is a path leading .... the river.
5.   You'll find the sports results .... the back page of the newspaper.
6.   I went for dinner with my fiancée last night and my boss was sitting .... a table right next to us.
7.   I grew up .... a small town .... Southwest England.
8.   We spent some days .... the Greek islands and then we flew .... Athens.
9.   I know he's married. I saw the ring .... his finger.
10.   You don't see any more children playing .... the streets.

7.   Use the right preposition to complete the sentences:
1.   Our headquarters are .... the corner of Oxford Road and Shaftesbury Avenue.
2.   Come over here! Don't' stand .... the corner.
3.   My office is .... the first floor, second door .... the left.

4.   .... your left-hand side, you see the Eiffel Tower.
5.   Please use the entrance .... the back.
6.   If you sit .... the sun too long you'll surely get burnt.
7.   It was really hot, but we were lucky to find a table .... the shade.
8.   It was wonderful! We had lunch .... the shade of the Acropolis.
9.   George is already .... a plane back to London.
10.   He was .... a train when I called him. I could tell by the noise.

8.   Use the right preposition to complete the sentences:
1.   Where is this beach? I cannot find it .... the map.
2.   London is .... the river Thames.
3.   The river Rhein flows .... the North Sea.
4.   It was a very slow train. It stopped .... every station.
5.   My dad is .... the hospital. Unfortunately he's very ill.
6.   My dad is .... the hospital. He went to see a friend of his.
7.   I felt feverish this morning so I decided to stay .... home and lie .... bed.
8.   George is a student .... the University of Manchester. He studies Operations Management .... the Department of Business Administration.
9.   Welcome .... England, welcome .... London! Enjoy your stay!
10. We got stuck .... a traffic jam .... our way .... the airport.

Prepositions (Mix)
9.   Use the right preposition to complete the sentences:
1.   Microsoft is racing to launch its new OS .... time for Christmas.
2.   I get my salary .... the end of every month.
3.   Our company is one of the biggest .... the world.
4.   Have you read any books .... J.K. Rowling?

5. I need to take some money out. I think I saw an ATM .... the end of the road.

6. Tim is .... holiday. He has gone to Bombay, ... the west coast of India.

7. You've got lipstick .... your collar. Have a look .... the mirror.

8. We went .... a party .... Linda's house .... Friday.

9. I've never been .... Tokyo. As a matter of fact, I've never been .... Japan.

10. Mozart died .... Vienna .... 1791 .... the age of 35.

10. Use the right preposition to complete the sentences:

1. Are you .... this photograph? I can see myself .... the left.

2. I wonder what's .... TV this evening. Do you have a TV guide?

3. We went .... the movies last night, but unfortunately our seats were .... the front row.

4. The light switch is .... the wall .... the door.

5. What time did you arrive .... work this morning?

6. I couldn't decide what to eat. There was nothing .... the menu that I liked.

7. I'm sorry but you cannot get in. You're not .... the list.

8. Wal-Mart is listed .... New York Stock Exchange.

9. How did you get here? .... foot or .... bus?

10. Are you paying cash or .... credit card?

E. Prepositions & Nouns / Prepositions & Adjectives / Prepositions & Verbs

Prepositions & Nouns

1. Use the right preposition to complete the sentences:

1. There are some differences .... British and American English.

2.	Everything can be explained. There is a reason .... everything.

3.	If I give you the camera, can you take a photograph .... me?

4.	Money isn't the solution .... every problem.

5.	There has been an increase .... the amount of city traffic.

6.	He didn't have any cash, so he signed a cheque .... EUR 300.

7.	The advantage .... working .... the public sector is that you feel secure.

8.	There are many advantages .... working .... the European Commission.

9.	When Paul was promoted, his attitude .... his colleagues changed dramatically.

10.	Unfortunately, I've lost contact .... my former classmates.

2.	Use the right preposition to complete the sentences:

1.	Last month, inflation was galloping .... a rate of 4%.

2.	.... resolution .... the Annual General Meeting, the company's share capital shall be increased .... EUR 100 mn .... the amount of EUR 200 mn .... the issuance of one million new shares .... a nominal value of EUR 100 each.

3.	What was the manager's reaction .... the news?

4.	John showed me a plan .... the new house he is building.

5.	The new CEO has big plans .... the company.

6.	The company's director rejected the workers' demands .... a rise .... wages.

7.	What was the answer .... question 3 .... the aptitude test?

8.	The fact that Jane has been offered a job has no connection .... the fact that her mother is the Human Resource Manager.

9.	Do you have a good relationship .... your colleagues?

10.   Nobody knows the cause .... his strange behaviour.

Prepositions & Adjectives
3.   Use the right preposition to complete the sentences:
1.   He was delighted .... the present I gave him.
2.   It was very nice .... you to give me a ride back home.
3.   Why are you always so rude .... the clients?
4.   It was a bit careless .... you not to cross-check the figures.
5.   I'm fed up .... my boss's inconsistent behaviour.
6.   Investors were disappointed .... the Q3 profits that the company posted.
7.   Investors were surprised .... the company's announcement to increase its share capital.
8.   I've been trying to learn Spanish but I'm not satisfied .... my progress.
9.   Linda doesn't look very well. I'm worried .... her.
10.   Are you still angry .... me .... what happened? I'm sorry .... what I've said.

4.   Use the right preposition to complete the sentences:
1.   The people next door were furious .... us .... making so much noise.
2.   Jill starts her new job tomorrow and she's quite excited .... it.
3.   I'm sorry .... the smell. I've been cooking snails.
4.   The man we interviewed was clever but we were not impressed .... his past experience.
5.   The letter I wrote was full .... mistakes.
6.   Our new Prime Minister is famous .... his ability to make quick decisions.
7.   I'm not really fond .... mountain climbing.
8.   I don't like flying. I'm afraid .... heights.
9.   You don't seem to be interested .... what the keynote speaker is saying.
10.   Do you know that Jane is engaged .... someone who's working in the same company?

5.   Use the right preposition to complete the sentences:
1.   I'm not ashamed .... what I've said. Actually, I'm proud .... it.
2.   I suggested we should go for a drink after dinner, but nobody was keen .... the idea.
3.   Are you aware .... the dangers .... smoking?
4.   During sales, all shopping streets in town are crowded .... people.
5.   I'm tired .... doing the same thing every day.
6.   A successful company attains maximum efficiency .... minimum cost.
7.   I don't think she is capable .... telling lies.
8.   I'm not surprised she's changed her mind. That's typical .... her.
9.   Our house is similar .... yours.
10.   It's so pathetic. He is 35 and he is totally dependent .... his parents.

Prepositions & Verbs
6.   Use the right preposition to complete the sentences:
1.   I like to listen .... some music while I study.
2.   I apologised .... my brother for the misunderstanding
3.   Look .... these flowers! Aren't they pretty?
4.   Do look .... my flowers while I'm on holidays, will you?
5.   I've been looking .... my glasses. Have you seen them?
6.   I don't know what this word means. Look it .... in the dictionary.
7.   I was waving hello to Samantha, but unfortunately she was looking ....
8.   She was so beautiful! I couldn't help staring .... her.
9.   I'm not leaving yet. I'm waiting .... the rain .... stop.
10.   Jane is always asking her parents .... money.

7.   Use the right preposition to complete the sentences:

1.   I've applied .... a job at the factory.
2.   All this company restructuring doesn't apply .... me.
3.   I've searched everywhere .... my keys but I cannot find them.
4.   Forget it. I don't want to talk .... what happened.
5.   There's no reason to be offended. I'm not laughing .... you, I'm laughing .... you.
6.   I'm leaving .... London tomorrow. Do you want me to bring you anything?
7.   He's so selfish. He doesn't care .... others.
8.   Have a nice trip! And take care .... yourself!
9.   I have a couple of hours to kill. Would you care .... a cup of coffee?
10.   She was so angry she threw a chair .... me.

8.   Use the right preposition to complete the sentences:
1.   Please don't shout .... me!
2.   Can I speak .... you for a moment?
3.   I feel so lonely. I need someone to talk ....
4.   Did you hear .... the company's plans to dismiss 300 employees?
5.   Have you heard .... the new striker that our football team got?
6.   Have you heard .... Jane lately? I haven't seen her .... a year.
7.   My associate complained .... me .... working long hours.
8.   He was complaining .... a strong pain in the chest, so he went to the hospital.
9.   I like this part of town. It reminds me .... the place where I grew up.
10.   I'm so glad you reminded me .... the meeting. I had totally forgotten it.

9.   Use the right preposition to complete the sentences:
1.   I'm dreaming .... the day I'll have my own yacht.
2.   Revenues soared .... EUR 2.48 mn .... EUR 15.12 mn .... just three years.
3.   Thank you for your offer. I'll think .... it.

4.	This was my best idea. I cannot think .... anything better.
5.	Nobody warned me .... the incidence of crime .... this part of town.
6.	John accused me .... being selfish.
7.	I don't approve .... your decision to walk away from home. Independence should not be sought .... the expense of family relations.
8.	I will never forgive them .... what they did.
9.	I'm so sorry about your father's demise. What did he die ....?
10.	I apologise .... being late. Thank you .... your patience.

10.	Use the right preposition to complete the sentences:
1.	The company's management is to blame .... the huge Q2 losses.
2.	Shareholders blamed the downturn of profits .... the inefficiency of the current management.
3.	The number of employees suffering .... strain injuries is rapidly increasing.
4.	You can rely .... Steve. He keeps his word.
5.	Nowadays, nobody can live .... 700 euros.
6.	I cannot live .... my parents anymore. I suffocate.
7.	Congratulations .... your achievement.
8.	Robert complimented me .... my English. He said I'm very fluent.
9.	Do you believe .... God or are you an atheist?
10.	Edward is a lawyer. He specialises .... company law.

F. Comparative & Superlative Forms / Countable & Uncountable Nouns / Word Order

Comparative & Superlative Forms
1.	Complete the sentences using the comparative form of the word in brackets:

1.   I was feeling tired last night, so I went to bed .... (early) than usual.
2.   Unfortunately, her illness was .... (serious) than I thought.
3.   You look .... (thin). Have you lost weight?
4.   I know him very well. Probably .... (well) than anyone else.
5.   He did pretty badly in the exam. Much .... (badly) than he thought.
6.   You're standing too close to the camera. Can you move a bit .... (far) away?
7.   Our manager is .... (interested) in saving costs than investing in new technology.
8.   You'd find your way around town .... (easily) if you had a map.
9.   The solution to the problem was .... (simple) than we thought.
10.   Let's move to the back of this café. It's .... (quiet) there.

2.   Complete the sentences using the comparative or superlative form of the word in brackets:
1.   We stayed at .... (cheap) hotel in town.
2.   Mexico is a big country but Canada is .... (large).
3.   What is .... (old) building in the city?
4.   I've got two sons and one daughter. My .... (old) son is 14 years old.
5.   This was the .... (delicious) meal I've ever had.
6.   Yesterday was .... (bad) day of my life.
7.   Everest is .... (high) any other mountain in the world.
8.   This company is multinational, one of .... (big) in the world.
9.   I prefer this chair to the other one. It's .... (comfortable).
10.   What's .... (quick) way to get to the airport?

Countable & Uncountable Nouns

3.	Complete the sentences using "a/an" where necessary. If no word is necessary, put a dash ("--"):
1.	Jim was listening to .... music when I arrived.
2.	We went to .... very nice restaurant last weekend.
3.	I brush my teeth with .... toothpaste.
4.	Can you tell me if there is .... bank near here?
5.	I don't like .... violence.
6.	What did you have for lunch. I smell .... garlic.
7.	We need .... petrol. I hope we find .... petrol station soon.
8.	Rachel has .... interview for .... job tomorrow.
9.	Do you take .... sugar in your coffee?
10.	It wasn't my fault. It was .... accident.

4.	Complete the sentences using "a/an" or "some" where necessary. If no word is necessary, put a dash ("--"):
1.	I've seen .... good films recently.
2.	What's wrong with you? Have you got .... headache?
3.	I know .... lot of people. Most of them are .... doctors.
4.	When I was .... child, I used to be shy.
5.	Would you like to be .... lawyer when you grow up?
6.	Do you collect .... stamps?
7.	What .... beautiful painting!
8.	.... birds, e.g. penguins, cannot fly.
9.	I've been walking for three hours. I've got .... sore feet.
10.	I don't feel very well this morning. I've got .... sore throat.

5.	Complete the sentences using "a/an" or "some" where necessary. If no word is necessary, put a dash ("--"):
1.	She is very beautiful. She's got .... blond hair, ... blue eyes and .... very cute nose.
2.	I suffocate. I need .... fresh air.
3.	It's a pity we haven't got .... camera. I'd like to take .... pictures of that beautiful church.
4.	I like taking .... pictures. That's why I've joined .... photography class.
5.	These are .... nice shoes. Where did you get them.

6.   You need .... visa for .... countries.

7.   William is .... teacher. His parents were .... teachers too.

8.   Do you enjoy going to .... concerts?

9.   When we got down town, ... shops were closed but most were still open.

10.   I don't believe him. He is .... liar. He's always telling .... lies.

Word Order

6.   Put the adjectives in brackets in the correct position:

1.   a table (wooden / round / beautiful):

....

2.   a ring (gold / unusual):

....

3.   shoes (nice / new):

....

4.   shoes (new / brown):

....

5.   a movie (old / American / black-and-white):

....

6.   a man (tall / young):

....

7.   clouds (white / big):

....

8.   a bag (small / plastic / red):

....

9.   a day (sunny / lovely):

....

10.   a painting (French / medieval / interesting):

....

7.   Put the parts of the sentence in the right order:

1.   (the party / very much / everybody / enjoyed):

....

2.   (quietly / the door / I / closed):

....

3.   (Diane / quite / well / German / speaks):

....

4.   (my grandmother / watches / all the time / television):

....

5.   (remembered / her name/ I / after a few minutes):

....

6.   (write / of the page / your name / at the top):

....

7.   (found / interesting / in the library / some / I / books):

....

8.   (a / hotel / new / opposite / the park / are building / they):

....

9.   (Sally / to the zoo / the kids / yesterday / took):

....

10.   (old / money / some / good / friend / of mine / borrowed / I / from / a): ....

8.   Put the parts of the sentence in the right order:
1.   (remember / never / can / I / her name):

....

2.   (I am / hungry / usually / when / I get / from work / home):

....

3.   (home / has / gone / John / early / probably / today):

....

4.   (we / for the bus / a long time / have to / always / wait):

....

5.   (read / with glasses / can / I / only):

....

6.   (my secretary / ever / in her office / when / need / I / her / is / hardly): ....

7.   (I / probably / will / be / tomorrow / leaving / early):

....

8.   (all / we / ill / after / felt / the meal):

....

9.   (Tom / by car / to work / goes / always):

....

10.   (to bed / really / you / go / shouldn't / so late):

....

Prepositions (Mix)
9.   Use the right preposition to complete the sentences:

1.   I hope you succeed .... finding the job you want.
2.   There was an accident in the port today. A small barge collided .... a big cruiser.
3.   You won't believe what happened .... me on my way back from work.
4.   I was trying to concentrate .... what our team leader was saying.
5.   Someone broke .... my office and stole some papers .... my desk.
6.   I ran .... my ex-girlfriend at the party.
7.   Fill the tank .... diesel, not unleaded gas.
8.   Maria translates medical texts .... English .... Greek.
9.   The company's equity capital was divided .... ten thousand shares.
10. I don't like alcohol, that's why I prefer refreshments .... spirits.

10.   Use the right preposition to complete the sentences:
1.   I wanted to pay .... my meal but he insisted .... treating me.
2.   My assistant at the office provided me .... all necessary info.
3.   I cannot believe Susan! She spent 400 euros .... shoes!
4.   I'm not very good .... cooking so I suggest we eat out.
5.   Let's go out. There is no reason .... staying .... home because of a drizzle.
6.   What do you think is the best solution .... the problem?
7.   There's been an increase .... the price of oil.
8.   He leads a lonely life. He doesn't have much contact .... people.
9.   I'm surprised .... the amount of work you completed over the weekend.
10.   He invested all his money .... treasury bonds.

G. Correct Use of Articles / Various Grammatical Issues

Subject-Verb Agreement (Singular vs. Plural)
1.   Choose the correct alternative:
1.   Economics is / are my favourite subject at the Uni.
2.   a. These jeans is / are too tight, let alone expensive.
        b. Don't worry. Money is / are not an issue.

3.	My glasses was / were broken. Thankfully, all the staff at the optician's was / were very helpful.
4.	The police want / wants to interview two men about the robbery.
5.	My family lives / live in England.
6.	Greece play / plays Scotland in a friendly game this weekend.
7.	Fortunately, the news wasn't / weren't as bad as we expected.
8.	The government wants / want to raise taxes and people is / are unhappy.
9.	I don't like hot weather. Thirty degrees is / are too warm for me.
10.	a. Your hair look / looks nice.
	b. Thank you. A number of friends has / have told me that.

"Some" vs. "Any"
2.	Complete the sentences using "some" or "any":
1.	They didn't pay us .... money.
2.	I am going out with .... friends of mine.
3.	Have you seen .... good films recently?
4.	I didn't have .... fruit, so I had to buy ....
5.	Can I have .... milk in my coffee, please?
6.	I was too tired to do .... work.
7.	You can cash these traveller's cheques at .... bank.
8.	Can you give me .... information about the new project?
9.	With this special ticket, you can travel on .... train you like.
10.	If you have .... questions, feel free to ask.

3.	Complete the sentences using "some-" or "any-" + "-body" / "-thing" / "-where":
1.	There is .... at the door. Can you go and see who it is?
2.	Does .... mind if I open the window?
3.	Would you like .... to eat? You haven't eaten .... all day.
4.	Quick, let's go! There's .... coming and I don't want .... to see us.
5.	Sally was upset about .... , so she refused to talk about ....

6.   .... can learn to send text messages.
7.   It's mid-August, so there is hardly .... in the office.
8.   Do you live .... near Jim?
9.   Let's go .... warm. I'm freezing out here.
10.   If .... phones, tell them I'm busy.

"Much" vs. "Many" / "Few" vs. "A few" / "Little" vs. "A little"
4.   Complete the sentences using "much", "many", "few", "a few", "little" or "a little":
1.   He isn't very popular. He has .... friends.
2.   Vicky is very busy these days. She has .... free time.
3.   Did you take .... photographs when you were on holiday?
4.   I'm not very busy today. I don't have .... to do.
5.   Listen carefully. I'm gonna give you .... advice.
6.   Do you mind if I ask you .... questions?
7.   The museum was very crowded. There were too .... people.
8.   The weather has been very dry recently. We've had .... rain.
9.   The weather has been very wet recently. We've had .... rain.
10.   Very .... animals can survive in the desert.

"Each" vs. "Every"
5.   Complete the sentences using "each" or "every":
1.   .... side of a square is the same length.
2.   The Olympic Games are held .... four years.
3.   .... parent worries about their children.
4.   There are eight teams in the qualifying round. .... team plays against the other seven at home and away.
5.   I understand most of what he says but not .... word.
6.   I get paid .... four weeks.
7.   Nick plays five-a-side .... Tuesday evening.
8.   .... of the five chapters is divided in two sections.
9.   There's a train to London .... hour.
10.   I saw a number of applicants. .... one had a different academic background.

"So" vs. "Such" vs. "Such a"

6.	Complete the sentences using "so", "such" or "such a":

1.	He's difficult to understand because he speaks .... quickly.
2.	I like Tom and Beth. They are .... nice people.
3.	It was a great holiday. We had .... good time.
4.	Everything is .... expensive these days, isn't it?
5.	It was .... boring film I almost fell asleep.
6.	There is no .... word as "blid".
7.	I couldn't believe the news. It was .... shock.
8.	I didn't expect the weather in Finland to be .... warm.
9.	I didn't realize you live .... long way from work.
10.	He looks .... tired after every exam.

"All" vs. "All of" / "Most" vs. "Most of"

7.	Complete the sentences using "of", "the" or "of the" where necessary. If no word is necessary, put a dash ("--"):

1.	All .... cars have wheels.
2.	Suzan is so annoying. She speaks all .... time.
3.	None .... this money is mine.
4.	Some .... people get angry very easily.
5.	I have lived in London most .... my life.
6.	Most .... days I get up before 7 o'clock.
7.	We've eaten most .... food we bought. There's very little left.
8.	George thinks that all .... museums are boring.
9.	Have you spent all .... money I gave you?
10.	The exam was very difficult. I could only answer half .... questions.

Correct Use of Articles

8.	Complete the sentences using "a/an" or "the" where necessary. If no word is necessary, put a dash ("--"):

1.	I don't usually like staying at .... hotels, but last summer we spent a few days at .... very nice hotel by .... sea.
2.	.... tennis is my favourite sport. I play once or twice .... week if I can, but I'm not .... very good player.
3.	I won't be home for .... dinner this evening. I'm meeting some friends after .... work and we're going to .... cinema.

4.	.... unemployment is very high at the moment and it's very difficult for .... people to find .... work.

5.	There was .... accident as I was driving .... home last night. Two people were taken to .... hospital. I think .... most accidents are caused by .... people driving too fast.

6.	William is .... economist. He used to work in .... financial strategy department of .... Lloyds Bank. Now he is working for .... American bank in .... United States.

7.	a. What's .... name of .... hotel you're staying at?

	b. .... Intercontinental. It's on .... Regent Street in .... city centre. It's close to .... airport.

8.	I have two brothers. .... older one is training to be .... pilot with .... British Airways. .... younger one is still at .... school. When he leaves .... school, he hopes to go to .... university to study .... management.

9.	This morning I bought .... newspaper and .... magazine. .... newspaper is in my bag but I don't know where I've put .... magazine.

10.	This morning I went to .... bank and then to .... post office. In .... afternoon, I have .... appointment with .... dentist. I'm afraid of .... doctors. I hope I get away with just .... filling.

9.	Complete the sentences using "a/an" or "the" where necessary. If no word is necessary, put a dash ("--"):

1.	Could you close .... door, please?

2.	.... sun is .... star.

3.	.... moon orbits around .... earth.

4.	.... black holes are .... result of .... stellar explosions, called .... supernovas.

5.	Tim lives in .... small house in .... suburbs.

6.	You shouldn't have spent all .... money I gave you. That was .... mistake.

7.	I've got .... problem. I need .... money.

8.	There is .... supermarket at .... end of .... street.

9.	.... policemen protect .... citizens. .... sense of security is instilled by means of .... frequent patrols in .... parts of town where .... crime thrives.

10.	.... meat costs EUR 8.00 .... kilo. Once .... week we have .... beef. .... butcher is .... friend of mine and I trust .... quality of his products.

10.	Complete the sentences using "a/an" or "the" where necessary. If no word is necessary, put a dash ("--"):
1.	a. Where did you have .... lunch?
	b. We went to .... restaurant.
2.	a. Did you have .... nice holiday?
	b. Yes, it was .... best holiday I've ever had.
3.	a. Do you often listen to .... radio?
	b. I haven't got .... radio. I'd rather watch
.... TV.
4.	a. Can you tell me where .... Room 418 is?
	b. Yes, it's on .... fourth floor.
5.	a. We stayed at .... most expensive hotel in
.... town.
	b. Why didn't you pick .... cheaper hotel?
6.	You'll find .... information you need at ....
top of .... page 27.
7.	a. How do your children come back from ....
school. By .... bus or on .... foot?
	b. .... school where they go to is very close to
.... hospital where I work, so I pick them on .... way back.
8.	I like to read in .... bed. .... book I'm reading
now is .... science fiction novel. .... books relieve all ....
stress from .... work.
9.	a. Look at .... apples on that tree!
	b. .... apples are very wholesome. ....
children should eat .... fruit but to tell .... truth, ...
parents don't provide them with .... balanced diet.
10.	a. There's .... piano in the corner. Do you play ....
piano?
	b. I come from .... family with .... strong
tradition in .... music. My dad plays .... guitar and I sing
.... songs that my uncle writes.
11.	.... brown bear is .... endangered species. In
.... Balkans alone, ... number of .... animals who have
become extinct is .... disgrace to .... international
community.

5. Tenses

Present Perfect

a)   They have moved into a new apartment.
b)   Have you ever visited Mexico?
c)   I have already seen that movie.
d)   I have never seen snow. The present perfect expresses the idea that something hap¬pened (or never happened) before now, at an unspecified time in the past. The exact time it happened is not important. If there is a specific mention of time, the simple past is used: I saw that movie last night.

 e)   We have had four tests so far this semester.
f)   I have written my wife a letter every other day for the last two weeks.
g)   I have met many people since I came here in June.
h)   I have flown on an airplane many times. The present perfect also ex-presses the repetition of an activity before now. The exact time of each repetition is not important.

i)   I have been here since seven o'clock.
j)   We have been here for two weeks,
k)   I have had this same pair of shoes for three years.
l)   I have liked cowboy movies ever since I was a child,
m)   I have known him for many years.
        The present perfect also, when used with for or since, expresses a situation that began in the past and continues to the pres¬ent.*
In the examples, notice the dif¬ference between since and for:
since + a particular time
for + duration of time

The present perfect has this meaning primarily for those verbs that are usually not used in any of the progressive tenses. This meaning is exactly the same as the meaning of the present perfect progressive tense.

Present Perfect Progressive

Right now I am sitting at my desk.

(a) I have been sitting here since seven o'clock.

(b) I have been sitting here for two hours.

(c) You have been studying for five straight hours. Why don't you take a break?

(d) He has been watching television since nine o'clock this morning.

(e) It has been raining all day. It is still raining right now.

This tense is used to indicate the duration of an activity that began in the past and continues to the present. When the tense has this meaning, it is used with time words such as for, since, all morning, all day, all week.

f)   I have been thinking about changing my major.

g)   All of the students have been studying hard.

h)   John has been doing a lot of work on his thesis. He should be finished by May.

i)   My back hurts, so I have been sleeping on the floor lately. The bed is too soft. When the tense is used without any specific mention of time, it expresses a general activity in progress recently, lately.

j)   I have lived here since 1975.

k)   I have been living here since 1975.

l)   He has worked at the same store for ten years.

With certain verbs (most notably live, work, teach) there is little or no difference in meaning between the two tenses when since or for is used.

Exercise 1:

Use the simple past or the present perfect. In some sentences either tense is possible but the meaning is different.

1.   I (not attend) ______________________________________ any parties since I came here.

2.   I (go) __________________to a party at Sally's apartment last Saturday night.

3.   Bill (arrive) ______________________________here three days ago.

4.   Bill (be) ____here since the 22nd.

5.   Try not to be absent from class again for the rest of the term. You (miss, already) ______________________________________ too many classes. You (miss) ______________________________________ two classes just last week.

6.   Last January, I (see) ____________________ snow for the first time in my life.

7.   In her whole lifetime, she (see, never) ______________________ snow.

8.   I (know) ______________________________ Greg Adams for ten years.

9.   So far this week, I (have) ______________________________ two tests and a quiz.

10.   Up to now, Professor Williams (give) ____________________ our class five tests.

11.   The science of medicine (advance) ____________________ a great deal in the 19th century.

12.   Since the beginning of the 20th century, medical scientists (make) ____________________ many important discoveries.

Exercise 2:

Use the present perfect progressive in the following.

1.   The boys are playing soccer right now. They (play) have been playing for almost two hours. They must be getting tired.

2.   Alex is talking on the phone. He (talk) ____________________on the phone for over a half an hour. He should hang up soon. Long distance is expensive.

3.   I'm trying to study. I (try) ____________________to study for the last hour, but something always seems to interrupt met I think I'd better go to the library.

Complete the following by writing two sentences. Use the present perfect progressive in the first sentence; then make another sentence that might typically follow in this situation.

4. The baby is crying. She Has been crying for almost ten minutes. I wonder what's wrong.

5. It's raining. It
____

6. I'm studying. I

____

7. I'm waiting for my friend. I
8. Bob is sitting in the waiting room. He

____

Exercise 3: Use the present perfect or the present perfect progressive. In some sentences, either tense may be used with little or no change in meaning.

1.   It (snow) ________________________________all day. I wonder when it stops.
2.   We (have) __________________three major snowstorms so far this winter. I wonder how many more we will have.
3.   It's ten p.m. I ___________________(study) for two hours and probably won't finish until midnight.
4.   I (write) ___________________ them three times, but I still haven't received a reply.
5.   I (live) ___________________ here since last March.
6.   The telephone (ring) ____________________ four times in the last hour, and each time it has been for my roommate.
7.   The telephone (ring) ___________________ for almost a minute. Why doesn't someone answer it?
8.   The little boy is dirty from head to foot because he (play) _____________ in the mud.

Exercise 4: Same as the preceding exercise.
1.   A: (Be, you) _________________ able to reach Bob on the phone yet? B: Not yet. I (try)_________________for the last twenty minutes, but the line (be) ___________busy.
2.   A: Hi, Jenny. I (see, not) _________________you for weeks. What (do, you) ___________________________ lately? B: Studying.
3. A: What are you going to order for dinner?
   B: Well, I (have, never) _________________pizza, so I think I'll order that.
4. A: What's the matter? Your eyes are red and puffy. (Cry, you)_____________________?
   B: No. I just finished peeling some onions.
4.   A: Dr. Jones is a good teacher. How long (be, he) _______________at the university?

186

B: He (teach) ___________________here for twenty-five years.

Exercise 5: What have they been doing?
Complete the sentences with the present perfect simple or the present perfect continuous.
Jane has been writing (write) a letter to a magazine. She hasn't finished it yet.
1.   Ben ___________________(look) for his pen-knife, but he hasn't found it yet.
2.   Jenny ___________________ (wait) for the bus for half an hour, but it hasn't arrived yet.
3.   Nick _________________ (play) a computer game for two hours and he's still playing.
4.   Mike hasn't finished painting his car yet. He _________________ (work) on it for two weeks.
5.   Amanda ___________________(not come) home yet. She has been shopping in town since 10 o'clock.
6.   Mike's car _________________(make) strange noises. Nick and Jane have cleaned all the parts.
7.   Ben has been drawing cartoons for two hours. He _________________ (not finished) yet.
8.   Amanda has been waiting for Jenny in town. Jenny _________________ (not arrive) yet.
9.   Jane has been knitting a pullover. She ___________________ (just finish) it.
10.   It _________________ (rain) all day and it hasn't stopped yet.
11.   Mr Blake has been marking tests all evening but he _______________ (not find) a perfect one yet.
12.   Trig ___________________(practise) the present perfect, but he hasn't got it right.
12. Rikin has been searching a suitable organic reaction to be demonstrated, but he ……………………….. (not get) a suitable one.
13. The train ………………………. (run) all day and it hasn't reached the destiny yet.

Think of a job or activity that you have started but have not finished, for example, something that you are making, reading or drawing. Write a short paragraph about it. Say how long you have been doing it.

Using the Present Perfect or the Past Simple, complete the following jokes:

1.   .... you .... (be) to America before?
No. This is my first time.
Did you know that Christopher Columbus
.... (find) America?
Really? I never knew it was lost!

2.   When you .... (sell) me this car this morning, you
.... (say) it was trouble-free. Since then, the brakes
.... (fail) and the door .... (fall) off.
    Well, sir, I did sell you the car but the trouble was free!

3.   Doctor, I .... (have) a sore stomach ever since I
.... (eat) three crabs last week.
.... they .... (smell) bad when you
.... (take) them out of their shells?
    What do you mean - took them out of their shells?

4.   Now, ... everyone .... (read) the
chapter on Lord Nelson for homework?
    Yes, sir.
    Kevin,. in which battle .... Lord Nelson
.... (die)?
    Er, his last one, sir?

5.   I .... (buy) this diamond ring from a man in the
street. It's for my girlfriend.
    Are they real diamonds?
    I hope so. If not, the man .... just.........................
(cheat) me out of £5.

6.   How's your sister?
    She .... (go) on a very strict diet to lose
weight.
    And how is she getting on?
    Fine. She .... (disappear) last
week.

7.   Mrs Smith is very upset. She thinks she .... (lose)
her cat.
    When .... she last......................... (see) it?
    Four days ago.
    Why doesn't she put an advertisement in the newspaper?
    Don't be silly. Her cat can't read.

8.   My dad .... never .... (visit) the dentist.
    My dad will never go back to the dentist.
    Why? What happened?
    The dentist.. (take) all his teeth out.
    What.......................... your dad .... (say)?
    Never again! Never again!
9.   Robert was fishing in a private lake. An old man came up to him and asked:
.... you .... (catch) anything?
    Yes. Three big fish since I .... (start) this morning.
    My name is Lord Arton and I own this lake. Oh. My name is Robert and I'm a terrible liar!

Past Perfect

A beggar stopped me the other day and said he hadn't had a bite for days. What did you do?   I bit him!

Peter had a very large garden and he had been digging it for about five hours when Mrs. Burns came along.
Oh, hello, Peter. What are you growing?
The sweat was running down Peter's face.
He looked up and said, "Tired!"

a.   My parents had already eaten by the time I got home.
b.   Until yesterday, I had never heard about it.
c.   The thief simply walked in. Someone had forgot¬ten to lock the door.
d.   He had arrived before we got there.
e.   He arrived before we got there.
f.   After the guests had left, I went to bed.
g.   After the guests left, I went to bed.
        The past perfect expresses an activity that was completed before another activity or time in the past.

If either before or after is used in the sentence, the past perfect is not necessary because the time relationship is already clear. The simple past may be used instead of the past perfect, as in (e) and (g).

Past Perfect Progressive

h.   The police had been look-ing for the criminal for two years before they caught him.

i.   The patient had been waiting in the emergency room for almost an hour before a doctor finally treated her.

j.   He finally came at six o'clock. I had been wait-ing for him since four-thirty.

k.   Her skin was sunburned because she had been lying on the beach all afternoon.

The past perfect progressive emphasizes the duration of an activity that was in progress before another activity or time in the past.

l.   When Judy got home, her hair was still wet because she had been swimming.

m.   Her eyes were red because she had been crying.

This tense also may express an activity in progress recent to another time or activity in the past.

Exercise 1: Use Simple Past or the Past Perfect
Are there some sentences where either tense is possible?

1)   He (be) ____ a newspaper reporter before he (become) _____________________________a business man.

2)   I (feel) _____________________________ a little better after I (take) ____________ the medicine.

3)   I was late. The teacher (give, already) _____________________________a quiz when I (get) _____________ to class.

4)   The anthropologist (leave) _____________________________the village when she (collect) __________________ enough data.

5)   It was raining hard, but by the time class (be) _________________over, the rain (stop) ___________________.

6)   Millions of years ago, dinosaurs (roam) _____________________ the earth, but they (become) _____________________extinct by the time humankind first (appear) _____________________.

7)   Class (begin, already) _________________ by the time I (get) _________________ there, so I (take, quietly) ___________________ a seat in the back.

8)   I (see, never) _______________________any of Picasso's paintings before I (visit) _________________ the art museum.

9)   I almost missed my plane. All of the other passengers (board, already) _________________ by the time I (get) _____________________ there.

10)   Yesterday at a restaurant, I (see) _____________________ Pam Donnelly, an old friend of mine. I (see, not) _______________________her in years. At first, I (recognize, not) _______________________her because she (lose) _______________at least fifty pounds.

Use had or hadn't to complete the following:

1)   When her daughter arrived home from a party, Mrs Thompson asked her if she (thank) _______________ her hostess. "No," she said. "The girl in front of me thanked her and the lady said 'Don't mention it' so I didn't."

2)   Here's your coffee, madam - it's a special coffee all the way from Brazil. Oh, I was wondering where you (go) ___________________.

3)   A stressed managing director went to his doctor for help in getting to sleep. The workers at his factory (go) _____________ on strike. They wanted better pay and conditions. The director (try) _____________ sleeping pills but they (not work) _____________. The doctor asked the director to lie quite still in bed at night and to count sheep. The following day the director returned to the doctor's surgery.
    Well, said the doctor. Any success?
    I'm afraid not, he said. By the time I (count) _____________ the thirty-first sheep they (all go) _________________ on strike for shorter hours and lower fences.

4)   Kenneth is so stupid. He phoned his teacher at school yesterday to say he couldn't come to school because he (lose) _________________ his voice!

5)	A doctor (just give) _______________ a boy an injection in his arm. He was about to put a bandage on his arm when the boy said, Would you mind putting the bandage on my other arm, doctor?

Why? I'm putting it over your vaccination so that the other boys will know not to bang

into It.

You don't know the boys in my school, doctor!

6)	Mum! Mum! Dad's fallen over a cliff. Is he okay? I don't know. He (not stop) __________________ falling when I left.

7)	A beggar stopped me the other day and said he (not have) _____________ a bite for days.

What did you do? I bit him!

8)	It was my grandmother's birthday yesterday. Is she old?

Well, by the time we lit the last candle on her birthday cake, the first one (go) ________

out!

9)	Harry Smith was sent to Central Africa by his company. He sent a postcard to his wife as soon as he arrived. Unfortunately it was delivered to another Mrs. Smith whose husband (die) _________________ the day before. The postcard read: ARRIVED SAFELY THIS MORNING. THE HEAT IS TERRIBLE.

Simple Future

[be going to]

a.	He will finish his work tomorrow.
b.	He is going to finish his work tomorrow.
c.	I will wash the dishes later.
d.	I am going to wash the dishes later.

Will or be going to is used to express future time. Shall may be used with I or we, but wil l /be going to is more com¬monly used.* In speech, going to is often pronounced "gonna."

e.	Bob will come soon. When Bob comes, we will see him.
f.	Linda will leave soon. Be-fore she leaves, she is going to finish her work.

g.   I will get home at 5:30. After I get home, I will eat dinner.
h.   The taxi will arrive in less than five minutes. As soon as the taxi ar¬rives, we will be able to leave for the airport.
i.   They are going to come soon. I will wait here until they come.
A clause is a grammatical struc-ture which has a subject and a verb. A "time clause" begins with such words as when, be¬fore, after, as soon as, until,
These words may be followed by a subject and verb:
When he comes, we will see him. When + subject + verb = time clause

A future tense is not used in a time clause. The meaning of the clause is future, but the simple present tense is used.

j.   I will go to bed after I finish my work.
k.   I will go to bed after I have finished my work.
        Occasionally, the present perfect is used in a time clause, as in (k). Examples (j) and (k) have the same meaning. The present perfect stresses the completion of the act in the time clause before the other act occurs in the future.

•   Shall is used much more frequently in British English than in American English.

Present Progressive

a.   My wife has an appointment with a doctor. She is seeing Dr. North next Tuesday.
b.   Sam has already made his plans. He is leaving at noon tomorrow.
c.   A: What are you going to do this
        afternoon?
    B: After lunch I am meeting a friend
        of mine. We are going shopping.
        Would you like to come along?
d. A: My car is in the garage for repairs.
    B: How are you going to get to work

tomorrow?

A: I am taking the bus.

The present progressive may be used to express future time when the idea of the sentence con¬cerns a planned event or definite intention.

(COMPARE: A verb such as rain is not used in the present progressive to indicate future time because rain is not a planned event.)

A future meaning for the present progressive tense is indicated either by future time words in the sentence or by the context.

Simple Present

e.	The museum opens at ten tomorrow morning.

f.	Classes begin next week.

g.	John's plane arrives at 6:05 next Monday.	Sometimes the simple present is used in sentences that contain future time words. The simple present is used primarily with verbs such as open/close, begin/end, arrive/leave and expresses an established fact.

(Note: In expressing future time, the present progressive is used in a much wider range of situations than the simple present.)

Future Progressive

a.	I will begin to study at seven. You will come at eight. I will be studying when you come.

b.	Right now I am sitting in class. At this same time tomor¬row, I will be sitting in class.

The future progressive expresses an activity that will be in prog¬ress at a time in the future.

c.	Don't call me at nine be¬cause I won't be home. I am going to be studying at the library.

The progressive form of be going to: be going to + be + -ing

(d) Don't get impatient. She will be coming soon, (e) Don't get impatient. She will come soon.

Sometimes there is little or no difference between the future progressive and the simple future, especially when the future event will occur at an indefinite time in the future, as in (d) and (e).

Future Perfect

a.   I will graduate in June. I will see you in July. By the next time I see you, I will have graduated.
b.   I will have finished my homework by the time I go out on a date tonight.

The future perfect expresses an activity that will be completed before another time or event in the future.
(Notice in the examples: by the time introduces a "time clause"; the simple present is used in a "time clause.")

Future Perfect Progressive

c.   I will go to bed at ten P.M. He will get home at mid¬night. At midnight I will be sleeping. I will have been sleeping for two hours by the time he gets home.

The future perfect progressive emphasizes the duration of an activity that will be in progress before another time or event in the future.

 d.   When Professor Jones re-tires next month, he will have taught for 45 years.
e.   When Professor Jones re-tires next month, he will have been teaching for 45 years. Sometimes the future perfect and the future perfect progres¬sive give the same meaning, as in (d) and (e). Also, notice that the activity expressed by either of these two tenses may begin in the past.

Usually there is little or no difference in meaning between will and be going to. Will and be going to indicate inevitability (i.e., they express a simple factual statement about a future activity or situation), but be

going to is used more frequently than will in spoken English when the speaker is expressing a definite plan or intention.
The present progressive is also sometimes used to express a future meaning. The future intention expressed by the present progressive is usually stronger than that ex¬pressed by be going to.

EXERCISE 1   Use the simple future/be going to* or the simple present.
1. I'm going to leave in half an hour. I (finish) will finish / am going to finish all of my work before I (leave) ____leave____.
2. I'm going to eat lunch at 12:30. After I (eat) ____________________ lunch, I (take)____ a nap.
3. I'll get home around six. When I (get) ________________________________ home, I (call) ________________________________ Sharon.
4. I'm going to watch a TV programme at nine. Before I (watch) ________________________ that programme at nine, I (write) ____________________________ a letter to my parents.
5. Gary will come soon. I (wait) ____________________________ here until he (come) ________
6. It will stop raining soon. As soon as the rain (stop) ____________________________, I (walk) ____________________________ to the drugstore to get some film.
7. The seasons are predictable. For example, when spring (come) ——— ——————— ____________ the weather (get) ____________________ warmer. This happens every year.
8. Right now it is winter. I'm tired of cold weather, but spring (come) __________________ soon. When spring (come) __________________ this year, I (go) __________________ to the park every day to enjoy the good weather.
9.   At a dinner party in the United States, people usually sit in the living room and (talk) ____________________ for a while before they (go) __________________ into the dining room.
10.   Tomorrow I'm going to give a dinner party. I have planned it very carefully. Before I (ask) ______________ my guests to come to the dining room, I (serve) ______________ drinks and hors d'oeuvres in the living room.
11.   A: Have you mailed your application yet?

B: Not yet. I
(fill)____ it out
later this evening. Then I (mail)_______________________________ it on
my way to class tomorrow.
12. A: (Be, Louise) ____at the
meeting tomorrow?
   B: No. She (be, not) _________________________________ there.
13.   Right now I am a junior. After I (graduate)
_________________________________ with a B.A., I   (intend)
_________________________________ to enter graduate school and work for an
M.A. Perhaps I (go)_________________________________ on for a Ph D.
after I (get) _________________________ my Master's degree.
14. A: How long (stay, you) _________________________________in this
country?
   B: I (plan)_________________________________ to be here for
about one more year.
I (hope)_________________________________ to graduate a year
from this June.
   A: What (do, you) _________________________________after you
_________________ (leave)
   B: I (return) _________________________ home and (get)
._______________ a job.

EXERCISE 2   Use the future progressive or the simple present.
1)   Right now I am attending class. Yesterday at this time, I was
attending class. Tomorrow at this time, I
(attend)_______________________ class.
2)   Tomorrow I'm going to leave for home. When I (arrive)
_______________ at the airport, my whole family
(wait)_______________________ for me.
3.   When I (get) _________________________ up tomorrow morning, the
sun (shine) _____________, the birds (sing) _____________, and my
roommate (lie, still) _________________________ in bed fast asleep.
4. A: When do you leave for Florida?
  B: Tomorrow. Just think. Two days from now I (lie)
_________________ on the beach
    in the sun.
  A: Have a good time. I (think)
_________________________________ about you.
5. A: How can I get in touch with you while you're out of town?

B: I (stay) _______________________________ at the Pilgrim Hotel. You can reach me there.

6.   Next year at this time, I (do) _______________________________ exactly what I am doing now. I (attend) _____________________________ school and (study) _____________________________ hard next year.

7. Look at those dark clouds. When class (be) _____________________________ over, it (rain, probably) _____________________________________.

8. A: Are you going to be in town next Saturday?

    B: No. I (visit) ____ my aunt and uncle in Chicago.

EXERCISE 3:   Use any appropriate tense.

1)   Ann and Andy got married on June 1st. Today is June 14th. Ann and Andy (be) _____________________________married for two weeks. By June 7th, they (be) _____________________________ married for one week. By June 28th, they (be) _____________________________ married for four weeks.

2)   This traffic is terrible. We're going to be late. By the time we (get) ———————— _____________________ to the airport, Bob's plane (arrive, already) _____________________, and he will be wondering where we are.

3)   The traffic was very heavy. By the time we (get)_____________________ to the airport, Bob's plane (arrive, already) _____________________________________.

    This morning I came to class at 9:00. Right now it is 10:00 and I am still in class. I (sit)

_____________________________________ at this desk for an hour. By 9:30 I (sit)

_____________________________ this desk for a half an hour. By 11:00 I (sit)

_____________________________ at my desk for two hours.

4)   I'm getting tired of sitting in the car. Do you realize that by the time we arrive in Phoenix, we (drive)

_____________________________ for twenty straight hours?

5)   Margaret was born in 1950. By the year 2010, she (live)_____________________________ on this earth for 60 years.

6)   Go ahead and leave on your vacation. Don't worry about this work. By the time you (get) _____________________________ back, we (take) _____________________care of everything.

7)   I don't understand how those marathon runners do it! The race began over an hour ago. By the time they reach the finish line, they (run) _______________________________ steadily for more than two hours. I don't think I can run more than two minutes!

8)   What? He got married again? At this rate, he (have._______________________ a dozen wives by the time he (die) _______________________________.

9)   We have been married for a long time. By our next anniversary, we (be) _______________ married for 43 years.

EXERCISE 4 -ORAL:

Discuss: What do you think the twenty-first century will be like?

Suggestions for discussion topics:

1. Means of transportation?
2. Sources of energy?
3. Population growth?
4. Food sources?
5. Extinction of animal species?
6. Weapon technology?
7. Exploration of the oceans; exploration of the earth's interior?
8. Space exploration; contact with beings from outer space?
9. Role of computers in daily life?
10. Long-term solutions to today's political crises?
11. Architecture?
12. Clothing styles?
13. International language?
14. International world government?
10)   15. International television; international communication via communication satellites?

Exercise 5: What will they have done?

Write a, b or c in the gap and read the completed sentences.

By the weekend they _____c_______ their newspaper.

a   will have been completing   b   have completed   c) will have completed

1   By Wednesday afternoon, Tom _______________ four people.

a will have interviewed b will interview c will be interviewed

2   By tomorrow night Jenny ______ four articles.

a will be written   b will have written   c won't have been writing

3   When the newspaper comes out, they _______ on it for six weeks.
a will work   b will have been working   c won't have been working
4   They hope that by the end of next week they _____ 2,000 copies.
a will be sold   b will have sold c won't have sold
5   Nick hopes that by the end of the year they _________ rich and famous.
a won't becomeb became   c will have become
6   By next month, Amanda ________ articles.
a   will have written   b   will have been writing   c   will write

Exercise 6: About you
Write the answers in full sentences. Use for + length of time.
How long will you have been learning English by the end of this school year?
By the end of this school year, I will have been learning English for three years.
1   How long will you have been living in your town by next summer?

____
____

2   How long will you have been living in your house or flat by next year?

____
____

3   How long will you have known your English teacher by the end of this school year?

____
____

4   How long will you have known your best friend by next summer?

____
____

5   How long will you have been watching your favourite TV programme by the end of this
    year?

____
6   How long will you have been attending your present school by the end of the school year?

Grammar: Use of Tenses

DREAMING THE GRAMMAR-DREAMS
Do you dream? Let me tell you about a dream I had two nights ago. I hadn't been dreaming for a long long time, in fact since last Christmas. Have you noticed my use of ago, for and since? Send me a message for help if you don't understand the use of the Past Perfect Continuous tense in the third sentence.

Anyway, it was a terrible nightmare. Terrible things were done to me: I was robbed, then I was beaten, and finally I was killed. But then the nightmare changed into a beautiful dream: I seemed to be in some sort of paradise, where all the people were very beautiful and nice, and I was constantly being hugged and kissed.

Exercise 1: Answer the questions in complete sentences:

1. What places have you visited since you came to Feldkirch? When?
2. What countries have you been to? When?
3. What programmess have you seen on television? What did you watch last night?
4. What are you doing right now? What is (. ....) doing? What am I doing?
5. What kind of shoes is (. ....) wearing?
6. What are you wearing today?
7. What will you be doing tonight at midnight? What were you doing last night at midnight?
8. What are you going to be doing at this time tomorrow?
9. What time are you coming to class tomorrow?
10. Where will you be living three years from now?
11. How long have you been going to school?
12. What have we been doing for the last five minutes?
13. How long have you been sitting in that chair?
14. How long will you have been sitting in that chair by the time class is over?

15. Where are you living? Where were you living five years ago?
16. How long are you going to be living in Vorarlberg? How long will you have been living here by the time you leave?
17. What have I been doing?
18. What have we been studying in class?

EXERCISE 2 Use any appropriate tense for the verbs in parentheses.
1)	John is in my English class. He (study) ____________________ English this semester. He (take, also) ____________________ a couple of other classes. His classes (begin) ____________________ at 9:00 every day.
2)	Yesterday John ate breakfast at 8:00. He (eat, already) ____________________ breakfast when he (leave) ____________________ for class at 8:45. He (eat, always) ____________________breakfast before he (go) __________ to class. I (eat, not, usually) ____________________breakfast before I(go) ____________________ to class. But I (get, usually) ____________________ hungry about midmorning. Tomorrow before I (go) ____________________ to class, I (eat) ____________________ breakfast.
3)	John is in class every morning from 9:00 to 12:00. Two days ago, I (call) ____________ him at 11:30, but I could not reach him because he (attend) ____________________ class at that time.
4)	Don't try to call John at 11:30 tomorrow morning because he (attend) ____________________at that time.
5)	Yesterday John took a nap from 1:00 to 2:00. I came at 1:45. When I (get) ____________ there, John (sleep) ____________________. - He (sleep) ____________________ for 45 minutes by the time I came.
6)	Right now John (take) ____________________ a nap. He (fall) ____________________ asleep an hour ago. He (sleep) ____________________ for an hour.
7)	Three days ago, John (start) ____________________ to read Farewell to Arms, a novel by Ernest Hemingway. It is a long novel. He (finish, not) ____________________ reading it yet. He (read) ____________________ it because his English teacher assigned it.
8)	Since the beginning of the semester, John (read) ____________________ three novels. Right now he (read) ____________________ A Farewell to Arms. He (read) ____________________that novel for the past three days. He

(intend) _________________________________ to finish it next week.
In his lifetime, he (read) ____
many novels, but this is the first Hemingway novel he (read, ever)

__________________________________.

9)   Tomorrow, after he (eat) _____________________________
dinner, John (go) _______________________to a movie. In other
words, he (eat) _________________ dinner by the time he (go)
_________________________________ to the movie.

EXERCISE 3: Use any appropriate tense for the verbs in parentheses.
1.   A: There is something I have to tell you.
B: Go ahead. I (listen) ———————————————————.
2.   A: Hi, Ann. (Meet, you) ___________________________ my friend,
George Smith?
B: No, I (have, never) ______________________________ . the pleasure.
A: Then let me introduce you.
3.   A: Stop! What (you, do)
____?
        B: I (try) _______________________ to get this piece of
toast out of the
toaster. It's stuck.
A: Well, don't use a knife. You
(electrocute)______________________________ yourself!
B: What do you suggest I do?
A: Unplug it first.
4   A: There's Jack.
B: Where?
A: He (lie) _______________________ on the grass under that
tree over there. B: Oh yes. I (see) _____________________________ him.
He (look, certainly) _________
_____________________________________ comfortable. Let's go talk to
him.
5.   A: (Take, you) _______________________________ Econ 120 this
semester?
        B: No, I ____.
        A: (Take, you, ever)
____ it?
        B: Yes, I ____.

A: When (take) ____________________you
____________________it?
B: Last semester.
A: Who (be) ________________ your professor?
B: Dr. Lee.
A: Oh, I have the same professor. What (be, he)
________________ like?
B: He (be) ____________________ very good.
6.   A: What's wrong with Chris?
B: While he (yawn)———————————————, a fly (fly)
____________ into his mouth.
A: I (believe, not) ________________________________ that! You (kid)

____
7   A: I (go) ____________________________ to a play last night.
B: (Be, it) ____________________ any good?
A: I thought so. I (enjoy) ____________________________ it a lot.
B: What (be, it) ____________________________?
A: Arsenic and Old Lace. I (see, never) ________________ it before.
B: Oh, I (see) ____________________________ that play too. I (see)

______
____________________ it a couple of years ago. It (be)
____________________ good, (be, not) ____________________
it?
8.   A: I was in your hometown last month. It looked like a nice
town. I (be, never)
____________________ there before.
B: What (do, you) ____________________ in that part of the country?
A: My wife and I (drive) ____________________ to Washington to
visit her folks.
9   A: May I borrow some money? My check (be)
____________________supposed to arrive yesterday, but I still (receive,
not) ____________________ it. I (need) ____________ to buy a book
for one of my classes, but I (have, not) ________________ any money.
B: Sure. I'd be happy to lend you some. How much (need,
you)____________________?
A: Five bucks {be} ____________________ enough. Thanks. I
(pay)____________
____________________ you back as soon as I (get)
____________________ my check.
10.   A: Hello?

B: Hello. May I speak to Sue?
A: She (be, not) _________________________________ in right now. May I take a
message?
B: Yes. This is Art O'Brien. Would you please ask her to meet me at the library
this afternoon? I (sit) _____________________________ at one of the study
booths on the second floor.

EXERCISE   4:   Use any appropriate tense for the verbs in parentheses.
1   My grandfather (fly, never) ____________________________ in an
airplane, and he has no intention of ever doing so.
2   Jane isn't here yet. I (wait) ____________________________ for her
since noon, but she still (arrive, not) __________________.
3   In all the world, there (be) _______________________________
only 14 mountains that (reach) __________________ above 8,000
meters (26,247 feet).
4   I have a long trip ahead of me tomorrow, so I think I'd better go
to bed. But let me say good-bye now because I won't see you in the
morning. I (leave, already) ________________ by the time you (get)
_________________________________up.
5   Right now we (have) _________________________________ a
heat wave. The tempera¬ture (be) _________________ in the upper
90's for the last six days.
6   Last night I (go) _________________________________ to a
party. When I (get) ___ _________________ there, the room was full of
people. Some of them (dance) __________________ and others (talk)
__________________. One young woman (stand)
__________________ by herself. I (meet,
never)__________________ her, so I
_________________________________ (introduce) myself to her.
7   About three yesterday afternoon, Jessica
(lie)__________________ in bed reading a book. Suddenly she (hear)
__________________ loud noise and (get) ____________ up to see
what it was. She (look) _________________________ out the window. A
truck (back, just) _________________________________ into her new car!
8   Next month I have a week's vacation. I (plan)
__________________ to take a trip. First, I (go) __________________ to
Madison, Wisconsin, to visit my brother. After I (leave)
__________________ Madison, I (go) __________________ to Chicago to

see a friend who (study) _____________________ at a university there. She (live) _____________________ in Chicago for three years, so she (know) _____________________ her way around the city. She (promise) _____________________ to take me to many interesting places. I (be, never) _____________________ in Chicago, so I (look) _____________________ forward to going there.

9   Yesterday while I (sit) _____________________ in class, I (get) _____________________ the hiccups. The person who (sit)_____________________ next to me told me to hold my breath. I (try)_____________________ that, but it didn't work. The instructor (lecture)_____________________ and I didn't want to interrupt him, so I just sat there trying to hiccup quietly. Finally, after I (hiccup)_____________________ for almost five minutes, I (raise) _____________________ my hand and (excuse) _____________________ myself from the class to go get a drink of water.

10   The weather has been terrible lately. It (rain)_____________________ off and on for two days, and the temperature (drop)_____________________ at least twenty degrees. It (be)_____________________ in the low 40's right now. Just three days ago, the sun (shine) _____________________ and the weather was pleasant. The weather certainly (change) _____________________ quickly here. I never know what to expect. Who knows? When I (wake) _____________________ up tomorrow morning, maybe it (snow) _____________________.

EXERCISE 5   Use any appropriate tense.

1)   On June 20th, I returned home. I (be)

____

2)   away from home for two years. My family (meet)

____

3)   me at the airport with kisses and tears. They (miss)_____________________________

4)   me as much as I had missed them. I (be) _____________________ very

5)   happy to see them again. When I (get) _____________________ the

6)   chance, I (take) _____________________ a long look at them. My little

7)   brother (be) _________________________________ no longer so little. He (grow)

8)   __________________ at least a foot. He (be)

____

9)   almost as tall as my father. My little sister (wear)

____

10)   a green dress. She (change) __________________ quite a bit, too, but

11)   she (be, still) __________________ mischievous and inquisitive. She

12)   (ask) __________________ me a thousand questions a minute, or so

13)   it seemed. My father (gain) __________,_________ some weight, and

14)   his hair (turn) __________________ a little bit grayer, but otherwise

15)   he was just as I had remembered him. My mother (look)

____

16)   a little older, but not much. The wrinkles on her face (be)

____

17)   smile wrinkles.

EXERCISE 6:   Use any appropriate tenses.
1)   On June 20th, I will return home. I (be) ____________________
2)   away from home for two years by that time. My family (meet)
3)   __________________ me at the airport with kisses and tears. They
4)   (miss) __________________ me as much as I have missed them. I
5)   (be) ————————————————————— very happy to see them again. When
6)   I (get) __________________ a chance, I (take) ___________
7)   a long look at them. My little brother (be, no longer)

____

8)   so little. He (grow) __________________ at least a foot. He (be)
9)   __________________ almost as tall as my father. My little sister
10)   (wear, probably) ______________________________ a green dress.
11)   She (change)__________________ quite a bit, too, but she (be, still)
12)   __________________ mischievous and inquisitive. She (ask, probably)

13) ______________________ me a thousand questions a minute, or so

14) it will seem. My father (gain, probably) ______________________ some

15) weight, and his hair (turn) ______________________ a little grayer, but

16) otherwise he will be just as I remember him. My mother (look)

17) ______________________ just the same. Perhaps she (look)

18) ______________________ a little older, but not much. The wrinkles on

19) her face (be) ______________________ smile wrinkles.

EXERCISE 7   Use any appropriate tenses.

1) Dear Ann,

2) I (receive) ______________________ your letter about two weeks

3) ago and (try) ______________________ to find time to write you back

4) ever since. I (be) ______________________ very busy lately. In the past

5) two weeks, I (have) ______________________ four tests, and I have

6) another test next week. In addition, a friend (stay)

____

7) with me since last Thursday. She wanted to see the city, so we (spend)

8) ______________________ a lot of time visiting some of the interesting

9) places here. We (be) ______________________ to the zoo, the art

10) museum, and the botanical gardens. Yesterday we (go)

____

11) to the park and (watch) ______________________ a balloon race.

12) Between showing her the city and studying for my exams, I (have, barely)

13) ———————————————————enough time to breathe.

14) Right now it (be) ______________________ 3 A.M. and I (sit)

15) ______________________ at my desk. I (sit) ______________

16) here five hours doing my studying. My friend's plane (leave)

17) ______________________ at 6:05, so I (decide)

____

18) not to go to bed. That's why I (write) ______________________ you at

19) such an early hour in the day. I (get) ______________________ a little

20)   sleepy, but I would rather stay up. I (take) ________________ a
21)   nap after I (get) ___________________ back from taking her to the
22)   airport.
23)   How (get, you) ___________________ along? How (go, your
24)   classes) ___________________? Please write soon.
Yours truly,

EXERCISE 8   Use any appropriate tense.
A: Hi, my name is Jose.
B: Hi, my name is Ali.
1)   Jose: (You, study) ___________________________________ at this university?
2)   Ali: Yes, I ___________________. _______________ you?
3)   Jose: Yes, I (be) ___________________ here since last September.
Before that I (study) _______________ English at another school.
4)   Ali: What (you, take) ___________________________?
5)   Jose: I (take) _______________________________ chemistry, math, psychology, and American history. What (take, you) _______________________________?
6)   Ali: I (study) ___________________________ English. I (need) ___________________________ to improve my English before I (take) _______________ regular academic courses next semester.
7)   Jose: How long (you, be) _______________________________here?
8)   Ali: I (be) ___________________________ here since the beginning of this semester. Actually. I (arrive) ___________________________in the United States six months ago, but I (study) ___________________________ English at this university only since January. Before that I (live) _______________ with my brother in Washington, D.C.
9)   Jose: You (speak) —————————————————— English very well. (You, study) ___________________ a lot of English before you (come) _______________ __ to the United States?
10)   Ali: Yes. I (study) ———————————————————— English for ten years in my own country. And also, I (spend) _________________ some time in Canada a couple of years ago. I (pick) ___________________________ up a lot of English while I (live) _______________ there.

11)   Jose: You (be) _______________________________lucky. When I (come) __________________ to the United States, I (study, never) __________________ any English at all. So I had to spend a whole year studying nothing but English before I (start) _______ school.

12)   Ali: How long (you, plan) ___________________________________ to be in the U.S.?

13)   Jose: I (be, not)_____________________________________ sure. Probably by the time I (return) __________________ home, I (be) ____________ here for at least five years. How about you?

14)   Ali: I (hope) ___________________to be finished with all my work in two and a half years.

EXERCISE 9:
.Put the verbs in brackets into the correct tenses.

1)   They ____ your lessons. (not like)

2)   While we _________________________________ to the station it __________________to snow, (drive)   (begin)

3)   Watch this runner. He _______________________________________ (win).

4)   After the centre forward ______________________________________ the first goal the fans ___________________ mad (score)   (go)

5)   I ___________________________________ a shooting star (never see)

6)   We ___________________________________ the results tomorrow. (know)

7)   Diana ____ Beethoven's moonlight sonata last night. (play)

8)   She ___________________________________ you are an old fool. (think)

9)   Bob _________________________________ three letters since breakfast. (write)

10)   Kate ____ in London (not live)

11)   She _________________________________ me an answer when I asked her. (not give)

12)   After Jane _____________________________________ a fashion magazine she ______________ the piano, (read)   (practise)

13)   Our landlady _________________________________ us a cup of tea last night. (give)

14)   Mr Brightwell _________________________________(phone) his secretary all day long .

15)   I _________________________________ any dressmaking since I left school, (not do)

16)   Mr Bellows _________________________ from the USA. (just arrive)

17)   Mr Brown _________________________________ a letter every day. (write)

18)   Mrs Mauldling _________________________________ the letter immediately after she _________________________________it (post) (finish)

19)   The Smiths _________________________________ yet. (not come)

20)   I _________________________________ two exercises, would you like to do the third? (correct)

21)   Richard usually_________________________________ a pullover but when I _______________ him last night he _________________________ a coat. (wear) (see) (wear)

22)   _________________________________to Mexico? (you, ever, be)

23)   I _________________________________ to Jane since last Monday. (not write)

24)   _________________________________to phone you last night? (Bob try)

25)   I _________________________________ this play before. (not see)

26)   Jeffrey thanked his father for what he _________________________________ for him. (do)

27)   Mary and Lizzy _________________________________ the poem all afternoon. (learn)

28)   Bob _________________________________ football all the afternoon. (play)

29)   They'd better come in. It _________________________________ to rain (begin)

30)   Bettie _________________________ his coat last night. (tear)

31)   The Second World War _________________________________ in 1939. (begin)

32)   Your coat _________________________________ there the whole afternoon. (lie)

33)   The postman ______________________________________ the post every day. (bring)

34)   She ____ you (soon forget)

35)   I __________________________________ a coat because it's too hot today. (not wear)

36)   Lizzie and Dolly ______________________________________ at six this morning, (wake up)

37)   We ____ an answer last night. (not get)

38)   My parents ______________________________________ in Berlin since 1980. (live)

39)   "How______________________________________ at school? -I __________________ very well (Bob get on) (believe)

40)   Jaqueline ______________________________ why I ______________________________ earlier. (wonder)   (write)

41)   ____ the film last night? (you see)

42)   We need not run. ____________________________________ the bus (you see). It ____________________ the bus station (just leave)

43)   I ____________________________________ a letter (write) when Fred ____________________ the room (enter)

44)   Peter ____ his best now. (try)

45)   I ____________________________________ the work tomorrow. (do)

46)   I couldn't answer the phone because I ____________________________ a shave. (have)

47)   I can't understand what you ____. The traffic is too noisy. (say)

48)   Mathews ____________________________________ an interesting play most of the evening. (watch)

49)   Peter suddenly ____________________________ that he ____________________________ his cap in the train, (realize) (leave)

50)   He ____ next week. (not come)

51)   Before he ______________________________ away he ____________________ a letter. (go) (write)

52) Bob ________________________________ tennis very well. (not play)

53) When I ________________________him he____________________ to Helen,   (see)   (talk)

54) You need an umbrella. It ____ (rain)

55) She ____________________ stay up later than nine yesterday, (mustn't)

56) I ________________________________ finish my work last night. (must)

57) We ____________________________ this letter before he ____________________ home (can translate)   (go)

58) John ____________________________ do it now. I ____________________________ it later, (not need)   (do)

.

6. Worksheets

Worksheet 1

Aspect
Definition
Aspect is a grammatical element that has to do with how an action, state of
being, or event as described by a verb relates to time. Aspect is often confused
with **tense**. While **tense** is concerned with when the action, state of being, or
event occurs (past, present, or future), **aspect** is concerned with how it occurs in
time. It is through aspect that we understand whether an action takes place at a
single point in time, during a continuous range of time, or repetitively.
Sometimes aspect is conveyed by a sentence's structure, through a combination
of particles, verbs, and verb phrases; other times, sentence structure may be used
for more than one aspect, so we rely on the overall sentence to understand its
temporal meaning.

Perfective and imperfective aspect
The most common distinction made regarding aspect is between the **perfective**
and **imperfective** aspects. While other languages mark the difference by using
two separate verb forms, English does not.
The **perfective aspect** can be conveyed through a variety of verb structures. It is
used when we draw attention to an action as a whole, summarizing it. The
perfective aspect may occur in past, present, or future actions and events. For

example:
- "I **ate** dinner."
- "I **swim** like a fish."
- "I **have** never **been** there before."
- "We **will help** you tomorrow."

The **imperfective aspect**, on the other hand, is used to draw attention to the

action as having an internal structure (rather than as a whole, complete action).

Like the perfective, this is the case regardless of *when* the event occurs. One instance of the imperfective is when we relate an action that is considered to

be in progress at the moment of speaking (or at the time of another event). This

is usually conveyed through the **continuous aspect**. For example:
- "I was washing dishes when she came through the door."

We also use the imperfective when we describe actions or events as occurring

repetitively, either now or in the past:
- "We used to go traveling a lot."
- "John runs five miles every day."

This is known as the **habitual** aspect.

Aspects of verb tenses

Traditionally, each verb tense is said to have four aspects, or temporal structures:

the *simple*, the *perfect*, the *continuous*, and the *perfect continuous*. These

traditional aspects of the tenses do not always coincide with theory on perfective

aspect and imperfective aspect—it should be remembered that certain structures

may express perfective aspect in some cases and imperfective aspect in others,

depending on the intended meaning.

Aspects of the present tense

The present tense is used for repeated actions, and for actions occurring or

having a result in the present. The different aspects of the present tense can be

found in the table below:

Aspect Structure Examples
Simple Subject + present verb
"I **go** shopping on
Tuesdays."
"She **runs** fast."
Perfect Subject + *have/has* + past
participle
"I **have eaten** here
before."
"She **has lived** here for a
long time."
Continuous Subject + *is/are* + present
participle
"We **are cooking** dinner."
"He **is singing** a song."
Perfect
Continuous
Subject + *have/has* + *been* +
present participle
"He **has been thinking**
about it."
"I **have been taking** an art
class."
Usually, the simple and the perfect aspects match up with the
perfective aspect in
grammatical theory. However, as mentioned, this is not always the case.
It could
be argued in this case that the simple aspect of the present tense
actually
corresponds with the imperfective aspect, since it is usually used to
convey
habitual acts, as in:
• "I go to school every day."
• "We go shopping on Saturdays."
Aspects of the past tense
Like the present, the past tense also has four traditional aspects, which
can be
found in the table below:
Aspect Structure Examples
Simple Subject + past verb

"I **went** shopping on
Tuesday."
"She **ran** fast."
Perfect Subject + *had* + past participle
"I **had eaten** here before."
"She **had lived** here for a
long time."
Continuous Subject + *was/were* + present
participle
"We **were cooking** dinner."
"He **was singing** a song."
Perfect
Continuous
Subject + *had + been* + present
participle
"He **had been thinking**
about it."
"I **had been taking** an art
class."
The simple and perfect simple tenses generally correspond with the perfective
aspect, while the continuous and perfect continuous correspond with the
imperfective aspect. Again, these do not always match up along clear lines, and
we should consider what the verb phrase conveys overall to decide whether the
sentence has perfective or imperfective aspect.

Aspects of the future tense
Although English does not have an inflected verb form for *future tense*,
there are
several structures that we use to convey future meaning, namely *will/would/be*
going to + verb. The different aspects of these structures are found in
the table:

Aspect Structure Examples
Simple Subject + *will/would/be going to* +
infinitive
"I **will go** shopping
on Tuesday."

" She **is going to run**
fast."
Perfect Subject + *will have* + past participle
"I **will have eaten**
before arriving."
"She **will have lived**
here for a long time."
Continuous Subject + *will/would/be going to* + be +
present participle
"We **are going to be**
cooking dinner."
"He **will be singing** a
song."
Perfect
Continuous
Subject + *will have/would have/be going*
to + have + been + present participle
"He**'ll have been**
thinking about it."
"I **would have been**
taking an art class."
Again, the simple and perfect aspects generally correspond with
perfective
aspect in the future, while the continuous and perfect continuous
structures
correspond with the imperfective.
Exercise

1. In grammar, **aspect** is concerned with __________ .
a) *when* events occur on a timeline
b) *how* events occur on a timeline
c) *why* events occur on a timeline
2. The **perfective aspect** is used when we view an action as __________.
a) a whole
b) a part
c) a continuous event
d) a habitual event
3. The **imperfective aspect** is used when we view an action as
__________.
a) habitual

b) in progress
c) a whole
d) A & B
e) all of the above
4. Which of the following sentences conveys the **continuous** aspect?
a) "I went to the doctor on Tuesday."
b) "She's going to take me on a vacation."
c) "They've been watching that TV all day."
d) "We haven't seen that movie yet."
5. Which of the following sentences uses the **perfect** aspect?"
a) "I was reading."
b) "He went home."
c) "She is eating."
d) "They have gone home."

Perfective and Imperfective Aspect

Definition

Aspect is a grammatical term that has to do with how an action, state of being,
or event unfolds in relation to time. The greatest distinction is made between the
perfective aspect, which focuses on actions and events as whole elements, and
the **imperfective** aspect, which deconstructs how an event is structured and
located in time.
While other languages may mark the difference with an inflected verb form,
English instead relies on a combination of particles, verbs, verb phrases, and
lexical clues to determine whether the overall meaning of the action is perfective
or imperfective.

Perfective aspect

The **perfective aspect** highlights actions, states, or events as a whole, presenting
the actions from an outside perspective as complete, bounded events.
The perfective aspect is encountered in all of the tenses—past, present, and
future—but it is easiest to illustrate in the past. For example:
• "I **went** to the supermarket yesterday." (**past simple tense**)

- "She **sang** in the choir." (past simple tense)
- "We **had eaten** already." (**past perfect tense**)

In all of the above examples, the action is presented as a complete event in the

past. We are simply told that the event occurred, with no clues as to *how often*

the actions happened or *how long* they took.

As mentioned, the perfective aspect also occurs in other tenses. For example:

- "I **have** a dog." (**present simple tense**)
- "She**'ll be** there soon." (**future simple tense**)
- "They **will have finished** by then." (**future perfect tense**)

Imperfective aspect

The **imperfective aspect**, on the other hand, is used when we focus on the

internal structures of an action, state, or event as it relates to time, such as being

continuous or habitual (repeating). Again, this has nothing to do with *when* the

event occurs, and, as with the perfective, there is no separate verb form in

English for the imperfective aspect.

Instead, it is expressed through different grammatical structures, which change

depending on what we are saying about the temporal structure of the action.

We sometimes classify these structures as the **continuous aspect** and the

habitual aspect, both of which are subclasses of the imperfective.

Continuous Aspect

The **continuous aspect**, also called the **progressive aspect**, is a subclass of the

imperfective that emphasizes the *progressive* nature of the verb, looking at it as

an incomplete action in progress over a specific period of time.

The continuous aspect does not indicate the duration of the action, nor how often

it occurs. It simply shows that the action or event is in progress, either at the time

of speaking, or at the time that another event occurs. It can be used with the past,
present, and future tenses, and it is usually conveyed using a form of the verb *be*
+ the present participle. For example:

Past

- "I **was talking** to my mother when you called."
- "They **had been living** here for a long time when they moved."

Present

- "I**'m cooking** dinner at the moment, so I'll have to call you back."
- "She**'s been playing** outside with her friends all day."

Future

- "He**'ll be sleeping** by 10 o'clock, hopefully."
- "Next month we**'ll have been living** in New York City for 10 years."

It should be noted that **stative verbs** do not normally occur using the *be* +
present participle structure. For example, you could not say "I **am knowing** John
a long time" or "She **is appearing** unwell."

Other constructions

There is disagreement over whether structures using *be* + the present participle
are the only structures that depict the continuous aspect. It is often argued, for
example, that the past simple often conveys the continuous aspect. For example:

- "I **stayed** up all night."
- "We **were** outside for hours."

Others would argue that since it is the additional information in the examples
above (*all night* and *for hours*) that gives the continuous aspect to the sentence
as a whole, the verb phrases themselves should not be considered to convey
continuous aspect.

Habitual Aspect

The **habitual aspect**, like the continuous aspect, is also a subclass of the
imperfective aspect. It is used when an action occurs repetitively and (usually)

predictably. English only has two *marked* ways of expressing habitual aspect:

would + base form of the verb (the infinitive without *to*) and *used to + base form*

of the verb. When we use these structures, we imply that the action occurred

habitually in the past, but does not anymore. For example:

- "When I was young I **used to walk** to school."
- "When I was young I **would walk** to school."

Although the meaning in the two examples above is the same, *used to* and *would*

are not always directly interchangeable. For example, *used to*, standing alone,

conveys habitual aspect, but *would* doesn't. Observe what happens if we remove

the time marker *when I was young*:

- "I **used to walk** to school."
- "I **would walk** to school."

When we remove *when I was young* from the examples, the example using *used*

to retains its habitual aspect, but the example with *would* doesn't. Since *would*

can also be used in conditional constructions, we need to include a time marker

to clarify when it is being used for the habitual past.

In addition, while *used to* can be used with both **action verbs** and **stative verbs**,

would can only be used with **action verbs**. For example:

✔ "When I was young, I **used to love** movies." (correct)

✖ "When I was young, I **would love** movies." (incorrect)

Other constructions

Although *used to + base form* and *would + base form* are the only structures that

explicitly mark habitual aspect, we often use other verb tenses to convey it as

well. For example, we often use the present simple tense to indicate habitual

actions, as in:

- "I **go** to school every day."

- "She **attends** karate class on Sundays."
- "They **work** six days a week."

However, other verb tenses can be used with an implied habitual aspect. For
example:

- "I **walked** to school every day for 10 years." (past simple tense)
- "I **had lived** in the same town my whole life before I decided to move to
Tokyo." (past perfect tense)
- "She **has eaten** the same sandwich for lunch for as long as I've known her."
(present perfect tense)

When the habitual aspect is unmarked, as above, it is often accompanied by a
time marker that clarifies how often the action occurs, such as *every day, on
Sundays, six days a week*, etc.

Future habits

English does not have an explicit habitual aspect marker for the future either.
Most often, we use the future simple tense along with a time marker to indicate
habit. For example:

- "I **will work** extra shifts every evening until I save enough money."
- "I **will go** for a run every day after school this year.
- "We **will eat** fruit and cereal every morning next month."

As with the alternate constructions of the perfective aspect, there is disagreement
over whether unmarked verb forms can be considered to express habitual aspect,
since it may simply be the additional information in the sentence that expresses
the habitual meaning, rather than the verb phrases themselves.

Exercise

1. Which of the following sentences conveys the **perfective aspect**?
a) "I have eaten breakfast already."
b) "I've been eating breakfast."
c) "I was eating breakfast."
d) "I used to eat breakfast in the late morning."

2. Which of the following sentences conveys the **imperfective aspect**?
a) "He finished his homework."
b) "He had already finished his homework."
c) "He will finish his homework later."
d) "He's finishing his homework."
3. Which of the following sentences conveys the **habitual aspect**?
a) "I attended a ballet lesson."
b) "I want to attend ballet lessons."
c) "I used to attend ballet lessons."
d) "I will attend a ballet lesson."
4. Which of the following sentences uses the **continuous** aspect?
a) "I used to watch a lot of TV."
b) "I watched a lot of TV yesterday."
c) "I will watch TV later."
d) "I've been watching a lot of TV."
5. Which of the following sentences is incorrect?
a) "I used to like sweets when I was little, but now I don't."
b) "I liked sweets when I was little, but now I don't."
c) "I would like sweets when I was little, but now I don't."
d) A & C

Aspects of the Present Tense
Definition
The **present tense** is combined with four traditional **aspects** to form the
structures that are known as the **present simple**, the **present
continuous** (or
present progressive), the **present perfect**, and the **present perfect
continuous**.
Although these structures are generally taught as individual "tenses" of
verbs,
they are actually a combination of the present tense and aspect. While
the **tense**
tells us when the action takes place in relation to time (in this case, the
present),
the added *aspect* gives us information about how the event takes place
in time.

Present Simple
The **present simple** structure is used to express facts and habits that are
true in
the present time. It is formed using the **bare infinitive** (the base form of
the

verb), or, in the case of the third person singular, the bare infinitive + "-s". For
example:
- "We **love** Thai food."
- "James **swims** on Sundays."
- "We **study** at the library every day."

Present Continuous

The **present continuous** is the combination of the present tense with the
continuous aspect. It is used for actions that are either in progress at the moment
of speaking, or will be in progress in the near future. It is formed using the
present form of the verb *be* (*are, am,* or *is*) + the present participle. For
example:
- "They**'re playing** outside." (in progress now)
- "Can I call you back? I**'m driving**." (in progress now)
- "We**'re eating** dinner with my in-laws tonight." (in progress in the future)

The continuous aspect is not usually used with **stative verbs**. For example, we
cannot say "I am knowing John many years" or "She is seeming sad."

Present Perfect

The **present perfect** is the combination of the present tense and the perfect
aspect. It is used for actions or states that began in the past but have an effect on
or relevance to the present, stressing the completion of the action. It is formed
using *have/has* + the **past** participle. For example:
- "She**'s** already **eaten**."
- "We**'ve seen** this movie."
- "I**'ve had** a bad cold this week."

Present Perfect Continuous

The **present perfect continuous** is the combination of the continuous and
perfect aspects with the present tense. It is used for actions that began in the past
and continue to have relevance in the present. The main difference between it

and the present perfect aspect is that the present perfect continuous aspect
emphasizes the progress of the action instead of its completion. Like the present
continuous, it is typically only used with **action verbs**, not with stative verbs.
The present perfect continuous is formed using *have/has + been* + the **present**
participle. For example:
- "We **have been waiting** for a long time."
- "My little sister **has been sitting** very quietly."
- "I**'ve been cleaning** all day."

Exercise

1. Which of the following is in the **present simple** form?
a) went
b) have been
c) goes
d) going
2. Which of the following is in the **present perfect** form?
a) saw
b) have seen
c) sees
d) seeing
3. Which of the following is in the **present perfect continuous** form?
a) has been going
b) had been going
c) had gone
d) goes
4. Which of the following is in the **present continuous** form?
a) sang
b) have sung
c) singing
d) been singing
5. Which of the following structures is used for **facts that are true at the moment of speaking**:
a) present simple
b) present continuous
c) present perfect
d) present perfect continuous

5. Which of the following sentences stresses the **completion** of an action that
occurred in the past but has relevance to the present?
a) "She buys everything we need."
b) "She's been buying everything we need."
c) "She bought everything we need."
d) "She has bought everything we need."

Aspects of the Past Tense

Definition

The **past tense** is combined with four traditional **aspects** to form the structures
that are known as the **past simple**, the **past continuous** (or past progressive), the
past perfect, and the **past perfect continuous**. Although these structures are
generally taught as individual "tenses" of verbs, they are actually a combination
of the past tense and aspect. While the **tense** tells us when the action takes place
in relation to the time (in this case, the past), the added *aspect* tells us how the
event takes place in time.

Past Simple

The **past simple** structure is used to express actions and events that were
completed at a given moment in the past. Whether the occurrence is of short or
long duration, the simple aspect emphasizes its completion. The past simple is
formed by adding "-d" or "-ed" to the end of **regular verbs**, but the past form of
irregular verbs must be memorized. For example:
- "They **lived** next door to us for years." (regular)
- "I **locked** myself out of the house this morning." (regular)
- "We *went* to a private school when we were young." (irregular)

Past Continuous

The **past continuous** is the combination of the past tense with the continuous
aspect. It emphasizes the progress of an action that occurred in the past, rather

than its completion. It is often used for actions that are interrupted by other
actions, and it is formed using the past form of the verb *be* (*was/were*) + the
present participle. For example:
• "They **were playing** outside when their father arrived."
• "I'm sorry I didn't answer the phone; I **was driving** when you called."
• "We **were eating** dinner when my in-laws told us the good news."
The past continuous usually occurs only with **action verbs**, not with **stative**
verbs. For instance, we cannot say "I was knowing John many years" or "She
was seeming sad."

Past Perfect

The **past perfect** is the combination of the past tense with the perfect aspect. It is
used for actions or states that began and were completed before another action in
the past took place. It is formed using *had* + the past participle. For example:
• "She **had** already **eaten** when she arrived."
• "We **had seen** the movie, but we watched it again."
• "I**'d had** a bad cold that week, but I went on my vacation anyway."

Past Perfect Continuous

The **past perfect continuous** is the combination of the continuous and perfect
aspects with the past tense. It is used for actions that took place before another
past action. The main difference between it and the past perfect structure is that
the past perfect continuous emphasizes the progress of the action instead of its
completion. It is also used to emphasize the action's strong effect on another
moment in the past. Like the past continuous, the past perfect continuous is
generally only used with action verbs, not stative verbs. It is formed using *had +*
been + the present participle. For example:
• "We **had been waiting** for a long time when the bus finally came."

• "My little sister **had been sitting** very quietly, but then she started to cry."
• "I**'d been cleaning** all day, so I was too tired to go out last night."
Exercise

1. Which of the following is in the **past simple** form?
a) sang
b) have sung
c) sing
d) singing
2. Which of the following is in the **past perfect** form?
a) was
b) had been
c) is
d) being
3. Which of the following is in the **past perfect continuous** form?
a) had been doing
b) has been doing
c) had done
d) does
4. Which of the following structures is used to emphasize general **completion** in
the past?
a) past continuous
b) past simple
c) past perfect
d) past perfect continuous
5. Which of the following sentences emphasizes the **progress** of a past action
that occurred before another action in the past?
a) "She sang in a band."
b) "She had been singing in a band at that point."
c) "She sings in a band."
d) "She has sung in a band."

Aspects of the Future Tense
Definition
Although English has no future tense in the strict sense (i.e., it has no verb form

specific to future meaning), we commonly refer to several structures that are
used for future meaning as belonging to the " **future tense**." The most common
of these structures begin with *will* or a form of the verb *be + going to.* For
example:
• "I **will** go with you."
• "I **am going to** send you an email."
While these verb markers tell us that the action takes place in the future, it is the
aspect of the verb that tells us *how* the event will be temporally structured. The
combination of the future marker and the aspect results in the verb structures that
we usually call the **future simple**, the **future continuous** (or future progressive),
the **future perfect**, and the **future perfect continuous**.
For the purpose of clarity, our example sentences will all use *will*, but it should
be remembered that, in each of the examples, we can replace *will* with another
modal verb of future meaning (*shall, might, would, could*, etc.) or with a form
of *be + going to*.
Future Simple
The **future simple** structure is the combination of the future tense and the simple
aspect. The future simple is used to express actions and events that will occur at
a given moment in the future. The simple aspect emphasizes the action or state
as a whole. The structure is formed using *will* + the base form of the verb (the
infinitive without *to*). For example:
• "We **will go** to a private school when we are older."
• "They **will move** next door to us soon."
• "I **will be** famous in the future."
Future Continuous

The **future continuous** structure is the combination of the future tense with the
continuous aspect. It is used to express actions and events that will be in
progress at a given moment in the future. The future continuous is formed using
will + be + the present participle. For example:
• "They **will be playing** outside when their father arrives."
• "I won't answer my phone later because I**'ll be driving**."
• "We **will be eating** dinner at 7 o'clock."
Like other structures that reflect the continuous aspect, it is usually only used
with **action verbs**, not with **stative verbs**. For example, we couldn't say "I will
be knowing John later" or "She will be seeming sad this evening."
Future Perfect
The **future perfect** is the combination of the future tense and the perfect simple
aspect. It is used to express actions and events that will be completed at a given
moment in the future. It is formed using *will* + *have* + the past participle. For
example:
• "She **will have eaten** before she arrives."
• "We **will have seen** that movie already."
• "I **will have spent** a lot of money after this weekend's festivities."
Future Perfect Continuous
Finally, the **future perfect continuous** is the combination of the perfect and
continuous aspects with the future tense. It is used to emphasize that an action
will be in progress until a given moment in the future, at which time the action
will stop. Like the future continuous, it is typically not used with **stative verbs**,
but only with action verbs. It is formed using *will* + *have* + *been* + the present
participle. For example:
• "We **will have been waiting** for a long time when the bus finally comes."

• "My little sister **will have been sitting** quietly for an hour when the movie
finishes."
• "I **will have been cleaning** all day when you arrive, so I'll be too tired to go
out."
Exercise

1. Which of the following is in the **future simple** form?
a) sing
b) will have sung
c) will sing
d) will be singing
2. Which of the following is in the **future perfect** form?
a) will watch
b) will have watched
c) will be watching
d) will have been watching
3. Which of the following is in the **future perfect continuous** form?
a) will have been doing
b) will have done
c) will be doing
d) will do
4. Which of the following structures is used to emphasize an action that will be
in progress at a particular moment in the future?
a) future simple
b) future continuous
c) future perfect simple
d) future perfect continuous
5. Which of the following sentences emphasizes the **completion** of a future
action before another action in the future?
a) "She'll have been doing all her work."
b) "She'll be doing all her work then."
c) "She'll do all her work."
d) "She'll have done all her work by then."
Mood
Definition

Grammatical **mood** refers to the way in which a verb is used to express certain
meaning by the speaker or writer. In linguistics, moods are broken down into
two main categories: **realis moods** (expressing what is real or true) and **irrealis**
moods (expressing what is unreal, hypothetical, or untrue).

Realis moods (the indicative mood)

The **indicative mood** is a type of grammatical **mood** used to express facts,
statements, opinions, or questions. It is the only **realis mood** used in English.

This mood is used in all verb tenses to form **declarative sentences** (i.e.,
statements or declarations) or **interrogative sentences** (i.e., questions). For
example:

- "She **graduated** last year with a doctorate in neuroscience." (declarative
sentence in the past simple tense)
- "He **is taking** his exam at the new testing center." (declarative sentence in the
present continuous tense)
- "**Are** you **going to give** your speech tomorrow?" (interrogative sentence in the
future simple tense)

The indicative mood is the most commonly used grammatical mood in English.

Irrealis Moods

The term **irrealis** means "unreal," and it refers to grammatical moods that reflect
what is not actually the case.

There are two irrealis moods in English: the **subjunctive mood** and the
imperative mood.

Subjunctive Mood

The **subjunctive mood** refers to verbs that are conjugated a certain way to
describe hypothetical or non-real actions, events, or situations. This is in
comparison to the **indicative mood**, which is used to express factual,
nonhypothetical
information.

We most commonly use the subjunctive mood to express wishes; to express
commands, suggestions, requests, or statements of necessity; or to describe
hypothetical outcomes that depend on certain conditions.
For example:
• "I wish I **didn't have to go** to work." (wish)
• "He demanded that they **leave** the room at once." (command)
• "I recommend that she **study** harder next time." (suggestion)
• "I ask that the audience **be** completely silent during the demonstration."
(request)
• "It's necessary that we **be** vigilant to avoid another disaster."
(statement of
necessity)
• "**If I had been more prepared**, I would have passed that test."
(hypothetical
condition)
There are very specific ways we conjugate verbs to create the
subjunctive
mood; continue on to that section to learn more.
Imperative Mood
Although we can use the subjunctive mood to express commands or
requests, it
is becoming less common in modern English. Instead, we usually use the
imperative mood to form **imperative sentences** when we want to issue
direct
orders, commands, or general instructions. It is considered an irrealis
mood
because the action being demanded has not actually happened (and
might not
happen).
When we make an imperative sentence, we use the infinitive form of
the verb
(without *to*), and we omit the subject of the verb.
For example:
• "Turn off the light before you leave."
• "Go to bed!"
As you can see, there are no subjects in the sentences above.

However, we do often use a **noun of address** (also called a **vocative**) instead,
which is a noun or noun phrase used to address the person to whom the command is directed. For example:
• "John, please turn out that light."
• "Stand up, Janet."
• "Be quiet, sir!"
• "You there, pay attention!"
To learn more about how we form and use sentences in the imperative mood, see
the section **Imperative Sentences** in the chapter on **Sentences**.

Other moods

The three true moods in English are the indicative, the subjunctive, and the
imperative.
However, there are two sub-categories that are sometimes described as moods in
different grammar guides: the "**emphatic mood**" and "**infinitive mood**." While
we do not consider them to be discrete grammatical moods in this guide, they are
worth mentioning for general reference.

Emphatic mood

The "**emphatic mood**" refers to the use of the **auxiliary verb** *do* to add emphasis to a verb that would otherwise not require an auxiliary.
We usually use emphatic *do* to stress the fact that something is the case.
For example:
• "Yes, I **do** know that we are meeting your parents tonight."
• "Well, she **does** have a Ph.D., after all."
We can also use *do* to add emphasis to demands or requests, as in:
• "**Do** be careful, John."
• "Oh, **do** be quiet!"
However, the use of *do* in such imperative sentences is now rather formal and
old fashioned.

Infinitive mood

The "**infinitive mood**" merely refers to a verb being put into its **infinitive form**
—that is, the base form with the particle *to*. For example:

• "**To be** loved is a wonderful thing."
In this case, the infinitive *to be* forms the infinitive phrase *to be loved*, which is
used as a noun and the subject of the sentence.
Infinitives have a variety of functions in a sentence, but none of them is as a true
verb, which is why we do not consider the so-called "infinitive mood" as belonging to any of the true grammatical moods in English.
Exercise

1. Which of the following moods is used to describe what is true or real?
a) Indicative mood
b) Subjunctive mood
c) Imperative mood
d) A & C
e) B & C
2. Which of the following moods is used to describe what is unreal, hypothetical,
or desired?
a) Indicative mood
b) Subjunctive mood
c) Imperative mood
d) A & C
e) B & C
3. Which of the following kinds of sentences can be made using the **indicative
mood**?
a) Declarative sentences
b) Conditional sentences
c) Interrogative sentences
d) Imperative sentences
e) A & C
f) B & D
4. Identify the grammatical mood used in the following sentence:
"I wish I were in Spain right now, instead of at home."
a) Indicative mood
b) Subjunctive mood
c) Imperative mood
d) Emphatic mood
5. Which of the following is **not** one of the true grammatical moods?

a) Indicative mood
b) Subjunctive mood
c) Imperative mood
d) Emphatic mood
e) Infinitive mood
f) A & B
g) C & E
h) D & E

Indicative Mood

Definition

The **indicative mood** is a type of grammatical **mood** used to express facts,
statements, opinions, or questions. It is the sole **realis mood** in English (as
opposed to the **irrealis moods**).

This mood can be used in the past, present, or future tense and in a **declarative**
sentence (i.e., a statement) or an **interrogative sentence** (i.e., a question). For
example:

• "She **graduated** last year with a doctorate in neuroscience." (declarative
sentence in the past indicative)

• "He **is taking** his exam at the new testing center." (declarative sentence in the
present indicative)

• "**Are** you **going to give** your speech tomorrow?" (interrogative sentence in the
future indicative)

The indicative mood covers a wide breadth of sentence structures and verb
tenses, and it is more commonly used than the **imperative** and **subjunctive**
moods (the two **irrealis moods** in English).

Function

Indicative-mood verbs function in many tenses and forms. The following
sections contain explanations for and various examples of declarative and
interrogative sentences in the **past indicative, present indicative**, and **future**

indicative.

Past indicative

Verbs in the **past indicative** describe things that have happened or are believed
to have happened at some point in the past.

Declarative sentences in the past indicative

In declarative sentences in the past indicative, the **past simple tense** and **past perfect tense** describe something that finished in the past, whereas the **past continuous tense** and **past perfect continuous tense** describe a continuous
action originating in the past. For example:

- "Verne **left** his house and **headed** to the airport." (past simple tense)
- "We **had lived** in Singapore for three years before returning to America." (past perfect tense)
- "She **was looking** online for a solution to her homework problem." (past continuous tense)
- "I **had been studying** philosophy at the time, but my real interest was in Japanese literature." (past perfect continuous tense)

Interrogative sentences in the past indicative

Interrogative sentences in the past indicative may use the past tense to inquire
about a past action or event. For example:

- "**Did** you **finish** the movie without me?" (past simple tense)
- "**Had** the candidate successfully **completed** the internship at the time?" (past perfect tense)
- "Where **were** they **training** for their race?" (past continuous tense)
- "Who **had** she **been spending** her time with when all this happened?" (past perfect continuous tense)

Present indicative

The **present indicative** describes things that are happening, are about to happen, or are believed to be happening.

Declarative sentences in the present indicative

In declarative sentences in the present indicative, the **present simple tense** and

present continuous tense describe habits or things occurring in the present or

near future, whereas the **present perfect tense** and **present perfect continuous**

tense describe experiences or things originating in the past and continuing into

the present. For example:

• "She **brings** her own lunch to work every day." (present simple tense)

• "The cashier **is counting** the customer's change." (present continuous tense)

• "I **have visited** every major theme park in the world." (present perfect tense)

• "They **have been staying** with my parents while the repairs are finished."

(present perfect continuous tense)

Interrogative sentences in the present indicative

Interrogative sentences in the present indicative may use the **present tense** to

inquire about a current or closely occurring action or event. For example:

• "What kinds of books **do** you normally **read**?" (present simple tense)

• "What **is** Mae **doing** right now?" (present continuous tense)

• "**Have** you **heard** that new song on the radio yet?" (present perfect tense)

• "Where **have** you **been working** these days?" (present perfect continuous

tense)

Future indicative

The **future indicative** describes things that will happen or things that it is

believed will happen. The *future tense* in English is not a unique verb inflection

(in comparison to the present and past tenses), but is approximated using the form *will* or *be going to* + the main verb.

Declarative sentences in the future indicative

Declarative sentences in the future indicative use the future tense to describe
things that will or are likely to occur at a future time. For example:

• "I **will try** to be more patient with children." (will)
• "Eugene **is going to compete** in a skiing competition next week." (be going to)

Interrogative sentences in the future indicative

Interrogative sentences in the future indicative use the future tense to inquire
about a future action or event. For example:

• "**Will** they **arrive** on time?" (will)
• "What **are** you **going to write** about for your thesis?" (be going to)

Exercise

1. The indicative mood can be used to express which of the following?
a) statements
b) opinions
c) questions
d) facts
e) All of the above
2. Which of the following sentences uses the **past indicative**?
a) "Jude is preparing breakfast for the guests."
b) "Have you ever been to Egypt?"
c) "The child was complaining about her missing toy."
d) "I won't be able to take time off from work."
3. Which of the following sentences uses the **present indicative**?
a) "She'll be busy at summer camp from June to August."
b) "He usually goes for a jog in the afternoon."
c) "Were you at the movie theater last night?"
d) "The two best friends hadn't seen each other in years."
4. Which of the following sentences uses the **future indicative**?
a) "Casey suffers from terrible migraines."
b) "They spent all day yesterday exploring the museum."
c) "Is he going to attend college or take a year off?"
d) "What country are you moving to with your family?"

Subjunctive Mood

Definition

The **subjunctive mood** refers to verbs that are used to describe hypothetical or
non-real actions, events, or situations. This is in comparison to the **indicative
mood**, which is used to express factual, non-hypothetical information. We most commonly use the subjunctive mood to express desires or wishes; to
express commands, suggestions, requests, or statements of necessity; or to
describe hypothetical outcomes that depend on certain conditions.

Using the Subjunctive Mood

Verbs do not have different forms to express the subjunctive mood in English.
Instead, they are **conjugated** a certain way depending on the meaning we wish
to achieve.

Expressing Wishes

When we a wish for something to be true, we conjugate the verb one degree into
the past to create the subjunctive mood. For example:

• Indicative mood: "It's Monday. I have to go to work."

• Subjunctive mood: "I wish it **weren't** Monday. I wish I **didn't have to go** to
work."

(Notice that the verb *be* always conjugates to **were** in the subjunctive mood,
regardless of whether it refers to a singular or plural noun.)

See the full section on **Expressing Wishes** to learn more about conjugating
wishes in different tenses.

Expressing Commands, Suggestions,
Requests, and Statements of Necessity

When we express actions that we demand, suggest, or request that someone else
take, or describe something that must be the case, we use the base form of the
verb—that is, the infinitive form without the word *to*.
For example:

• "He demanded that they **leave** the room at once." (command)

- "I recommend that she **study** harder next time." (suggestion)
- "I ask that the audience **be** completely silent during the demonstration."
(request)
- "It's necessary that we **be** vigilant to avoid another disaster."
(statement of
necessity)

The biggest difference between the subjunctive and indicative mood in this case
is that the verb does not change according to who is taking the action. For
instance, it is *she **study**, the audience **be**,* and *we **be*** in the subjunctive, while it
would be *she **studies**, the audience **is**,* and *we **are*** in the indicative mood.

Note that when we issue direct demands using **imperative sentences** (as in, "Do
your homework!" or "Please close the window."), we are no longer using the
subjunctive mood—instead, we are using what's known as the **imperative
mood**.

Conditional Sentences

Conditional sentences are used to describe hypothetical scenarios that require a
certain condition or conditions to be met. They use what's known as the
conditional mood and are generally constructed using *if* to identify the
conditions that must be met.

There are four "degrees" of conditionals, all of which vary in structure and
meaning. We'll give a brief synopsis of the different conditionals below; see the
section on **Conditional Sentences** to learn more about how they are formed and
used.

Zero Conditional

The zero conditional is used to talk about something that is generally true. For
instance:

• "If you throw a ball in the air, it comes back down." (Always true: A ball will
come back down every time you throw it in the air.)

First Conditional

The first conditional is very similar in structure to the zero conditional, except
that we now use the **future simple tense** (*will* + bare infinitive) to describe a
probable or intended result of the condition. For example:

• "If I see him, I **will** tell him."

• "If I win the lottery, I **will** buy a new house."

Second Conditional

We use the second conditional to speak about a hypothetical situation or
outcome resulting from the condition. Unlike the first conditional, we generally
use the second conditional to talk about things that cannot or are less likely to
happen.

To create the second conditional, we use the **past simple tense** after the *if* clause,
followed by *would, could* or *might* + the bare infinitive for the result of the
condition. For example:

• "If you had a phone, you **could call** me every day."

• "If I were older, I **might stay up** all night long."

Third Conditional

Third conditionals are used to establish a hypothetical situation in the past,
followed by a hypothetical outcome that did not really happen—typically, the
outcome is the opposite of what actually happened.

To form the third conditional, we use the **past perfect tense** for the *if* conditional
clause, and *would/could/should/might have* + the **past participle** of the verb for
the hypothetical outcome.

• "**If I had been more prepared**, I would have passed that test."

• "If I **hadn't overslept**, I **wouldn't have been late** for work."

Exercise

1. Which of the following is **not** something we use the subjunctive mood to
express?
a) A wish
b) Commands, suggestions, requests, and statements of necessity
c) Conditionals
d) Factual, non-hypothetical information
2. How are verbs conjugated to express **wishes** in the subjunctive mood?
a) Shifted one tense into the future
b) Shifted one tense into the past
c) Into the base form of the verb
d) Into the infinitive form of the verb
3. How are verbs conjugated to express **commands** in the subjunctive mood?
a) Shifted one tense into the future
b) Shifted one tense into the past
c) Into the base form of the verb
d) Into the infinitive form of the verb
4. Which of the following words is used to indicate a **conditional** sentence?
a) if
b) were
c) will
d) wish
5. Which of the following sentences is in the subjunctive mood?
a) "I'm going out for a walk later."
b) "It's really important that you be still during the procedure."
c) "Please don't be so noisy!"
d) "She will be studying tonight, so she can't come to baseball practice."
Subjunctive Mood - Expressing Wishes
Definition
One of the most straightforward ways of using the **subjunctive mood** is when
we want to describe a wish for something to be different than it is or was. We
generally construct these sentences using the word *wish*, followed by the verb of

the desired action.
Creating the subjunctive mood
When we express wishes, we create the subjunctive mood by moving the main
verb of the sentence one tense back in the past. We'll look at some examples of
these tense shifts below, but here is a quick reference to remember how each
tense moves back in the past:
present simple tense —> past simple tense
present continuous tense —> past continuous tense
present perfect tense —>past perfect tense
present perfect continuous tense —>past perfect continuous tense
past simple tense —> past perfect tense
past continuous tense —> past perfect continuous tense
past perfect tense —>past perfect tense (no further shift possible)
past perfect continuous tense —>past perfect continuous tense (no
further shift possible)
Present tense wishes
As we can see above, for a wish about a situation in the present, we use the **past
tense** equivalent of the verb:
• Situation: "It's Monday. I have to go to work." (present simple tense)
• "I wish it **weren't** Monday. I wish I **didn't have to go** to work." (past simple
tense)
**Conjugating *be* in the subjunctive
mood**
You might be more inclined to say "I wish it **wasn't** Monday," because this
sounds like the natural subject-verb agreement resulting from "It is
Monday."
However, the verb *be* always conjugates to **were** in the subjunctive mood,
regardless of whether it refers to a singular or plural noun.
Although it is becoming increasingly common to use *was* in everyday writing
and speech, you should always use ***were*** when talking about wishes or desires,
especially in formal, professional, or academic contexts.

Be is the only verb that conjugates irregularly to reflect the subjunctive mood for
wishes and desires. For all other verbs, we simply move them back one tense in
the past as normal.
For example:
• Situation: "I can't speak French, but would like to."
• Desire: "I wish I **spoke** French."
When we use **auxiliary verbs**, we move these back a tense instead of the main
verbs:
• "I wish I *could* speak French."
We can also use the subjunctive mood within the same sentence as verbs in the
indicative mood:
• "I *can't speak* French, but **I wish I** *could*."
**Examples of other present tense
wishes**
• Situation: "It *is raining* outside." (present continuous tense)
• Desire: "I wish it **weren't raining**." (past continuous tense)
• Situation: "He *has lived* in New York City his whole life." (present perfect
tense)
• Desire: "He wishes he **had lived** somewhere else at some point." (past perfect
tense)
• Situation: "My assistant *has been organizing* the filing cabinet." (present
perfect continuous tense)
• Desire: "I wish he **had been working** on something more important." (past
perfect continuous tense)
Past tense wishes
For past wishes, we go back in the past one tense further. For instance:
• Situation: "I'll miss my appointment because I *left* the house late." (past simple
tense)
• "I wish I **had left** the house earlier." (past perfect tense)
As with the present tense, we can also have sentences that use both the
indicative

mood and the subjunctive mood. For instance:
• "I *forgot* to set an alarm; I wish I **hadn't**."
Examples of other past tense wishes
• Situation: "I *was living* in Canada when I met you." (past continuous tense)
• Desire: "I wish I **had been living** in America when I met you." (past perfect
continuous tense)
• Situation: "He *had started* smoking again." (past perfect tense)
• Desire: "They all wished he **hadn't started** smoking again." (past perfect tense
—no further shift possible)
• Situation: I *had been working* outside when you called. (present perfect
continuous tense)
• Desire: "I wish I **hadn't been working** outside when you called." (past perfect
continuous tense)
Wishes about others' behavior
When we talk about someone's continued behavior that we wish were different,
we either use *would* + the desired verb, or simply the past tense of the verb.
For example:
Your son is always leaving his clothes lying around the bedroom floor.
• "I wish he **would pick up** his clothes off the floor when I asked him to."
or
• "I wish he **picked up** his clothes off the floor when I asked him to."
Your mother always whistles when she is in the house.
• "I wish she **wouldn't whistle** in the house like that."
or
• "I wish she **didn't whistle** in the house like that."
In the examples above, both constructions of the subjunctive are acceptable,
though the *would* construction is more conventional. If we want to imply that we
find a certain behavior annoying, we tend to use the *would* construction.
If only* instead of *wish

To express a desire that is more fanciful, unrealistic, or that we consider to be
ideal, we can use *if only* instead of *I wish* to add more emphasis to the desire.
(Note that the subjunctive verb still goes back one tense in the past.)
For example:
- "I hate being cold all the time. **If only I lived** in a hot country."
- "**If only I were** rich—I would spend my whole life traveling."
- "We're spending two weeks in the French alps next month; **if only I could**
ski!"
Exercise

1. Which verb conjugates **irregularly** when describing wishes in the subjunctive
mood?
a) can
b) will
c) be
d) have
2. For a situation in the present perfect tense, what verb tense would we use for a
wish in the subjunctive mood?
a) present perfect continuous tense
b) past simple tense
c) past continuous tense
d) past perfect tense
3. Which of the following sentences is **correctly** conjugated for a wish in the
subjunctive mood?
a) "I wish I weren't short."
b) "I wish I wasn't short."
c) "I wish I won't be short."
d) "I wish I'm not short."
4. Which of the following phrases can be used instead of *wish* to describe an
ideal or fanciful desire?
a) if so
b) if only
c) if possible

d) if hopefully

5. Which auxiliary verb can we use when we express a desire about someone
else's behavior in the subjunctive mood?

a) will

b) would

c) could

d) should

Voice

Definition

Voice, also known as **diathesis**, is a grammatical feature that describes the
relationship between the *verb* and the *subject* (also known as the *agent*) in a
sentence. More specifically, voice describes how the verb is expressed or written
in relation to the agent.

There are two main types of voice: **active voice** and **passive voice**. A third type
of voice called **"middle" voice** also exists but is less commonly used. Here are
some examples of the three types of voice:

- "She **wrote** a novel." (active voice)
- "The house **was purchased** by an elderly couple." (passive voice)
- "The cat **licked** itself." ("middle" voice)

Active voice

A verb is in the **active voice** when the agent of the verb (the person or thing that
performs the action specified by the verb) is also the subject of the sentence. The
active voice is the most common type of voice in both spoken and written
English, and is generally considered to be the **default voice**.

Not all active-voice verbs are required to take an *object*. Any object present,
however, must come after the verb (which always comes after the agent). For
example:

- "The boy **sang** a song." (with an object, *a song*)
- "I **am watching** a movie." (with an object, *a movie*)

- "Vivian **sings** well." (without an object)

Passive voice

A sentence uses the **passive voice** when the subject is acted upon by the verb.

Passive-voice sentences are structurally opposite to active-voice sentences, with the object (now the subject* of the sentence) coming before the verb and the verb coming before the agent of the action. A passive-voice verb is used in the past participle form preceded by the auxiliary verb *be*, and the preposition *by* is inserted before the agent to form a **prepositional phrase**. For example:

- "*Angie **will perform** a famous piano piece tomorrow night.*" (active voice)
- "A famous piano piece **will be performed** *by Angie* tomorrow night." (passive voice)
- "*Thousands of people **have already read** his new book.*" (active voice)
- "His new book **has already been read** *by thousands of people.*" (passive voice)

(*When converting a sentence from active to passive, the original *object* becomes the new *subject* due to its position at the beginning of the sentence. At the same time, the *agent* changes into the object of a *prepositional phrase*.)

Unlike active-voice, passive-voice sentences **do not** require agents. If an agent is unknown or irrelevant, you may eliminate the prepositional phrase containing the agent. For example:

- "The light bulb was patented **by Thomas Edison** in 1880." (with agent)
- "The light bulb was patented in 1880." (without agent)
- "The wedding venue has been decided on **by the bride and groom**." (with agent)
- "The wedding venue has been decided on." (without agent)

"Middle" voice

The term **"middle" voice** describes a type of voice that is a combination of sorts
between the active and passive voices. The middle voice is not clearly defined in
the English language; that is, it does not have a verb form specific to it. It does,
however, contain several odd or irregular verb usages that are said to correspond
most closely with the middle voice of other languages.
In most "middle"-voice sentences, the agent performs the verb's action on itself.
To compensate for the lack of a middle-voice verb form, these verbs are typically followed by a **reflexive pronoun**. For example:
• "My girlfriend always **checks** herself in the mirror before we go out."
• "The dog **bit** itself on the tail."
"Middle" voice can also be used to describe some **intransitive verbs**. These
verbs syntactically appear active (*agent + verb*) but function more similarly to
verbs in the passive voice. In other words, the agent is being acted upon (like the
passive voice) despite its position in front of the verb (as in the active voice). For
example:
• "The **lasagna *cooked*** in the oven for several hours." (The verb *cook* is acting
upon the agent *lasagna*.)
• "The **bicycle *broke*** without warning." (The verb *break* is acting upon the agent
bicycle.)
Exercise

1. Which of the following voices is typically regarded as the **default voice**?
a) passive voice
b) active voice
c) "middle" voice
d) none of the above
2. Which of the following choices contains the **correct** word order for an **activevoice**

sentence?
a) agent – verb – object
b) verb – agent – object
c) agent – verb – reflexive pronoun
d) subject – verb – prepositional phrase
3. Which of the following choices contains the **correct** word order for a
passivevoice
sentence?
a) agent – verb – object
b) verb – agent – object
c) agent – verb – reflexive pronoun
d) subject – verb – prepositional phrase
4. Which of the following sentences uses the **"middle" voice**?
a) "Her parents had chosen the school she would attend."
b) "I was blinded by a bright light."
c) "He threw a birthday party for himself."
d) "All of our food burned."

Active Voice

Definition

The **active voice** is a type of grammatical **voice** in which the *subject* of a
sentence is also the **agent** of the verb—that is, it performs the action
expressed
by the verb. In active-voice sentences, the agent always comes before
the verb.
For example:
• *"My friend* **bought** a new car." (*My friend* performed the action
bought.)
• *"She* **enjoys** watching movies." (*She* performs the action *enjoys*.)
• *"Barney* **is talking** to his sister." (*Barney* is performing the action
talking.)
A *direct object* is not always required for active-voice verbs. When an
object is
included, however, it must come directly after the verb. For example:
• *"I* **am drinking** some tea." (with a direct object, *some tea*)
• *"The boy* **hid** his report card from his parents." (with a direct object,
his report
card)
• *"Dr. Johnson* **will speak** at the convention." (without a direct object)
When to use the active voice

Typically, the active voice is preferable to the **passive voice**, as it requires fewer

words and expresses a clearer relationship between the verb and its agent. The

active voice is generally thought of as the **default voice** in spoken and written

English.

The following sections contain circumstances in which you should always try to

use the active voice over the passive voice.

When there is no direct object

Because passive-voice sentences require direct objects (which are turned into

subjects when converted from active to passive voice), sentences without direct

objects must be active. For example:

- *"That man* **has painted** for more than 40 years."
- *"We* **departed** immediately after the grand finale."
- *"The kids* **chatted** for several minutes."

We can see how these sentences cannot be put in the passive voice, because there

is no direct object to become the subject. Take, for instance, the first sentence:

- "For more than 40 years, **has been painted** *by the man*." (**What** has been

painted?)

It no longer makes any sense when structured in the passive voice, so it must

remain active.

When the agent is important

The active voice is commonly used to emphasize the importance of an agent in a

sentence. By using the active voice, we can highlight an agent's *responsibility*

for or *involvement* with a particular action. The examples below demonstrate the

differences between an **important agent** (active voice) and an **unimportant**

agent (passive voice):

- *"The employees* **drink** lots of coffee before work every day." (active voice—
describes the employees in relation to the act of drinking coffee)
- "Lots of coffee **is drunk** *by the employees* before work every day." (passive
voice—describes the act of drinking coffee in relation to the employees)
- *"Sir Isaac Newton* **discovered** gravity more than 300 years ago." (active voice
—emphasizes Newton's responsibility for the discovery of gravity)
- "Gravity **was discovered** *by Sir Isaac Newton* more than 300 years ago."
(passive voice—emphasizes the discovery of gravity over Newton's
involvement)

When the agent is known or relevant

You should always use the active voice if an agent is identifiable or contains
information that is relevant to the rest of the sentence. For example:
- "**Shawn stole** a menu from the restaurant." (The speaker knows or is familiar
with Shawn.)
- "**A veterinarian found** an abandoned puppy by the road." (The speaker knows
that it was a *veterinarian* who found the puppy and believes the information is
relevant.)
- "**Dr. Li opened** *the hospital* in 1989." (The speaker knows the name of the
person who started the hospital and the information is relevant to the
conversation.)

On the other hand, when an agent is unknown or irrelevant, we usually switch to
the passive voice and eliminate the agent altogether. For example:
- "A menu **was stolen** from the restaurant."
- "An abandoned puppy **was found** by the road."
- "The hospital **was opened** in 1989."

When expressing an authoritative tone

The active voice may also be used to stress the authority of an agent. This

authoritative tone is a strategy commonly used in copywriting, advertising, and
marketing in order to convince consumers of the beneficial effects of a product
or service. It may also be used to establish a command or to more strongly
emphasize an agent's responsibility for an action. For example:
• "Brushing your teeth at least twice a day **is recommended** *by dentists*."
(passive voice)
• *"Dentists* **recommend** brushing your teeth at least twice a day." (active voice—
emphasizes the authority of the *dentists*)
• "All of your broccoli **must be eaten** *by you* before dessert is served." (passive
voice)
• *"You* **must eat** all of your broccoli before dessert is served." (active voice—
emphasizes your responsibility to eat your broccoli)
When the agent is an ongoing topic
Agents that can perform multiple actions may be treated as **topics**. Making an
agent an ongoing topic places emphasis on that agent instead of the actions it
performs. When an agent acts as a topic, it usually remains the primary *subject*
in most active-voice sentences used to describe or refer to it. This can be seen
most prominently in works of fiction, in which protagonists typically perform
numerous actions throughout a story.
For example, look at how the passage below describes a fictional protagonist
named Caroline:
"*Caroline* **jumped** back and gasped. *She* **was** afraid of spiders and **despised** the
feeling of their silky webs on her skin. But *she* **knew** it was time to face her
fears. Sighing and brushing herself off, *Caroline* slowly **continued** down the

path toward the hill."
Exercise

1. In the following active-voice sentence, which word is the **agent** of the verb?
"Damien built a bookshelf with his own two hands."
a) built
b) bookshelf
c) Damien
d) hands
2. Which of the following active-voice sentences does **not** contain a **direct
object**?
a) "She reads a chapter from her book before bed every night."
b) "Mom already made plans for the weekend."
c) "The tornado caused severe damage to the neighborhood."
d) "Tomorrow night I will be dining with my friends."
3. In which of the following cases should you always use the **active voice**?
a) When the agent is known or relevant
b) When the agent is an ongoing topic
c) When there is no direct object
d) A & B
e) B & C
f) All of the above
4. Which of the following sentences uses the **active voice**?
a) "The town was founded over 400 years ago."
b) "The father surprised his children by bringing home a kitten."
c) "Her car has been missing since last week."
d) "I will be visited by my grandfather tomorrow."
Passive Voice
The **passive voice** is a type of grammatical **voice** in which the *subject* is acted
upon by the *verb*. In passive-voice sentences, the subject is the **receiver of the
action** (i.e., what would be the *direct object* in an **active-voice** sentence). For
example:
• "The concert **was attended** by many young people." (The subject *the concert*

receives the action of *attended*.)
• "The necklace **is being made** by a child." (The subject *the necklace* receives
the action of *being made*.)
Passive-voice verbs are always preceded by the auxiliary verb *be* and are in their
past participle forms. While the receiver of the action comes before the verb,
the person or thing performing the action (known as the *agent*) comes after the
verb and is preceded by the preposition *by* to form a **prepositional phrase**. For
example:
• "The lights **were turned off** *by the janitor*." (*The lights* is the subject, but *the
janitor* performs the action *turned off*.)
• "Final exams **will be taken** *by students* on Friday." (*Final exams* is the subject,
but *students* performs the action *taken*.)
• "Letters to Santa **are sent** *by children* every year." (*Letters to Santa* is the
subject, but *children* performs the action *sent*.)
**Converting the active voice into the
passive voice**
You may only convert a sentence from the active voice into the passive voice if
there is a **direct object**. As we've seen, this direct object becomes the
subject in
the passive voice. For example:
• "*A high school track and field star* **won** the race." (active voice)
• "The race **was won** *by a high school track and field star*." (passive voice)
• "*Local businesses* **are handing out** pamphlets near the mall." (active voice)
• "Pamphlets **are being handed out** *by local businesses* near the mall." (passive
voice)
If an active-voice sentences does **not** contain a direct object, it **cannot** be

converted into the passive voice, as the sentence will lack coherency without a

subject. For example:

• *"The kids* **are playing** outside." (active voice)

• "**Is being played** *by the kids* outside." (**What** is being played by the kids?)

Converting the passive voice into the
active voice

You may only convert a sentence from the passive voice into the active voice if

there is an identifiable **agent** of the verb. In the active voice, this agent becomes

the *subject*. For example:

• "This blanket **was knitted** *by my grandmother*." (passive voice)

• "*My grandmother* **knitted** this blanket." (active voice)

• "The deer **was being chased** *by a bear*." (passive voice)

• "*A bear* **was chasing** the deer." (active voice)

If a passive-voice sentences does **not** contain an agent, it **cannot** be converted

into the active voice, as the sentence will lack coherency without a subject. For

example:

• "The Great Pyramid of Giza **was constructed** more than 4,000 years ago."

(passive voice)

• "**Constructed** the Great Pyramid of Giza more than 4,000 years ago." (**Who**

constructed the Great Pyramid of Giza?)

When to use the passive voice

The passive voice is less commonly used than the active voice because it is

wordy and often lacks clarity; however, there are several cases in which using

the passive voice may be necessary or preferable.

The following sections contain various circumstances in which you might wish

to use the passive voice instead of the active voice.

When the receiver of the action is
important

The passive voice may be used to emphasize the importance of the receiver of
the action. (In contrast, the active voice typically emphasizes the importance of
the *agent*.) The examples below demonstrate the differences between an
important receiver of the action (passive voice) and an **important agent**
(active voice):

- "The school dance **will be organized** *by the science teachers* this year."
(passive voice—emphasizes the *activity* in relation to the organizers)
- "*The science teachers* **will organize** the school dance this year." (active voice
—emphasizes the *organizers* in relation to the activity)
- "She **is always being praised** *by her parents*." (passive voice—
emphasizes *she*
in relation to *her parents*)
- "*Her parents* **are always praising** her*." (active voice—emphasizes *her
parents* in relation to *her*)

(*When the pronoun *she* is converted into an object, it becomes *her*.)

**When the agent is unknown,
irrelevant, or implied**

Occasionally, the agent of an action may be unknown or irrelevant to the rest of
a sentence, or it may already be heavily implied through the action or receiver of
the action. In these cases, the agent may be eliminated altogether (which can
only be done with the passive voice—**not** the active voice). For example:

- "My missing wallet **was returned** to a lost-and-found." (unknown agent—we
don't know who returned the missing wallet)
- "A popular play **is being performed** at the local theater." (irrelevant agent—
the names of the performers are irrelevant)
- "Bathing suits **are usually sold** in the summer months." (implied agent—we
can assume that the agent is *clothing stores* or something similar)

When softening an authoritative tone

Because the passive voice places less emphasis on the *responsibility of
the agent*

and more emphasis on the *receiver of the action*, we can use the passive voice to
express commands in a softer, less authoritative tone than those expressed
through the active voice. For example:
• "*Inexperienced mountaineers* **should not attempt** Mount Everest." (active
voice—emphasizes inexperienced mountaineers' responsibility to avoid the
mountain)
• "Mount Everest **should not be attempted** *by inexperienced
mountaineers*."
(passive voice—emphasizes the difficulty or danger of the mountain)
If the agent is clearly implied, it may be eliminated for the sake of
conciseness:
• "*You* **need to finish** this project by tomorrow." (active voice)
• "This project **needs to be finished** *by you* by tomorrow." (passive
voice with
agent)
• "This project **needs to be finished** by tomorrow." (passive voice
without
agent)
**When expressing a professional,
neutral, or objective tone**
Various forms of writing, including scientific reports and instruction
manuals,
use the passive voice to express a professional, neutral, or objective
tone.
Typically, the receiver of the action functions as the primary **topic**
throughout
the text. The agent is usually removed due to irrelevance or to avoid a
sense of
subjectivity. For example:
• "The experiment **was conducted** over the course of two weeks."
• "Once Part A **has been inserted** into Part B, tighten the screws with a
screwdriver."
• "Adverse reactions to the medication **should be assessed and treated**
*by a
medical professional*."
Exercise

1. In the following passive-voice sentence, which group of words is the **receiver**
of the action?
"The large monument was erected by the construction crew last spring."
a) the large monument
b) was erected
c) by the construction crew
d) last spring

2. Which of the following passive-voice sentences does **not** contain an **agent** of
the verb?
a) "The homework assignment was completed last Thursday."
b) "Frank was struck by lightning."
c) "Her poem will be read aloud by her teacher."
d) "This desk was assembled by my aunt."

3. Which choice **correctly** converts the following active-voice sentence into the
passive voice?
"You should congratulate your sister on her academic achievement."
a) "Your sister should congratulate on her academic achievement."
b) "Your sister should be congratulated on her academic achievement."
c) "Your sister should congratulate on her academic achievement by you."
d) "Your sister on her academic achievement should be congratulated."

4. In which of the following cases should you use the **passive voice**?
a) When softening an authoritative tone
b) When the agent is important
c) When expressing a neutral or professional tone
d) A & B
e) A & C
f) All of the above

5. Which of the following sentences uses the **passive voice**?
a) "You can get to Vienna from Salzburg by train."
b) "The elementary school is by the park."
c) "I learned Korean by watching dramas."
d) "This scarf was crocheted by my friend."

Middle Voice

The so-called **middle voice** is an approximate type of grammatical **voice** in which **the subject** both performs and receives the action expressed by the verb.

In other words, the subject acts as both the **agent** and the **receiver** (i.e., the

direct object) of the action. For example:

• *"He* **injured** himself playing rugby." (*He* is the agent and *himself* is the receiver of the action.)

• *"The cat* **is scratching** itself." (*The cat* is the agent and *itself* is the receiver of the action.)

Middle-voice verbs follow the same syntactic structure as in the **active voice** (*agent + verb*), but function semantically as **passive-voice** verbs. As a result, the middle voice is described as a combination of the active and passive voices.

Because there is no verb form exclusive to the middle voice, it is often categorized as the active voice since it uses the same verb structure in a sentence. The following examples highlight the similarities between the two:

• *"Some snakes* **have tried to eat** inedible things." (active voice)

• *"Some snakes* **have tried to eat** themselves." (middle voice)

• *"The man* accidentally **hit** his face." (active voice)

• *"The man* accidentally **hit** himself in the face." (middle voice)

How to identify the middle voice

We can distinguish the middle voice from the active voice by determining whether there is a **reflexive pronoun** after the verb (in the direct object position) or an **intransitive verb** acting upon the agent.

When the direct object is a reflexive pronoun

Because the agent is also the receiver of the action in the middle voice, we can clarify this connection by inserting a reflexive pronoun after the verb. The reflexive pronoun assumes the role of the **direct object** and indicates that the agent is acting upon itself. For example:

• *"The child* **warmed** herself by blowing into her hands." (*Herself* is a reflexive pronoun that refers to *the child*.)

• *"Small dogs* tend to **hurt** themselves when playing with bigger dogs." (*Themselves* is a reflexive pronoun that refers to *small dogs*.)

Many middle-voice verbs are **transitive verbs** and therefore require a direct

object in the form of a reflexive pronoun. Without a reflexive pronoun, the receiver of the action becomes unclear, and the sentence loses coherence. For example:
• *"The child* **warmed** by blowing into her hands." (**What** or **whom** did the child warm?)
• *"Small dogs* tend to **hurt** when playing with bigger dogs." (**What** or **whom** do small dogs tend to hurt?)
Reusing the agent instead of adding a reflexive pronoun will affect the coherence of the sentence or even change its meaning altogether:
• *"The child* **warmed** the child by blowing into her hands." (implies *the child* warmed a different child)
• *"Small dogs* **tend to hurt** small dogs when playing with bigger dogs." (implies
small dogs tend to hurt other small dogs)
Likewise, using a **personal pronoun** instead of a reflexive pronoun will change or confuse the meaning of the verb's action:
• *"The child* **warmed** her by blowing into her hands." (implies *the child* warmed a different child)
• *"Small dogs* **tend to hurt** them when playing with bigger dogs." (indicates an unspecified object of the verb *hurt* other than *small dogs*)
However, there do exist certain verbs for which the reflexive pronouns are implied and may therefore be eliminated. For example:
• *"My father* **is shaving** himself in the bathroom." (with the reflexive pronoun *himself*)
• *"My father* **is shaving** in the bathroom." (without reflexive the pronoun)
• *"She* always **stretches** herself before doing yoga." (with the reflexive pronoun
herself)
• *"She* always **stretches** before doing yoga." (without reflexive the pronoun)
When the verb is intransitive and
acting upon the agent
Certain **intransitive verbs** can be used to modify an agent (usually an inanimate object) that is also the receiver of the action. In the middle voice, this type of verb does **not** take a reflexive pronoun (or any direct object). For example:
• *"My sister's lunch* **is cooking** on the stove." (*Cook* is an intransitive verb indicating **what** is being cooked.)

• *"This car **doesn't drive** smoothly anymore."* (*Drive* is an intransitive verb indicating **what** is being driven.)
• *"Her engagement ring **broke** in half."* (*Break* is an intransitive verb indicating **what** is being broken.)
However, active-voice verbs can also be intransitive and are expressed identically to middle-voice verbs. For example:
• *"The boy **laughed** when he heard the joke."* (*Laugh* is an intransitive verb
indicating **who** is laughing.)
• *"Someone **is crying** in the hallway."* (*Cry* is an intransitive verb indicating **who** is crying.)
You can determine whether an intransitive verb is in the active voice or the middle voice by changing the verb into the **passive voice**. Doing so will convert
the intransitive verb into a *transitive verb* and the agent into the *receiver of the action*. If the meaning of the sentence stays roughly the same, it is in the middle
voice. If the meaning changes dramatically or lacks coherence, it is in the active
voice. For example:
• *"My sister's lunch **is cooking** on the stove."* (original)
✔ "My sister's lunch **is being cooked** on the stove." (passive voice)
Because *cook* can be converted into a transitive verb in the passive voice without
altering the meaning of the original sentence, the original sentence must be in the
middle voice.
Here is another example:
• *"The boy **laughed** when he heard the joke."* (original)
✖ "The boy **was laughed** when he heard the joke." (passive voice)
When converted into the passive voice, the original sentence loses coherence;
therefore, it must be in the **active voice**.
Exercise

1. Which of the following is the **correct** word order for a middle-voice sentence?
a) agent – verb – reflexive pronoun

b) subject – verb
c) subject – reflexive pronoun – verb
d) A & B
e) A & C
f) None of the above
2. Which of the following sentences is in the **middle voice**?
a) "Brianna wants to see the world for herself."
b) "The mountain appeared vaster than the sky itself."
c) "I can't contain myself when I'm excited about something."
d) "Children are encouraged to play by themselves."
3. Which of the following sentences is in the **active voice**?
a) "He can never control himself when he's angry."
b) "Edmund is shaving in the upstairs bathroom."
c) "What's cooking for dinner tonight?"
d) "You should always stretch your muscles before exercising."
4. Which of the following sentences is **not** in the middle voice?
a) "The child exhausted her by playing too many games."
b) "The man saw himself in the mirror."
c) "Joanna entertained herself by whistling."
d) "The employees dedicated themselves to their work."

Answers
 Aspect: 1-b, 2-a, 3-d, 4-c, 5-d
Perfective and Imperfective Aspect: 1-a, 2-d, 3-c, 4-d, 5-c
Aspects of the Present Tense: 1-c, 2-b, 3-a, 4-c, 5-a, 6-d
Aspects of the Past Tense: 1-a, 2-b, 3-a, 4-b, 5-b
Aspects of the Future Tense: 1-c, 2-b, 3-a, 4-b, 5-d
Mood: 1-a, 2-e, 3-e, 4-b, 5-h
Indicative Mood: 1-e, 2-c, 3-b, 4-c
Subjunctive Mood: 1-d, 2-b, 3-c, 4-a, 5-b
Subjunctive Mood - Expressing Wishes: 1-c, 2-d, 3-a, 4-b, 5-b
Voice: 1-b, 2-a, 3-d, 4-d
Active Voice: 1-c, 2-d, 3-f, 4-b
Passive Voice: 1-a, 2-a, 3-b, 4-e, 5-d
Middle Voice: 1-d, 2-c, 3-d, 4-a

Worksheet 2

Past Tense

Definition

The **past tense** is used to describe or indicate an action that began in the past.

Depending on how we form the past tense, it might describe actions that

happened or were completed in the past, were occurring at the same time as

something else in the past, or continued to happen until or near the present time.

There are four forms of the past tense that can accomplish these tasks. We will

give a brief summary of each below. To learn more about each of them, you can

go to the appropriate section.

Past Simple Tense

The **past simple tense** (also called the **simple past tense**, or simply the **past**

simple) is used to express completed actions. It is known as the past *simple*

because it does not require any auxiliary verbs to complete its meaning; its

structure is simply the past-tense form of the verb. The past simple tense only

uses the **auxiliary verb** *did* when it is used in a question or becomes negative.

Examples

- "I **went** to the park yesterday."
- "I ***did not* eat** the cookie."
- "I **called** my sister over an hour ago, but she **didn't call** back."
- "**Did** they **mow** the lawn yet?"
- "What **did** you **wear** last night?"

Past Continuous Tense

Also called the **past progressive**, the **past continuous tense**, is used to describe

something that was in progress at a certain moment in the past and either

finished in the past or continued until the present moment.

It is called the *past continuous* because it uses the past tense of the auxiliary verb
be (*was* or *were*) followed by the **present participle** of the main verb (which is
used to describe an action that is or was *continuously* happening).
Examples
• "We **were working** on our assignment when our parents came home."
• "The phone rang as they **were leaving**."
• "She **was still writing** her thesis at 2 o'clock in the morning."
• "My roommates **were fighting** all the time, so I decided to move out."
• "His memory **was fading** as he got older."
• "Sorry I'm so muddy; I **was working** in the garden."
Past Perfect Tense
The **past perfect tense** expresses the idea that something occurred before
another action in the past. It can also show that something happened before a
specific time in the past. To form the past perfect, we use *had* (the past tense of
the auxiliary verb *have*) + the **past participle** of the main verb.
Because we use the past perfect to highlight two separate points in the past, we
often use the conjunctions *before, when, because, until,* or *by the time* to specify
the order in which they occurred in time.
Examples:
• "The film **had already ended** when I switched on the TV."
• "Unfortunately, he **had left** his keys in the house when he left."
• "The construction **had been going** quite smoothly before the earthquake."
• "I **hadn't dreamed** of living in Ireland before I visited the country."
• "**Had** you ever **ridden** on a tractor before working on the farm?"
• "What **had** you **done** that forced you to move abroad?"
Past Perfect Continuous Tense
The **past perfect continuous tense** (also called the **past perfect progressive**
tense) is used to describe an action that began and was still in progress in the
past before another past action started.

We usually use the present perfect continuous tense to emphasize the duration of
the past action before the second action or event occurred. We can also use it to
talk about a past action that caused or resulted in a past event or situation.
To form the past perfect continuous, we use *had been* + the **present participle** of
the main verb.

Examples

• "We **had been waiting** for a long time before the bus finally came."
• "I ***had been*** **working** on the ranch for more than half my life when I retired."
• "I**'d been cleaning** all day, so I was too tired to go out last night."
• "She ***had been*** **traveling** around Europe when she heard about her mother's
illness."
• "He ***hadn't been*** **feeling** well, so he went to lay down."
• "I was covered in mud as I***'d been*** **digging** in the back yard."
• "He needed to study harder, because he ***hadn't been*** **doing** very well on his
exams."
• "Where ***had*** you ***been*** **staying** at the time of the incident?"

The Subjunctive Mood

So far, we've seen examples of the past tense being used to describe what did or
did not actually happen. This is known as the **Indicative Mood**.
However, we can also use the past tense to describe hypothetical scenarios,
conditions, and desires—this is known as the **subjunctive mood**, one of the
Irrealis Moods in English.

Expressing Wishes

We generally use one of the past tenses to describe a wish or desire for a
hypothetical alternative, even if it is for something in the present or the future.
For example:
• "I wish it **weren't** Monday."
• "I wish I **hadn't agreed** to work on Sunday."

• "We both wish you **weren't moving** to Europe for college."
Conditional Sentences
We can also use the different past tenses to create **conditional sentences**, which
describe possible (but unreal) outcomes based on hypothetical conditions. For
example:
• "If I **won** the lottery, I would buy a new house."
• "If you **were** older, you could stay up as late as you want."
• "If I **didn't live** in London, I could never speak English so well."
• "If she **had been** there, she could have helped you."
• "What might you have done **had** you **known** the truth?"
• "**Had** you **been listening**, you would have heard that the report was needed on
Monday."
• "I might have lost my job if my brother **hadn't been working** in the head
office at the time."
Go to the sections related to the **subjunctive mood** if you want to learn more
about using the past tense to describe hypothetical actions, events, and situations.
Exercise

1. Which of the following **cannot** be described by one of the past tenses?
a) An action that began in the past and will continue into the future
b) An action in the past that was interrupted by another past action
c) An action that began and ended in the past
d) Things that began in the past and continued until the present moment
e) A & D
f) None of the above
2. Which form of the past tense is used to indicate the **cause** of a past result?
a) Past simple tense
b) Past continuous tense
c) Past perfect tense
d) Past perfect continuous tense
3. Which of the following sentences uses one of the past tenses?

a) "I regret to inform you that I shall be submitting my resignation soon."
b) "They've been trying to get a loan."
c) "She had been spending some time with her father."
d) "He'll have been working in this factory for nearly 30 years next March."
4. Which form of the past tense does the following sentence use?
"I hadn't considered her as a possible candidate for the job."
a) Past simple tense
b) Past continuous tense
c) Past perfect tense
d) Past perfect continuous tense
5. When do we use the past tense to describe a wish or desire?
a) For things happening in the past
b) For things happening in the present
c) For things happening in the future
d) All of the above

Past Simple Tense
Definition
The **past simple tense** (also called the **simple past tense**, or simply the **past
simple**) is used to express completed actions. We often use the past simple with
an adverb or adverbial phrase that specifies a time from the past, such as
yesterday, last year, an hour ago, etc.
Structure
This tense is known as the past *simple* because, like the **present simple
tense**, it
does not require any auxiliary verbs to complete its meaning; its structure is
simply the **subject** + the past tense form of the verb.
For example:
• "I **went** to the park."
The speaker's action of going to the park has been completed. The verb
go is
therefore put in the simple past tense, *went*.
However, we do not know anything about *when* the action was
completed. We

often add adverbs or adverbial phrases that provide additional information about
past time, which can be placed at the beginning or end of the sentence. If
appearing at the beginning of the sentence, these adverbs are often set apart by
commas (although this is not necessary if the information is only one or two
words). However, this information can't come between the subject and the verb,
and it usually does not come between the verb and any information that is
necessary to complete the verb's meaning (such as its **direct object** or an
adverbial complement). For example:
✔ "I *went* to the park yesterday." (correct)
✔ "Yesterday I *went* to the park." (correct)
✔ "Yesterday, I *went* to the park." (correct)
✘ "I yesterday *went* to the park." (incorrect)
✘ "I *went* yesterday to the park." (incorrect)
In more stylized writing, however, adverbials relating to time will *sometimes*
come between a verb and its complement, which gives them extra emphasis in
the sentence. For example:
• "I *wrote* over an hour ago to my sister, but have yet to hear a reply."
Notice that the tone becomes much more formal and the sentence sounds a bit
more convoluted. In most cases, it is best to avoid this structure.
Types of sentences
Positive (affirmative) sentences
The types of past simple tense sentences we've looked at so far have all been
examples of **positive sentences**, also known as **affirmative sentences**. These tell
the reader what *did* happen. We can also create negative, interrogative, and
negative interrogative sentences in the past simple tense; however, the structure

of the sentence changes slightly in each case.

Negative sentences

In contrast to positive sentences, negative sentences in past simple tense tell the
reader what *did not* happen. To form negative sentences in the past simple tense,
we must use the auxiliary verb *did* (the past tense of *do*) together with *not* before
the main verb of the sentence. The main verb, meanwhile, goes back to present
simple tense, which is the infinitive form of the verb without *to*. For example:
- "I ***did not* eat** the cookie."
- "She ***didn't* enjoy** the movie."
- "He ***didn't* have** to leave so early."

Interrogative sentences (questions)

Like negative sentences, we have to use the auxiliary verb *did* to make
interrogative sentences (sentences that ask questions) in the past
simple tense.
In this case, however, *did* comes before the subject, rather than the
verb.
We can see this construction more clearly if we compare affirmative vs.
interrogative constructions:
- Affirmative: "**I *went*** to the park."
- Interrogative: "***Did* you *go*** to the park?"
- Affirmative: "**Janet *saw*** a great movie on Friday."
- Interrogative: "***Did* Janet *see*** a movie on Friday?"
- Affirmative: "**They *mowed*** the lawn already."
- Interrogative: "***Did* they *mow*** the lawn yet?"

With question words

We can also use question words (such as *who/whom, what, where*, etc.)
before
did if we are asking for specific information. For example:
- "*Who/whom* **did** you **see**?"
- "*What* **did** you **wear** last night?"
- "*When* **did** they **arrive**?"

Additionally, we can use *who* without the auxiliary *did* in interrogative
sentences
in the past simple tense. In this case, it is functioning as an **interrogative**

pronoun and acts as the subject of the sentence. Because we no longer need *did*
to complete the sentence's meaning, we use the past tense of the main verb once
again.
- "*Who* **went** to the movie with you?"
- "*Who* **left** their wallet behind?"

Negative interrogative sentences
Negative interrogative sentences also ask a question, but they imply that the
speaker expects the answer to be (or believes the answer *should* be) "yes." We
form these by adding the auxiliary verb *did* before the subject of the sentence
and the word *not* after the subject. *Did* and *not* are very often contracted, in
which case *didn't* comes before the subject:
- "***Didn't*** you **go** to Europe last year?"
- "**Did** Jessie ***not* try** the cake **we baked** for her?"
- "**Did** I ***not* tell** you to clean your room an hour ago?"
- "***Didn't*** he **say** he was leaving in the morning?"

Other types of sentences
The types of sentences we've covered above are the most common uses of the
past simple tense. However, there are a couple of other ways we can use the past
simple to express specific meanings.

**Emphatic *did* – the past emphatic
tense**
There is another way that we can form a positive sentence in the past simple
tense. It is known as the **past emphatic tense**, and it is formed by using *did*
before the main verb, which is in present tense. It is the same construction as
negative sentences in the past simple tense, except that we leave out the word
not.
This form places special emphasis on the *fact* that something happened in the

past, which is usually used as a means of explanation or to convince someone of
something. For example:
- "But I'm telling you, **I *did* clean my room** when you asked me to!"
- "John was in a sorry state last night. I suppose **he *did* have a lot to drink**."

We can hear the emphasis that is placed on the word *did* in these sentences if we
read them aloud, and it is this stress that creates the explanatory intonation in the
text.

Using the past simple tense for hypotheticals (the subjunctive mood)

If we are expressing a wish or desire, we usually use the past tense; for a present
wish, we use the past simple.

For example:
- "I wish it **weren't/wasn't** Monday."
- "I wish I **didn't have to** go to work."

This is an example of what's called the **subjunctive mood** in English, which is
used for expressing things that are hypothetical or not objectively factual. To
learn more about how the past simple tense is used in this way, see the section on
subjunctive mood under the chapter on **Mood**.

Exercise

1. What do we **primarily** use the past simple tense for?
a) To express what will happen
b) To express what did happen
c) To express what did not happen
d) To express what should have happened

2. In which of the following types of sentences do we need the auxiliary verb *did*
to make the past simple tense?
a) Negative sentences
b) Interrogative sentences
c) Positive sentences
d) A & B

e) B & C

3. Select the sentence below that is **correct**:

a) "I knew where to go."

b) "He didn't studied hard enough."

c) "But I did washed the dishes!"

d) "I wish it isn't raining."

4. Where does the auxiliary verb *did* appear in an **interrogative sentence** that

does **not** use question words?

a) Immediately before the main verb

b) Immediately after the main verb

c) Immediately before the subject

d) Immediately after the subject

5. Which of the following sentences is **not** in the past simple tense?

a) "He found a way of keeping possession of the house."

b) "We didn't travel to Rome after all."

c) "Well, you can be sure that he does have a solution in mind."

d) "Did he not know that we were coming?"

Past Continuous Tense

Definition

Also called the **past progressive**, the **past continuous tense** is used to describe

something that was in progress at a certain moment in the past.

It is called the *past continuous* because it uses the past tense of the auxiliary verb

be (*was* or *were*) followed by the **present participle** of the main verb (which is

used to describe an action that is or was *continuously* happening).

Structure

To form the past continuous, we order the sentence like this: subject + **was/were**

+ **present participle of main verb**.

For example:

• "I **was** *working*."

• "She **was** *reading* a book."

These sentences are both complete, but they give very little information. Often,

the past continuous tense is used with additional information to convey a more

complete story about what surrounded a continuous action or event.

Functions of the past continuous

There are a number of functions for which we use the past continuous tense in
speech and writing. Let's look at some examples of these various functions.

Before and after another action or
event happened

• "We **were busy working** on our assignment when our parents came home."

• "I **was watching** the lovely sunset as a flock of birds soared by."

Interrupted by another action or
event

• "He **was having** the most wonderful time on the beach when the weather
suddenly turned awful."

• "As they **were leaving**, the phone rang."

Before and after a certain time

• "Two years ago, I **was working** at a bar in New York City."

• "She **was still up writing** her thesis at 2 o'clock in the morning."

For a certain length of time (whether
specific or undefined)

• "My head **was throbbing**." (undefined length of time)

• "You **were eating** that sandwich for an hour!" (specific length of time)

Repeatedly and frequently

• "My parents **were fighting** all the time when I decided to leave.

• "I **was often worrying** we wouldn't be able to afford the wedding in the
months leading up to it."

A source of irritation

We can also indicate that things that happened repeatedly were a source of
irritation by using the **adverbs of frequency** *always* or *constantly*, as in:

• "My ex-husband **was *always* leaving** dirty dishes in the sink."

• "The old boss **was *constantly* berating** employees over silly issues."

To show development, growth, or
other change(s) over time

• "Things **were changing**; there was no denying that."

• "I thought her condition **was improving**, but I guess not."

• "His memory **was fading** as he got older."

Narrating a story or describing an

atmosphere
• "As they walked into the sunshine, the birds **were singing** and the breeze **was**
softly blowing."
• "I **was working** in a New York City bar when all of this took place."
Sentence types
All of the examples above have used the past continuous in **positive**
sentences.
As with the other tenses, we can use the past continuous in negative, imperative,
and negative imperative sentences, with slight changes in structure as a result.
Negative sentences
To make a sentence negative in the past continuous, we simply add "not"
between the auxiliary verb (*was/were*) and the present participle of the main
verb. *Not* is often contracted with the auxiliary verb to make *wasn't/weren't*.
For example:
• "I *was not* feeling well."
• "The kids *weren't* sleeping when we got home."
• "She *wasn't* working for two years after the baby was born."
Interrogative sentences (questions)
To form an interrogative sentence (i.e., one that asks a question) in the past
continuous tense, simply invert the subject with the verb.
For example:
• Positive: "**I *was* sleeping** when you called."
• Interrogative: "***Were you sleeping*** when I called?"
• Positive: "**They *were* watching** a movie last night."
• Interrogative: "***Were* you watching** a movie last night?"
• Positive: "**She *was* working** on her thesis at the time."
• Interrogative: "***Was* she working** on her thesis at the time?"
Negative interrogative sentences
Negative interrogative sentences also ask a question, but they imply that the
speaker expects the answer to be (or believes the answer *should* be) "yes." We

form these by adding the word *not* after the subject. *Was/were* and *not* are very
often contracted into *wasn't/weren't*, in which case they both come before the
subject:
- "***Was* she *not* looking** for a new place to live?"
- "***Weren't* you watching** a movie last night?"
- "***Wasn't* he keeping** track of the inventory?"

Exercise

1. Which of the following **auxiliary verbs** is used to form the past continuous
tense?
a) can
b) do
c) be
d) will
2. What *form* of the **main verb** is used in the past continuous tense?
a) present participle
b) past participle
c) future participle
d) infinitive form
3. Which of the following sentences is in the past continuous tense?
a) "I had been watching a movie when they walked in."
b) "He knew a lot of people who had seen the movie."
c) "She was waiting to hear from her sister in New York."
d) "I am certainly trying to find a solution."
4. Which of the following sentences is **not** in the past continuous tense?
a) "I was always trying to find the best opportunities."
b) "They left without saying goodbye."
c) "Weren't we looking for something just like this?"
d) "Sure, he's doing his best, but is it good enough?"

Past Perfect Tense

Definition

The **past perfect tense** expresses the idea that something occurred before
another action in the past. It can also show that something happened before a
specific time in the past.
Consider these two sentences, for instance:

- "When she arrived at the airport, she realized she **dropped** her passport."
- "When she arrived at the airport, she realized she **had dropped** her passport."

She arrived at the airport in a moment in the past, but the moment she dropped

her passport happened before this past moment. Because the first sentence only

uses the **past simple tense**, it sounds as if both moments happened at the same

time in the past, and the sentence becomes confusing. By using the **past perfect**

tense in the second sentence, we are able to distinguish that one event happened

earlier than the other.

Structure

To form the past perfect tense, we use *had* (the past tense of the auxiliary verb

have) + the **past participle** of the main verb.

Because we use the past perfect to highlight two separate points in the past, we

often use the conjunctions *before, when, because, until,* or *by the time* to specify

the order in which they occurred in time.

An action or event before another

action or event

If we are highlighting that the action or event in the **past perfect tense** came

before *another* action or event, this second verb is often (but not always) in the

past simple tense. For example:

- "When I *turned on the TV*, the film **had ended**."
- "I **had dreamed** of living in Ireland even before I *visited* the country."
- "She *was sad when she left* the house she **had lived in** for so many years."
- "Unfortunately, he **had not taken** his keys before he *left* the house."

Notice that the past perfect can appear in a sentence either before or after a later

action or event. Regardless of its position, the past perfect always refers to an earlier time.

This is especially important to remember when using the conjunction *when*,
because it will help distinguish between events that happened simultaneously in
the past and events that happened sequentially. For example, consider these two
subtly (but distinctly) different sentences:

• "Mary *cooked* dinner when the kids *came* home."
• "Mary **had cooked** dinner when the kids *came* home."

In the first sentence, it sounds like Mary started cooking at the same time as the
kids arrived home. By using the past perfect in the second sentence, it is made
clear that Mary had already cooked dinner before the kids arrived.

Omitting the past perfect

The past perfect is not always necessary, however, when we use the conjunctions
before or *after* to link two clauses of past events. This is because these two
words already specify an order of time. If this is the case, both verbs can be in
the past simple tense. For example:

• "I **packed** a bag of snacks before I *left* for the airport." (correct)
• "I **had packed** a bag of snacks before I *left* for the airport." (correct, but not
necessary)

Although not absolutely necessary, the past perfect still gives a greater sense of
time than the past simple alone. The first sentence above is completely correct
and easy to understand. The second sentence is equally correct, but it lets us
know that the earlier event did not happen *immediately* before the later one. In
this particular example, it gives the impression that the speaker had the foresight
to pack a bag of snacks, rather than simply doing so just before he or she left for
the airport.

This distinction is subtle, and its impact on the sentence is somewhat minor, but

using the past perfect tense in this way creates a more rich and nuanced meaning.

An action or event before a specific point in time

If we are talking about a past perfect action that came before a certain point in

time in the past, then we use an adverbial prepositional phrase to specify exactly

when we are talking about.

For example:

- "*Until that afternoon,* she **had never considered** living abroad."
- "The construction **had gone** quite smoothly *before the earthquake.*"
- "I **had expected** to be married *by this morning.*"
- "I **hadn't used** a hammer *before working in construction.*"

(Note that, in the last example, "working in construction" acts as the object of

the preposition *before*. *Working* is a gerund in this case, so it does not have to be

in the past simple tense, as with the other verbs we examined in the previous

section.)

Other types of sentences

All of the above sentences are either **positive sentences** (also known as **affirmative sentences**) or **negative sentences**—as we can see, the negative

sentences are formed by simply inserting *not* or *never* between *had* and the past

participle of the main verb.

However, there is another way we can construct negative sentences in the past

perfect. We'll briefly look at how this is used, and then we'll examine the other

types of sentences that can be made in the past perfect tense.

Negative sentences – alternative construction

Most of the time, we make the past perfect negative by simply adding *not* or

never after the auxiliary verb *had*.

If we want to emphasize that something never happened before a given time,
event, or action in the past, we can also place the word *never* before the verb
had. In this case, both *never* and *had* come before the subject of the clause. For
instance:
• "***Never had* I felt** so alive."
• "***Never had* she imagined** that love like this could exist."
If we want to add even more emphasis, we can also include the word *before*
between *never* and *had*, as in:
• "***Never before had* she seemed** so beautiful to him."
Such sentences are much more literary in style—they typically would not be
found in academic, professional, or colloquial speech or writing. Because of this
literary usage, the construction is also primarily used with **stative verbs** (e.g.
feel, imagine, appear) as opposed to **action verbs**. For example, the statement
"never before had I run so far" sounds rather over-embellished or hyperbolic.
Finally, you may have noticed that none of the above sentences include another
action, event, or point in time to which the past perfect is referring. This again is
due to the literary usage of such a construction. In such cases, the past perfect
often alludes to something that has already been mentioned elsewhere in the
narrative.

Interrogative sentences (questions)
To form interrogative sentences (sentences that ask questions) in the past perfect,
the auxiliary verb *had* again comes before the subject, which is then followed by
the past participle of the main verb. Most of the time, we use the word *ever*

before the main verb to ask if something had happened or been the case at any

time before something else. It is usually constructed with the conjunction or

preposition *before*.

For example:

• "***Had* you ever been on** a tractor *before starting work on the farm*?"

• "*Before the war*, **had you ever considered** living abroad?"

Negative interrogative sentences

Negative interrogative sentences also ask a question, but they imply that the

speaker expects the answer to be (or believes the answer *should* be) "yes." We

form these by adding the word *not* or *never* after the subject.

Had and *not* are very often contracted, in which case *hadn't* comes before the

subject.

Negative interrogative sentences in the past perfect are not very common in

everyday speech and writing. Like the alternative use of *never* that we looked at

above, it would be more common to hear them in a story or narrative. For

example:

• "I began to panic. It was nearly midnight. ***Hadn't* the train arrived yet**?"

Negative interrogative sentences in the past perfect might also occur if someone

is asking another person a question about a story they are telling. For example:

• Person A: "It was nearly midnight by the time I got home, with still more work

ahead of me."

• Person B: "***Hadn't* you at least gotten** close to finishing by then?"

• Person A: "No, I was barely even halfway done!"

Exercise

1. We use the past tense of which **auxiliary verb** to form the past perfect?

a) be

b) will
c) have
d) do
2. Which of the following is **not** something we use the past perfect tense to
describe?
a) An action or event before a specific point in time
b) An action in the past that was happening until recently
c) An action or event before another action or event
d) A hypothetical situation in the past that might have led to a different outcome
3. Which of the following types of sentences is *more likely* to be found in **literary writing** when it is in the past perfect tense?
a) Negative interrogative
b) Conditional
c) Positive
d) Interrogative
4. Which of the following sentences is in the past perfect tense?
a) "I had been hitchhiking for miles before someone picked me up."
b) "I have seen some weird things out here on the road."
c) "Unfortunately, I hadn't eaten before I left home that day."
d) "I felt awful by the time I finally got home."
5. Which of the following is **not** in the past perfect tense?
a) "Had she ever been in this bar before today?"
b) "He hadn't seen her when he first came in."
c) "Never before had he met someone so interesting."
d) "He had a strong hope that they would meet again."

Past Perfect Continuous Tense

Definition

The **past perfect continuous tense** (also called the **past perfect progressive tense**) is used to describe an action that began and was still in progress in the past before another past action started. In contrast to the **past perfect tense,** which describes a past action that finished before the second action started, the past perfect continuous emphasizes the continuous progress of that action.

We usually use the present perfect continuous tense to emphasize the duration of
the past action before the second action or event occurred. We can also use it to
talk about a past action that caused or resulted in a past event or situation.

To form the past perfect continuous, we use *had been* + the **present participle** of
the main verb. It is nearly identical in structure to the **present perfect continuous tense**, except that the **modal auxiliary verb** *have* is now in the past
tense. For example:

- "We **had been waiting** for a long time when the bus finally came."
- "My little sister **had been sitting** very quietly, but then she started to cry."
- "I**'d been cleaning** all day, so I was too tired to go out last night."

Like the **past continuous tense**, the past perfect continuous is generally only
used with **action verbs**, not **stative verbs**.

Using the Past Perfect Continuous

Actions interrupted in the past

The most common use of the past perfect continuous tense is to describe an
action that was in progress in the past before another past action or event
occurred. When the second action happens, it interrupts and marks the completion of the first one. For example:

- "I ***had been* teaching** English in Tokyo when the earthquake hit."
- "They***'d been* living** in New York before she got the job in Washington, D.C."
- "She ***had been* traveling** around Europe when she heard about her mother's illness."

Past durations of time

When we use the past perfect continuous tense in this way, we often describe the
duration of the continuous past action. The meaning is very similar to the
present perfect continuous tense in this way. However, whereas the present

perfect continuous describes an action that was happening up until the present

moment, the past perfect continuous highlights an action that was finished when

another action or event in the past occurred. Consider, for example, these two

sentences:

• "She *has been* waiting for over an hour for him to arrive." (present perfect

continuous tense)

• "She *had been* waiting for over an hour for him to arrive." (past perfect

continuous tense)

The meaning of both sentences is quite similar. However, in the first sentence,

she began waiting an hour ago in the past, and is still waiting; in the second

sentence, *she* began waiting an hour ago in the past, but the waiting was

completed, either when he arrived or when she decided to stop waiting.

Here are some other examples using the future perfect continuous tense:

• "I *had been* working on the ranch for more than half my life when I retired."

• "She *had been* studying Japanese for four years by the time she moved to the

country."

• "When the teacher came back, we *had been* reading for half an hour."

Cause of past results

We can also use the past perfect continuous to indicate that the continuous action

that finished in the past was the cause of a condition, situation, or event in the

past. Used in this way, the past continuous action was not interrupted by a

second action or event. For example:

• "She was very sweaty because she *had been* running for nearly an hour."

• "I didn't have any energy to play with the kids because I *had been* working so

hard all the week."
• "I could tell you **had been** swimming all morning because you looked like a

prune!"

We can also use the past perfect continuous in this way without an expression of

duration, as in:

• "He **had been** feeling unwell, so he went to lay down."

• "I was covered in mud as I **had been** digging in the back yard."

Past continuous vs. Past perfect

continuous

We can use the **past continuous tense** in a similar way to show causation, but

the difference is that the past continuous describes an action that finished just

now or very recently, while the past perfect continuous describes an action that

may have finished further in the past. For example:

• "My eyes were tired because I **was** working on the computer." (past

continuous)

The action finished just now or very recently.

• "My eyes were tired because I **had been** working on the computer." (past

perfect continuous)

The action likely finished at a point further in the past.

With action verbs

Because it describes continuous, dynamic action, the past perfect continuous can

only be used with **action verbs**; it cannot be used with **stative verbs** (such as

linking verbs or **verbs of the senses**), which describe non-continuous actions.

For stative verbs, we can only use the **past simple** or **past perfect** tenses. For

example:

✔ "We **were** married for 10 years before we had kids." (correct—past simple

tense)

✔ "We ***had* been** married for 10 years before we had kids." (correct—past
perfect tense)

✖ "We ***had been* being** married for 10 years before we had kids." (incorrect—
past perfect continuous tense)

✔ "By the next morning, it all **seemed** like just a bad dream." (correct—past
simple tense)

✔ "By the next morning, it all ***had* seemed** like just a bad dream." (correct—
past perfect tense)

✖ "By the next morning, it all ***had been* seeming** like just a bad dream."
(incorrect—past perfect continuous tense)

Other types of sentences

So far we've only looked at **affirmative** sentences—**declarative
sentences** that
describe an action that **did** happen. Let's look at some of the other
types of
sentences we can make with the past perfect continuous.

Negative sentences

Sentences in the past perfect continuous tense can be made negative by
using the
word *not* after *had*; the two words are often contracted into *hadn't*. For
example:

• "I didn't mind her coming over; I ***hadn't been* getting** much work done
anyway."

• "She ***hadn't been* living** there for very long before she had to move
back
home."

• "He needed to study harder, because he ***hadn't been* doing** very well
on his
exams."

We generally do not use *never* with the past perfect continuous tense.

Interrogative sentences

When we make questions with the past perfect continuous tense, the
subject and
the auxiliary verb *had* are inverted. For example:

• "Where ***had* you *been* working** at the time of the incident?"

• "***Had*** she ***been*** living in Italy for a long time?"
• "Why ***had*** they ***been*** telling me I was doing a good job if they were planning
on firing me?"
We can also make interrogative sentences negative by adding *not* between the
subject and *been*, or we can contract *had* and *not* into *hadn't*:
• "***Hadn't*** you ***been*** writing a novel before you got this job?"
• "***Had*** he ***not been*** feeling well at the time?
• "You had plenty of money, so why ***hadn't*** you ***been*** paying your bills?"
As we see in the first example, a negative interrogative question can sometimes
be used rhetorically, implying that the speaker expects the answer to be "yes."

Conditional sentences

Conditional sentences describe a hypothetical action or outcome that might
happen if a certain condition is or was met. Conditional sentences that use the
past perfect continuous tense are known as **third conditionals**, which establish a
hypothetical situation in the past followed by a hypothetical outcome that did not
really happen.
There are two ways we can use the past perfect continuous to form conditional
sentences. We can either use the normal form in a conditional clause that begins
with *if*, or we can invert *had* with the subject to create a conditional clause,
which adds a bit more formality to the tone of the sentence.
For example:
• "If I ***had still been*** living there when the earthquake hit, I probably would have
lost everything I owned."
• "We would have gone hiking on Saturday if it ***hadn't been*** snowing in the
mountains."
• "***Had*** you ***been*** listening, you would have heard that the report was needed on

Monday."
• "I could have lost my job *had* my brother *not been* working in the head office
at the time."
Exercise

1. What form of the **main verb** is used to create the past perfect continuous
tense?
a) infinitive
b) base form
c) present participle
d) past participle
2. Which of the following is a function of the past perfect continuous
tense?
a) To describe how long something had been happening by a specific
point in the
past
b) To indicate the cause of a past result
d) To indicate a continuous action that began in the past and continues
into the
future
d) To indicate a continuous action that finished in the present
e) A & B
f) B & C
g) C & D
3. Where does *not* appear in a **negative sentence** in the past perfect
continuous
tense?
a) After the subject
b) After *had*
c) After *been*
d) After the present participle of the main verb
4. Which of the following uses the past perfect continuous tense to
form a
conditional sentence?
a) "Had you been waiting for long before your brother arrived?"
b) "I hadn't been studying for more than an hour when they closed the
library."

c) "Had we been digging just a few feet from here, we would have hit a gas
line."
d) "He had been living in Rome for eight years, so he spoke perfect
Italian."
5. Which of the following types of verbs **cannot** be used in the past perfect
continuous tense?
a) action verbs
b) stative verbs
c) factitive verbs
d) conditional verbs
e) A & B
f) B & C
g) C & D

Future Tense (Approximation)
Definition
Grammatically speaking, there are no **future tenses** in the English
language;
verbs do not inflect (conjugate) a certain way to reflect future actions.
There are
really only **aspects of the future tense**—that is, ways of expressing the
future
using other grammatical elements and constructions.
To talk about other future events or actions, we use different sentence
constructions to achieve a future point of view. This is most often
accomplished
by using the **modal auxiliary verb** *will* or the verb phrase *be going to*.
These
constructions make up what are commonly referred to as the **future
tenses**.

Future Simple Tense
The future simple tense is used in a few different ways to describe
things that
have not happened yet—it can be used to predict something, to make
promises,
to describe a future fact, to describe unplanned actions, or to offer to
do
something.

The simplest way we create the future simple tense is by using *will*/*be going to* +
the base form (the **infinitive** without *to*) of the main verb of the
sentence. For
example:
- "I *will* **walk** to work."
- "The president *will* **be** in Portland tomorrow."
- "Don't worry, I**'m going to pay** for the coffee."
- "I **am going to** drive to work tomorrow, if you want a ride."

Future Continuous Tense

The **future continuous tense** (also known as the **future progressive**) is
used to
describe an unfinished action occurring in the future; this action can
either begin
in the future, or it can already be in progress in the present and
continue into the
future. We can also use the future continuous tense to make predictions
about an
action we think will still be happening in the future.

To form the future continuous, we usually use *will*/*be going to* + the
auxiliary
verb *be* + the **present participle** of the main verb. For example:
- "I **will be running** 10 miles tomorrow."
- "This is your captain speaking; the plane **will be landing** *in 10
minutes*."
- "We **are going to be buying** our own house *soon*."
- "They**'ll be sleeping** by the time we return home."
- "In 10 years, people **are going to be consuming** even more natural
resources."

Future Perfect Tense

We use the **future perfect tense** to say that something will finish or
complete at
a specific point in the future. We also often include durations of time to
indicate
how long something has been happening once a future moment in time
is
reached.

In addition, we can use the future perfect tense to make a present
prediction

about something that we believe has or should have happened in the past.

The most common way we create the future perfect tense is by using *will + have*

+ the **past participle** of the verb. For example:

• "This June, I **will have lived** in New York for four years."

• "You **will have heard** by now that the company is going bankrupt."

• "She**'ll have slept** for the whole day if she doesn't get up soon!"

(We can also use *be going to* instead of *will*, but this construction is less common

and cannot be used to make a present prediction about a past action.)

Future Perfect Continuous Tense

Like the **future perfect tense**, we use the **future perfect continuous tense** (also

known as the **future perfect progressive tense**) to indicate how long something

has been happening once a future moment in time is reached, emphasizing the

continuous nature of the action. It can also be used in this way to indicate the

cause of a possible future result.

The most common way we create the future perfect continuous tense is by using

will + have been + the **present participle** of the verb. For example:

• "By June, I **will have been living** in New York for four years."

• "She's going to miss half the day because she**'ll have been sleeping** for so

long!"

• "By the time I get there, she **will have been waiting** for over an hour."

• "I **will have been working** on this ranch for more than half my life when I turn

40."

• "I'm not going to have any energy to play with the kids because I**'ll have been**

working so hard this week."

(Like the future perfect tense, we can also use *be going to* instead of *will*, but this

construction is less common.)

Using *shall*

In addition to *will* and *be going to*, the modal verb *shall* can also be used to form
each of the future tenses. Although *will* is generally preferred in modern English
(especially American English), using *shall* adds an additional degree of politeness or formality to the sentence sometimes lacking with *will* or *be going*
to.

Exercise

1. Which of the following **cannot** be described by the future tenses?
a) Things that began in the past and will continue into the future
b) Things that we believe have already happened
c) Things that are going to happen in the future
d) Things that began in the past and continued until the present moment
e) A & C
f) B & C
g) None of the above
2. Which form of the future tense is used to indicate the cause of a possible
future result?
a) Future simple tense
b) Future continuous tense
c) Future perfect tense
d) Future perfect continuous tense
3. Which of the following sentences does **not** use one of the future tenses?
a) "I regret to inform you that I shall be submitting my resignation soon."
b) "They're going to see if they can get a loan."
c) "She had been spending some time with her father."
d) "He'll have been working in this factory for nearly 30 years next March."
4. Which form of the future tense does the following sentence use?
"I won't be coming here ever again!"
a) Future simple tense
b) Future continuous tense
c) Future perfect tense
d) Future perfect continuous tense

Future Simple Tense
Definition
English verbs do not have unique forms for the future tense; instead, we use
different sentence constructions to describe actions that will occur in the future.
There are two ways we do this for the **future simple tense**.
The simplest way we create the future simple tense is by using the **modal verb**
will + the bare infinitive (without *to*) of the main verb of the sentence, as in, "I
will walk to work."
We can also form the future simple tense by using *be going to* + the bare
infinitive of the main verb, as in "I **am going to walk** to work." However, the
usages of this construction are slightly different.
For now, we will focus on *will* constructions; a little later on, we'll look at how
going to can be used to create subtle differences in meaning.
Uses of the future simple tense – *will*
constructions
The future simple tense can be used in a few different ways to describe things
that have not happened yet. The structure of the sentence does not change,
though, so we generally rely on context or other parts of the sentence to create
these differences in meaning.
To predict something
Example:
• "I think it **will rain** today."
This is a prediction; it may be based on fact (i.e., because there are dark storm
clouds), or perhaps on current, less tangible evidence (i.e., it "feels" like rain is
coming).
• "Our team **will win** the game."
This is also a prediction, which may or may not be based on facts or past

experience. We often use the future simple tense for simple predictions that are
based on desires.

To make promises

Example:

• "I **will definitely come** to the party. You have my word."
• "I**'ll wash** the dishes later."

Neither of these is a prediction; each is an assurance that something is going to
happen. The adverb *definitely* in the first sentence solidifies this promise, while
later in the second sentence lets the reader/listener know when the dishes will be
washed.

To describe a future fact

Example:

• "The president **will be** in Portland tomorrow."
• "I **will drive** to work tomorrow, if you want a ride."

These are neither predictions nor promises, but rather are factual statements of
thing that are going to happen.

Unplanned actions or decisions

We can also use the future simple when we decide to do something at the
moment of speaking, rather than something that was already planned or decided.

For example:

• Person A: "There's no milk left."
• Person B: "I **will get** some the next time I'm out."
• Person A: "The TV isn't working, so you won't be able to watch the football
game."
• Person B. "I**'ll just read** a book instead."

To offer to do something

Example:

Imagine you see your neighbor coming out of the supermarket carrying two
heavy shopping bags. You might say:

• "I**'ll help** you. Give me one of the bags and I **will carry** it for you."

If your friend is low on money when you are both out at a coffee shop, you
might say:

- "Don't worry, I**'ll pay** for the coffee."

Negatives

We can achieve strong negative meanings for most of the above uses by adding
not or *never* to *will*, as in:

- "Our team **will never win** the game." (negative prediction)
- "I **won't wash** the dishes later." (negative promise; also used for refusals)
- "He **won't drive** to work tomorrow." (negative future fact)

However, we generally don't put unplanned decisions or offers in the negative
with the *will* construction, because the sentence ends up describing a negative
promise, a refusal, or a negative future fact:

- "I**'ll never read** a book." (negative promise)
- "I **won't pay** for the coffee." (refusal or negative fact)

Interrogative sentences (questions)

To form questions in the future simple tense, we simply move *will* before the
subject of the sentence. For example:

- "**Will** it **rain** today?" (question of a prediction)
- "**Will** you **come to the party**?" (question of an intention, promise, or assurance)
- "**Will** the president **be** in Portland tomorrow?" (question of a future fact)
- "**Will** you **get** some milk the next time you are out?" (an unplanned request,
phrased as a question)

We can also use *shall* instead of *will* in questions when making offers, as in:

- "**Shall** I **carry** that bag for you?"
- "**Shall** I **get** some milk the next time I'm out?"

This makes the question more formal and polite.

***Going to* constructions**

In several of the cases we looked at above, we can use *be going to* in place of
will.

For example:
- "I think it **is going to rain** today."
- "I **am going to come** to the party."
- "The president **is going to be** in Portland tomorrow."

***Going to* for intended future actions**

Unlike the *will* construction, we do not use *going to* to describe unplanned
decisions or offers; instead, we use this construction to express intended, preplanned
actions, as in:
- Person A: "There's no milk left."
- Person B: "I**'m going to get** some the next time I'm out."
- Person A: "I don't have any cash."
- Person B: "Don't worry, I **am going to pay** for the coffees."

This is also the case if we use *going to* in one of our previous examples that
described a future fact:
- "I**'m going to** drive to work tomorrow, if you want a ride."

When we used the *will* construction, we were describing something that is
considered a concrete fact; now, however, it expresses a planned intention. We
can see this in other examples as well:
- "She**'s going to play** soccer later." (She has already decided that this is what
she wants to do later.)
- "He **is going to make** a cake for us tomorrow." (This is his plan of action.)

We can also use *going to* when something is certain or very likely to happen, but
not in the immediate future.

For example:
- "Look at those black clouds. It**'s going to rain**." (This is very likely due to the
evidence of the weather.)
- "My mama told me that she**'s going to have** a baby." (This is a certainty, but it
will not happen right away.)
- "Hurry up! We**'re going to be** late." (This is also evident and very likely.

Although it will happen soon, it will not happen immediately.)
Finally, children often use the *going to* construction when they speak about what
they want to be when they grow up, as in:
• "When I grow up, I'**m going to be** a police officer." (At this moment, that is
what I intend to be.)
Interrogative sentences using *going to*
To form interrogative sentences in the future simple tense using the
going to
construction, we simply put the linking verb *be* before the subject of the
sentence. This is also the case if we use question words. For example:
• "**Are** you **going to see** Jennifer later?"
• "**Is** it **going to rain**?"
• "***What** **are** you **going to say** to him?"
• "***Where** **are** they **going to stay**?"
Exercise

1. Which **modal auxiliary verb** is commonly used to create the future
simple
tense?
a) can
b) do
c) will
d) would
2. What is the **main** function of the *going to* construction (as compared
to the
will construction)?
a) To express intended action
b) To express certainty in predictions
c) To express an unplanned decision
d) To make a refusal
3. What is the following sentence describing?
"I'll drive to the airport to pick you up, if you like."
a) A prediction
b) An unplanned action
c) A future fact
d) An offer
4. What **other** auxiliary verb can be used **instead** of *will* in interrogative
sentences in the future simple tense?

a) can
b) shall
c) would
d) going
5. Which construction would we **most likely** use to describe something that is
certain or very likely to happen, but not in the immediate future?
a) will + bare infinitive
b) be going to + bare infinitive
c) Either A or B
d) Neither A nor B

Future Continuous Tense

Definition

The **future continuous tense** (also known as the **future progressive**) is used to
describe an unfinished action occurring in the future. This action can either
begin in the future, or it can already be in progress in the present and continue
into the future.

Structure

As with all so-called future tenses, English verbs do not inflect into a unique
"future form"—rather, we must use auxiliaries and participles in other tenses to
describe future events or actions.

To form the future continuous, we use *will be* **or** *is/are going to be* + the **present**
participle of the main verb.

For example:

• "I **will be running** 10 miles tomorrow."
• "He **is going to be leaving** the company soon."

Much of the time, either construction may be used with no appreciable
difference in the meaning of the sentence. However, as with the **future simple**
tense, we sometimes use the *will be* construction for actions or events that are
more certain to happen, whereas the *going to be* construction can be used to
imply an *intended* action or event.

Using the future continuous tense
The future continuous is primarily used in three ways:
1. To say that something will be in progress from a certain moment in the future.
2. To predict that something will be in progress at some point in the future (i.e.,
not starting at a specific time).
3. To describe something that is expected or predicted to continue happening
from the present for an uncertain amount of time into the future.
Let's look at examples of each of these uses.
From a certain point in the future
In this usage, we describe something that will definitely be happening in the
future—that is, it is not a prediction or an expectation. Because it is a certainty,
we often reference specific points in time.
For example:
• "This is your captain speaking; the plane **will be landing** *in 10 minutes*."
This means that it will begin to land progressively starting 10 minutes from now.
• "Please make your way to checkout counters, as the store **will be closing** *in five minutes*."
This means that in five minutes' time, the store will begin to close.
• "I just wanted to let you know that I**'ll be arriving** in Milan *on Saturday*."
In this example, the action of *arriving* will begin on Saturday.
We can also use more vague references in time, so long as they are not too vague
or too far in the future. For instance:
• "I need to get this report finished, as the boss **is going to be leaving** *shortly*."
The progressive future action is going to begin happening (it is not a prediction),
but the time frame is not exact.
We can see, however, that this can easily turn into a prediction when we use
vague time references:

• "We **will be buying** our own house *soon*."
• "Our kids **are going to be leaving** for college *eventually*."
Predictions of future actions
The future continuous is often used to predict actions that we think or presume
will be happening at an uncertain or generic point in the future.
• "Don't call Paul after 7 PM; he**'ll be having** dinner."
We predict that this will be in progress at some point after 7 o'clock.
• "In 10 years, people **are going to be consuming** even more natural resources."
We predict this to be in progress at a certain point in the future. Even though a
specific time is referenced, it is far enough in the future that we can assume this
isn't a certainty.
• "By the time we arrive home, they**'ll be sleeping**."
Again, we predict this action will be in progress at a future point (when we
arrive home); we have reason to believe this, but it is not an absolute certainty.
In progress now and into the future
We can also use the future continuous to predict that an event or action is
currently happening, and that it will continue for an uncertain amount of time
into the future. For example:
• "Don't call the house now, as John **will be sleeping**."
We predict this to be in progress now, and that it will continue to be happening in
the near future.
If we want to describe something that is definitely happening now and will (or is
expected to) continue to happen in the future, we use the adverb *still* after *will* or
before *going*. For instance:
• "I'm so behind on this assignment. The sun is going to rise and I **will** *still* **be**
working on it."
• "No matter who is elected, we**'re still going to be dealing** with the effects of

the recession for years to come."

Types of sentences

So far, we've looked at examples of positive sentences using the future continuous tense. As with the other tenses, we can also form negative, interrogative, and negative-interrogative sentences.

Negative sentences

We form the negative of the future continuous by adding **not** after *will* or before

going in the sentence. (*Will* and *not* are often contracted to *won't*.)

We form the negative to achieve the opposite meaning of all the uses we've

looked at so far. For example:

• "Contrary to our previous announcement, the store **will not be closing** in five

minutes." (negative certainty of a future action)

• "Don't bother trying to get a hold of Paul after 7; he **won't be taking** calls

then." (negative prediction of a future action)

• "I may be behind on this assignment, but I **am not going to be working** past 5

o'clock." (negative intention of allowing a current action to progress into the

future)

Interrogative sentences (questions)

We create questions in the future continuous by inverting *will* or *be* with the

subject. This is also the case if we use question words—*what, where, when, etc.*

(An exception is the word *who*, which becomes the subject of the sentence but

remains at the beginning.)

We most often use interrogative sentences in the future continuous tense to

politely inquire about information:

• "**Will** you **be joining** us after dinner?"

• "*What* **will** they **be doing** in Mexico?"

• "*Who* **is going to be performing** at the concert?"

Negative interrogative sentences

Negative interrogative sentences also ask a question, but they imply that the speaker expects the answer to be (or believes the answer *should* be) "yes."

Again, in the future continuous, this is done to create a polite inquiry. We form these by using the interrogative form we looked at above, and adding

the word *not* after the subject. However, this is considered a formal construction

—more often in modern English, *will* and the forms of *be* are contracted with *not*

to create *won't, isn't,* or *aren't,* all of which come before the subject.

- "**Will** you ***not*** **be joining** us after dinner?" (more formal, but less common)
- "***Won't*** we **be leaving** after the concert?" (less formal, but more common)
- "**Is** he ***not*** **going to be studying** for an exam?" (more formal, sometimes used for emphasis)
- "**Aren't** you **going to be working** next week?" (less formal, but more commonly used)

We do not use question words with negative interrogative sentences in the future continuous tense.

Exercise

1. Which auxiliary verb is often used to create the future continuous tense?
a) will
b) be
c) have
d) A & B
e) A & C
f) All of the above

2. Which of the following is **not** a usage of the future continuous tense?
a) To say that something will be in progress from a certain moment in the future.
b) To say that something will end sometime in the near future.
c) To predict that something will be in progress at some point in the future.
d) To describe something that is happening in the present and will continue into

the future.

3. What form does the **main** verb take in the future continuous tense?

a) Infinitive

b) Past participle

c) Present participle

d) Present tense

4. Which of the following sentences uses the future continuous tense?

a) "I told him we will be coming home on Saturday."

b) "She said she'll work weekends while Mike is out sick."

c) "They said they would be arriving at 8 PM."

d) "I'm traveling to France next week."

5. Which of the following sentences **does not** use the future continuous tense?

a) "I'm sure he'll be trying as best he can to be there tomorrow."

b) "That no-good snitch is going to be sleeping with the fishes by the morning."

c) "She told him she would be working at the warehouse this week."

d) "I heard Daniel is going to be moving to Canada soon!"

Future Perfect Tense

Definition

We use the **future perfect tense** to say that something will finish or be completed at a specific point in the future. We also often include durations of

time to indicate how long something has been happening once a future moment

in time is reached.

In addition, we can use the future perfect tense to make a present prediction

about something that we believe has or should have happened in the past.

The most common way we create the future perfect tense is by using the **modal**

auxiliary verb *will* + *have* + the **past participle** of the verb. For example:

• "This June, I ***will have*** lived in New York for four years."

• "You ***will have*** heard by now that the company is going bankrupt."

• "She***'ll have*** slept for the whole day if she doesn't get up soon!"

Functions of the Future Perfect

Actions completed in the future

We often use an adverbial expression of a future point in time with the future

perfect tense to describe when an action will be completed or accomplished.
This adverbial phrase can occur either before or after the future perfect verb. For
example:
• "With the way you're spending money, you **will have** gone through your
savings in less than a month."
• "After this next race, I **will have** **completed** 10 triathlons."
Future spans of time
The future perfect tense is often used to indicate a point in the future at which a
certain action or situation will have been happening for a given length of time.
For example:
• "It's hard to believe that by next month we**'ll have** **been** married for
10 years."
• "I **will have** **worked** on this ranch for more than half my life when I
turn 40."
As we can see above, the adverbial phrase expressing the **duration** of time ("for
10 years," "for more than half my life") usually comes after the future perfect
tense construction. The expression of the future **point** in time (the point at which
the duration is accomplished) can appear either before or after the future perfect
tense.
Present predictions of past actions
We also use the future perfect for a present prediction of something we believe
has already happened in the past. If we include adverbials related to time, we
generally include expressions related to the **present time** rather than the future.
For example:
• "You **will have** **seen** on page 18 how to set up the computer."
• "Your mother **will have** **left** the dentist's by now."
• "At this stage, everyone **will have** **heard** the rumors already."
Other sentence types

Negative sentences

To describe something that will **not** be completed at a point in the future, we

make the future perfect tense negative by adding *not* after the modal verb *will*

(usually contracted as *won't*). For example:

• "Why are you going to the airport so early? Her flight **will not have arrived**

yet."

• "At this rate, I **won't have** **finished** half of the work I need to get done by

tomorrow."

Interrogative sentences

We can ask whether an action will be complete in the future by inverting *will*

with the subject, as in:

• "**Will** they **have read** the memo ahead of the meeting?"

• "**Will** you **have had** something to eat before you arrive?"

We can also ask about specific aspects of a future action by using different

question words or phrases. Remember, we still invert *will* with the subject in this

case:

• "What **will** we **have learned** from such tragic events as these?"

• "Who **will have** **prepared** the notes for the seminar?"

• "How much money **will** we **have** **spent** trying to get this car working?"

• "How long **will** you **have worked** there before your maternity leave begins?"

Other constructions

Although we most commonly use the modal verb *will*, there are two other ways

we can form the future perfect tense: *be going to* and *shall*.

Be going to

Be going to can only form the future perfect tense when it is used to describe an

action that finishes in the future—in this way, it is interchangeable with *will* in

meaning.

We usually contract *be* with the subject when we use *be going to*. For example:

• "She**'s going to have won** nine championship titles by the time she's 25."
• "If you keep reading at that pace, you**'re going to have finished** the book
before the rest of the students."
However, using *be going to* can sometimes result in an awkward construction,
and it is not as common as *will*. We also **cannot** use the *be going to* construction
when talking about something that we predict to have happened in the past.

Shall
We can also use the modal verb **shall** instead of *will* to form the future perfect
tense in formal speech or writing. Unlike *be going to*, we can use *shall* for all
uses of the future perfect. For example:
• "By next spring, I **shall have lived** on my own for nearly a decade."
• "The students **shall have finished** their evaluations this time next week."
• "You **shall have heard**, no doubt, the unflattering remarks made about my
character."
However, this creates a very formal tone that is not common in modern English;
as a result, *will* + *have* + past participle remains the most common construction
of the future perfect tense.

Exercise

1. Which of the following **modal auxiliary verbs** is used to create the future
perfect tense?
a) would
b) may
c) will
d) can
2. Which of the following is **not** a function of the future perfect tense?
a) To say that something will be completed or achieved at a specific point in the

future

b) To indicate how long something will have been occurring by a specific point
in the future

c) To make a present prediction about something that happened in the past

d) To indicate a continuous action that began at a specific point in the future

3. How does the structure of the future perfect tense change in an **interrogative**
sentence?

a) *will* inverts with the subject

b) *have* inverts with the subject

c) *will* inverts with a question word

d) *have* inverts with a question word

4. For what purpose can we use *shall* instead of *will* to form the future perfect
tense?

a) To make the sentence a question

b) To make the sentence more formal

c) To make a present prediction about something that happened in the past

d) To indicate an intention to do something in the future

5. When are we **not** able to use *be going to* instead of *will* to form the future
perfect tense?

a) When saying that something will be completed or achieved at a specific point
in the future

b) When indicating how long something will have occurred by a specific point in
the future

c) When making a present prediction about something that happened in the past

Future Perfect Continuous Tense

Definition

Like the **future perfect tense**, we use the **future perfect continuous tense** (also
known as the **future perfect progressive tense**) to indicate how long something

has been happening once a future moment in time is reached. It can also be used
in this way to indicate the cause of a possible future result.
The most common way we create the future perfect continuous tense is by using
the **modal auxiliary verb** *will + have been +* the **present participle** of the verb.
For example:
- "By June, I ***will have been*** living in New York for four years."
- "She's going to miss half the day because she***'ll have been*** sleeping for so
long!"

Using the Future Perfect Continuous
The future perfect continuous tense is used in a very similar way to the **future**
perfect to describe the duration of a completed future action. They both carry
the same meaning when used in this way, but the future perfect continuous
emphasizes the continuous nature of the action. Consider, for example, these two
sentences:
- "By the time I get there, she ***will have*** waited for over an hour." (future perfect
tense)
- "By the time I get there, she ***will have been*** waiting for over an hour." (future
perfect continuous tense)
The meaning is technically the same in both examples above; however, the
second sentence stresses the fact that *she* was continuously waiting during the
future period *by the time I get there*. The change in meaning is subtle, but it adds
greater depth to the sentence. Here are some other examples using the future
perfect continuous tense:
- "I ***will have been*** working on this ranch for more than half my life when I turn
40."

• "She**'ll have been** studying Japanese for four years by the time she graduates."

• "When the teacher comes back, we**'ll have been** reading for nearly two

hours."

With action verbs

Because it describes continuous, dynamic action, the future perfect continuous

can only be used with **action verbs**; it cannot be used with **stative verbs** (such

as **linking verbs** or **verbs of the senses**), which describe non-continuous actions. For stative verbs, we can only use the future perfect tense instead. For

example:

✔ "Next month we**'ll have** been married for 10 years." (correct)

✘ "Next month we**'ll have been** being married for 10 years." (incorrect)

✔ "By tomorrow morning, this all **will have** seemed like just a bad dream."

(correct)

✘ "By tomorrow morning, this all **will have been** seeming like just a bad

dream." (incorrect)

Cause of future results

We can also use the future perfect continuous to indicate that the continuous

action that finishes in the future will be the cause of something in the future. For

example:

• "I bet he'll be hungry because he **will have been** studying straight through

lunch."

• "I'm not going to have any energy for the kids because I**'ll have been** **working**

so hard this week."

• "You're going to look like a prune since you **will have been** swimming all

afternoon!"

Other sentence types

Negative sentences

To describe something that will **not** be completed over a certain span of time
into the future, we make the future perfect continuous tense negative by adding
not after the modal verb *will* (usually contracted as *won't*). For example:
• "Why are you bringing your book to the airport? We ***won't have been*** **waiting**
for very long before her plane arrives."
• "He ***will not have been*** **working** here for very long if he is fired over this
incident."
However, it's not very common to make negative constructions of the future
perfect continuous tense.

Interrogative sentences
We can ask whether an action will be completed in the future after a certain
duration by inverting *will* with the subject, as in:
• "***Will*** they ***have been*** **searching** for us for very long?"
• "***Will*** she ***have been*** **working** in Japan for the whole time she's lived there?"
We can also ask about specific aspects of a future action by using different
question words or phrases. Remember, we still invert *will* with the subject in this
case:
• "Who***'ll have been*** **writing** the notes for the class while the teaching assistant
is absent?"
• "How long ***will*** you ***have been*** **working** there before your maternity leave begins?"

Other constructions
Although we most commonly use the modal verb *will*, there are two other ways we can form the future perfect continuous tense: *be going to* and *shall*.

Be going to
Be going to is interchangeable with *will* in meaning when we make the future perfect continuous tense. However, using *be going to* can sometimes result in a
wordy, awkward construction, and it is not as common as *will*.

We usually contract *be* with the subject when we use *be going to*. For example:

• "She*'s going to have been* **working** for nearly 18 hours by the time she's finished with her shift tonight."

• "I*'m going to have been* **reading** this book for nearly six months if I don't finish it soon!"

Shall

We can also use the modal verb ***shall*** instead of *will* to form the future perfect continuous tense in more formal speech or writing. For example:

• "By next spring, I ***shall have been*** **living** on my own for nearly a decade."

• "The students ***shall have been*** **reading** their books for the entire period."

• "You ***shall have been*** **hearing**, no doubt, the unflattering remarks made about

my character.

However, this creates a very formal tone that is not common in modern English.

Among the three options available, *will* is the most common way to construct of

the future perfect continuous tense.

Exercise

1. What form of the **main verb** is used to create the future perfect continuous tense?

a) infinitive

b) base form

c) present participle

d) past participle

2. Which of the following is a function of the future perfect continuous tense?

a) To indicate how long something will have been occurring by a specific point in the future

b) To indicate the cause of a future result

c) To make a present prediction about something that happened in the past

d) To indicate a continuous action that began at a specific point in the future

e) A & B

f) B & C
g) C & D
3. Where does *not* appear in a **negative sentence** in the future perfect continuous tense?
a) After *will*
b) After *have*
c) After *been*
d) After the present participle of the main verb
4. Which of the following is the **most common** way to form the future perfect tense?
a) *be going to have been* + the present participle of the main verb
b) *will have been* + the present participle of the main verb
c) *shall have been* + the present participle of the main verb
d) Each is equally common
5. Which type of verb **cannot** be used in the future perfect continuous tense?
a) action verb
b) factitive verb
c) conditional verb
d) stative verb
e) A & B
f) B & C
g) C & D

Answers
Past Tense: 1-a, 2-d, 3-c, 4-c, 5-d
Past Simple Tense: 1-b, 2-d, 3-a, 4-c, 5-c
Past Continuous Tense: 1-c, 2-a, 3-c, 4-b
Past Perfect Tense: 1-c, 2-b, 3-a, 4-c, 5-d
Past Perfect Continuous Tense: 1-c, 2-e, 3-b, 4-c, 5-b
Future Tense (Approximation): 1-d, 2-d, 3-c, 4-b
Future Simple Tense: 1-c, 2-a, 3-d, 4-b, 5-b
Future Continuous Tense: 1-d, 2-b, 3-c, 4-a, 5-c
Future Perfect Tense: 1-c, 2-d, 3-a, 4-b, 5-c
Future Perfect Continuous Tense: 1-c, 2-e, 3-a, 4-b, 5-d

Worksheet 3

Tense
Definition
Grammatical **tense** refers to the conjugation of a verb to reflect its place in time
—that is, when the action occurred.
There are technically only two grammatical tenses in English: the **past** and the
present. Verbs in their basic form inherently describe the present time, and they
can be conjugated into a unique form that describes the past. We can then use
auxiliary verbs and verb **participles** to create different **aspects** of the past and
present tenses, which describe if an action is or was continuous, or if it began at
an earlier point in the past.
However, verbs do **not** have a specific conjugated form to reflect the future, and,
for this reason, English is considered not to have a true future tense.
Nevertheless, although English has no future tense in the strict sense, we
commonly refer to several structures that are used for future meaning as
belonging to the "future tense." The most common of these structures begin with
will or *be going to*. For the sake of consistency, we will be referring to such
constructions as the **future tense** in this chapter.
Summary of the Main Tenses
Below, we'll provide a very brief summary of each of the variations of the
present, past, and future tenses. Go to the individual sections to learn more about
each variation.
The Present Tense
Present Simple Tense
The present simple tense (also called the **simple present**) is used to express
express

habits, facts, and timetables.

Structures of the present simple tense

Affirmative: The base form of the verb. It is usually conjugated for the thirdperson
singular by adding "-s" or "-es" to the end of the verb (except for **irregular verbs**).

Question: Use the **auxiliary verb** *do* (or *does* for the third-person singular)
before the main verb.

Negative: Use *do not* (contracted as *don't*) or *does not* (contracted as *doesn't*)
before the main verb.

Examples:

"I **go** to work every day."

"He **works** in finance."

"I **don't go** out very often."

"**Do** you **eat** breakfast every morning?"

"The sun **rises** in the East."

"The sun **doesn't** rise in the West."

"The train **leaves** at 9:30 tomorrow morning."

"It **doesn't leave** from platform 12."

"**Does** the train for Detroit **leave** at 9 AM tomorrow?"

With the verb *be*

The **linking verb** *be* has three different conjugations for grammatical person in
the present tense: *am* (first-person singular); *are* (first-person plural, second
person, and third-person plural); and *is* (third-person singular). *Be* does not need
do when making questions or negative statements in the present simple tense.

Affirmative: "I **am** from the United States."

Question: "**Is** he **Canadian**?"

Negative: "They **are not** British."

Present Continuous Tense

The present continuous tense (also called the **present progressive tense**) is used
for something in progress at the moment of speaking; it describes something that

is happening in the present moment and also for expressing future arrangements.

It can only be used with **action verbs**.

Structures of the present continuous tense

Affirmative: The **auxiliary verb** *be* plus the **present participle** of the main

verb. We conjugate *be*, rather than the main verb, for grammatical person.

Question: Invert *be* with the subject of the sentence.

Negative: Use *not* after auxiliary *be* (contracted as *isn't* or *aren't*; *am not* is not

normally contracted) before the present participle of the main verb.

Examples:

Present moment

Affirmative: "John **is sleeping** at the moment."

Question: "**Am** I **wearing** the right uniform?"

Negative: "Jack **isn't coming** to the movie with us."

Present moment

Affirmative: "The managers **are working** on the new project."

Question: "**Are** you still **reading** that book?"

Negative: "I **am not living** in New York anymore."

Future arrangement

Affirmative: "We**'re flying** to Spain tomorrow."

Question: "**Are** you **meeting** Tom for lunch on Wednesday?"

Negative: "They**'re not having** the party on Saturday anymore."

Present Perfect Tense

The present perfect tense (sometimes called the **present perfect simple tense**) is

used to give general information about something that happened at an indefinite

point in the past. We also use the present perfect with the prepositions *for* and

since when we speak about something that started in the past and is still true

now.

Structures of the present perfect tense:

Affirmative: The **auxiliary verb** *have* plus the **past participle** of the main verb.

Have conjugates as *has* for the third-person singular.

Question: Invert *have/has* with the subject of the sentence.

Negative: Use *not* after *have/has* (often contracted as *haven't/hasn't*) before the
past participle of the main verb. We can also use *never* instead of *not*.

Examples:

"I **have lived** in Italy for many years."

"She **has been** here since 8 o'clock."

"**Have** you **been** here since this morning?"

"We **haven't been** to the movies in a long time."

"I**'ve lost** my pen."

"**Have** you **seen** my jacket anywhere?"

"She **hasn't been** in work for a few weeks."

"I **have seen** this movie already."

"**Have** you ever **tried** Indian food?"

"She **has never flown** on an airplane before."

Present Perfect Continuous Tense

We use the present perfect continuous tense (also called the present perfect
progressive tense) to talk about that which began in the past and is still
happening in the present. We often use it to emphasize the length of time that has
passed while something is happening. We can also use it to talk about something
that has been happening lately or only finished very recently. It can only be used
with **action verbs**.

**Structures of the present perfect
continuous tense**

Affirmative: The auxiliary verb *have* (or *has* with third-person singular
subjects) + *been* + the present participle of the main verb.

Question: Invert *have/has* with the subject of the sentence.

Negative: Use *not* after *have/has* (often contracted as *haven't/hasn't*) before the
past participle of the main verb.

Example:

"I**'ve been writing** for over an hour."

"How long **have** you **been writing** for?"

"They **haven't been living** in Spain for very long."

"She's tired because she**'s been working** a lot."

"That bag looks new. **Have** you **been shopping**?"

"He **hasn't been sleeping** a lot lately."

The Past Tense

Past Simple Tense

We use the past simple tense to express finished actions. It is often used with an

expression of past time to give more complete information.

Structures of the past simple tense

Affirmative: The past-tense conjugation of the verb. This is generally accomplished by adding "-d" or "-ed" to the end of the verb, but there are many

specific forms for **irregular verbs**.

Question: Use *did* (the past tense of the **auxiliary verb** *do*) before the main

verb. *Did* does not conjugate differently for third-person singular.

Negative: Use *did not* (often contracted as *didn't*) before the main verb.

Examples:

"She **worked** in finance before this job."

"We **lived** in China for six years after I **graduated** from college."

"They **didn't watch** the movie last night."

"I **went** to the park yesterday."

"**Did** he **wake up** early yesterday morning?"

"I **didn't go** to the supermarket this morning."

With the verb *be*

The **linking verb** *be* has two different conjugations for grammatical person in

the past tense: *was* (first-person and third-person singular) and *were* (first-person

plural, second person, and third-person plural). *Be* does not need *did* when

making questions or negative statements in the present simple tense.

Affirmative: "I **was** their accountant at the time."

Question: "**Were** you in the military?"

Negative: "He **was not** serious."

Past Continuous Tense

The past continuous tense (also called the **past progressive tense**) is used for

something in progress at a certain moment in the past. It can only be used with

action verbs.

Structures of the past continuous tense

Affirmative: *Was* or *were* (the past tense of the auxiliary verb *be*) followed by
the **present participle** of the main verb.

Question: Invert *was/were* with the subject.

Negative: Add *not* after *was/were* (often contracted as *wasn't/weren't*).

Examples:

"I **was reading** a book when they arrived."

"What **were** you **talking about when I arrived?"**

"She was worrying we wouldn't be able to afford the wedding."

"I **was not feeling** well."

"**Were you sleeping** when I called?"

"My ex-husband **was always leaving** dirty dishes in the sink."

"I guess things **weren't improving**."

Past Perfect Tense

The past perfect tense expresses the idea that something occurred before another
action in the past. It can also show that something happened before a specific
time in the past.

Structures of the past perfect tense

Affirmative: *Had* (the past tense of the auxiliary verb *have*) + the **past
participle** of the main verb.

Question: Invert *had* with the subject of the verb.

Negative: Add *not* after *had* (often contracted as *hadn't*). We also often make the
past perfect negative by using the word *never* instead of *not*.

Examples:

"The movie **had already ended** when I turned on the TV."

"I was sad to leave the house I **had lived** in for so many years."

"Until this morning, I **had never been** on a plane.

"**Had** you ever **been** on a tractor before working on our farm?"

"I **hadn't eaten** Parmesan cheese before going to Italy."

"I **hadn't ever ridden** on a rollercoaster before going to the
amusement park yesterday."

Past Perfect Continuous Tense

The past perfect continuous tense (also called the **past perfect
progressive**

tense) is used to express something that began and was in progress until a

moment in the past or until another past action occurred.

Structures of the past perfect

continuous tense

Affirmative: *Had + been* + the **past participle** of the main verb.

Question: Invert *had* with the subject of the verb.

Negative: Add *not* after *had* (often contracted as *hadn't*).

Examples:

"When I arrived at the bus stop, the other people there **had been waiting** for nearly an hour."

"How long **had** you **been standing** there before they let you in?"

"We **hadn't been talking** for very long before she had to leave."

"I saw that it **had been raining** outside."

"My eyes were tired because I ***had been* working** on the computer."

"***Had*** she ***been* living** in Italy for a long time?"

"He ***had been* feeling** unwell, so he went to lie down."

The Future Tense

The most common constructions of the **future tenses** use the **modal auxiliary**

verb *will* or the verb phrase *be going to*. We can also use the modal verb *shall* to

create the future tense, but this is generally reserved for more formal or polite

English, and it is not very common in everyday speech and writing, especially in

American English.

Future Simple Tense

We use the future simple tense to describe an intended action, make a prediction,

state future facts, make promises, or offer to do something.

Structures of the future simple tense

Affirmative: The modal verb *will* or the verb phrase *be going to* + the base form

of the verb. If using *be going to*, we must conjugate *be* to reflect grammatical

person in the present tense (*is, am,* or *are*).

Question: Invert the subject with *will* or *be*.

Negative: Add *not* after *will* (often contracted as *won't*) or between *be* and

going.
Examples:
"The Queen **will be** in Rome tomorrow."
"I **will definitely arrive** on time."
"He**'ll help** you with that heavy suitcase."
"She **won't do** her homework."
"**Will** they **be** late?"
"I **am going to wash** my hair after dinner."
"We **aren't going to join** the gym after all."
"I think it**'s going to rain** tomorrow."
"**Are** you **going to mow** the lawn today?"
Future Continuous Tense
The future continuous tense (also known as the **future progressive**) is used to
describe an unfinished action occurring in the future. This action can either
begin in the future, or it can already be in progress in the present and continue
into the future. The future continuous can only be used with **action verbs**.
Structures of the future continuous tense
Affirmative: The modal verb *will* or the verb phrase *be going to* + the auxiliary
verb *be* + the **present participle** of the main verb. If using *be going to*, we must
conjugate *be* to reflect grammatical person; we do **not** conjugate *be* before the
present participle, however.
Question: Invert the subject with *will* or *be*.
Negative: Add *not* after *will* (often contracted as *won't*) or between *be* and
going.
Examples:
"You shouldn't call their house now; they **will be sleeping**."
"I**'ll be flying** to Boston tomorrow, so I can't come to lunch."
"People **are going be consuming** even more natural resources by the year 2030."
"We **won't be leaving** until the evening."
"**Is** she **going to be working** from home now?"

"I**'m not going to be living** in New York for much longer."
"**Will** you **be graduating** this year?"
Future Perfect Tense
We use the future perfect tense to say that something will finish or complete at a
specific point in the future, often indicating how long something will have been
happening once a future moment in time is reached. We can also use the future
perfect to make a prediction that something has or should have happened in the
past.
Structures of the future perfect tense
Affirmative: The modal verb *will* + the auxiliary verb *have* + the **past participle** of the main verb. We can also use *be going to* instead of *will*, but it is
less common with the future perfect tense.
Question: Invert the subject with *will*.
Negative: Add *not* after *will* (often contracted as *won't*).
Examples:
"By October we **will have lived** in this house for 20 years."
"After this next race, I **will have completed** 10 triathlons."
"You **will have heard** by now that the company is going bankrupt."
"**Will** they **have read** the memo ahead of the meeting?"
"Why are you going to the airport so early? Her flight **will not have arrived** yet."
"How long **will** you **have worked** there before your maternity leave begins?"
Future Perfect Continuous Tense
Like the future perfect, we use the **future perfect continuous tense** (also known
as the **future perfect progressive tense**) to indicate how long something has
been happening once a future moment in time is reached; the emphasis is on the
continual progression of the action. It can also be used to indicate the cause of a
possible future result. We can only use the future perfect continuous with **action**
verbs.

Structures of the future perfect continuous tense

Affirmative: The modal verb *will* + the auxiliary verb *have* + *been* + the **present**

participle of the main verb. We can also use *be going to* instead of *will*, but it is

less common with the future perfect continuous tense.

Question: Invert the subject with *will*.

Negative: Add *not* after *will* (often contracted as *won't*). However, it is not very

common to make negative constructions of the future perfect continuous tense.

Examples:

"She**'ll have been waiting** for nearly an hour by the time we arrive."

"I **will have been living** in this country for 10 years this November."

"He's not going to have any energy for the kids because he**'ll have been working** so hard this week."

"**Will** they **have been looking** through our tax returns for the last few years?"

"How **will** he **have been coping** on his own for all these years?"

"He **won't have been sleeping** for very long, but I have to wake him up."

Indicative Mood vs. Subjunctive Mood

All of the above tenses that we've looked at have been in what's called the

Indicative Mood (also known as the **Realis Mood**), which is used to talk about

what is factual or really happening.

There is also another mood in English called the **subjunctive mood**, which deals

with things that are not objective facts, such one's state of mind, opinions,

beliefs, intentions, desires, and so on. It is one of the **Irrealis Moods**, so called

because they deal with what is not objectively real.

The subjunctive mood has all of the tenses that the indicative mood deals with,

but it is used in much more specialized circumstances. When we talk about verb

tense in this chapter, we will be focusing on the **indicative mood**; to learn about
the subjunctive mood and its tenses, go to the section on the **Irrealis Moods** in
the chapter about **Grammatical Mood**.
Exercise

1. How many grammatical tenses does English **technically** have?
a) one
b) two
c) three
d) four
2. Identify the tense form that is made using the following structure:
Had + been + the **past participle** of the main verb
a) Present continuous tense
b) Past perfect tense
c) Present perfect tense
d) Past perfect continuous tense
3. Which of the following sentences uses the **future simple tense**?
a) "John goes for a walk every morning."
b) "The train is leaving tomorrow at 10 AM."
c) "Her flight is going to arrive a little later than expected."
d) "I will be working for my Uncle this summer."
4. Which of the following sentences uses the **present perfect tense**?
a) "I have lived in this town my entire life."
b) "She had been staying with a friend for a few weeks."
c) "We'll have worked something out by the time you get here."
d) "They have been saying the same thing for years."
5. Which of the following is **not** used to create the **future tense**?
a) will
b) shall
c) do
d) be going to
Present Tense
Definition
The **present tense** is mostly used to identify the action of a verb as taking place
in the present time. However, depending on which way we form the present

tense, it can also be used to describe things that happened in the past, or even
certain events that are planned to happen in the future.
There are four forms of the present tense that can accomplish these tasks. We
will give a brief summary of each below, but go to the appropriate section to
learn about them more in-depth.
Present Simple Tense
The **present simple tense** is used to describe that which is done habitually, that
which is generally true, that which is always the case, or that which is scheduled
to happen. It is made up of only the basic form of the verb: the infinitive (+ -(e)s
if used with the third-person singular). It is called "simple" because it does not
rely on any modal or auxiliary verbs to accomplish its meaning.
Examples:
• "I come from Berlin."
• "The train leaves at 2 PM."
• "He has breakfast every morning."
• "We like ice cream."
Present Continuous Tense
(Progressive)
The **present continuous** or **present progressive tense** is used to speak about
actions that are currently happening. It can also be used to describe actions or
events that are planned for the future, but which are not definitively fixed in
time.
We create the present continuous tense by using the **present participle** (*-ing*
form) of the "main" verb after the present-tense form of the auxiliary linking
verb "be." The present participle creates the **continuous** forms of verbs, which is
where "present continuous" gets its name.
Examples:

- "She is running for president next year."
- "They are not watching television."
- "We are eating ice cream."
- "Are you reading that book?"

Present Perfect Tense

Present perfect tense (sometimes called the **present perfect simple tense** is

used to talk about things that happened sometime in the past, but which are not

given a specific time or date.

We form the present perfect by using the present tense of the auxiliary verb

"have" (or *"has,"* if used with third-person singular pronouns) along with the

past participle of the "main" verb. Using forms of an auxiliary verb (such as

"have") together with the past participle of the main verb is called the **perfect**

aspect in English, which is where the "present perfect" gets its name. (To learn

more about the *perfect* and other aspects, see the chapter on **Aspect**.)

Examples:

- "I have seen that movie already."
- "She's been to Prague."
- "He has lost his keys."
- "Jenny's lived in Dubai for 10 years!"

Present Perfect Continuous Tense

The present perfect continuous is used in a very similar way to the present

perfect simple tense. It is used to talk about that which began in the past and is

still happening in the present, with an emphasis on the continued action and/or

the amount of time it is taking. We can also use it to talk about something that is

only temporary, has been happening lately, or only finished very recently.

The **present perfect continuous tense** (sometimes called the **present perfect**

progressive tense) is formed by using the present tense of the auxiliary verb
"have" (or *"has,"* if used with third-person singular pronouns) along with "been"
(the *past participle* of the linking verb "be") and the present participle (-*ing*
form) of the "main" verb.

Examples:
- "I have been living in New York City."
- "We have been walking for four hours!"
- "They have been working in the shop for 10 years."
- "Bill has been coming into work late a lot."
- "I'm so sweaty because I have been exercising."

Exercise

1. What can the present tense be used to describe?
a) Things are happening in the present moment in time.
b) Things that happened at an unspecified time in the past.
c) Things that will happen in the future.
d) Things that began in the past and are still happening now.
e) A & C
f) B & D
g) All of the above
h) None of the above
2. Which form of the present tense is used to describe a habit or general truth?
a) Present Simple
b) Present Continuous
c) Present Perfect
d) Present Perfect Continuous
3. Which of the following is **not** in the present tense?
a) I hear that he is living in Saudi Arabia.
b) They haven't been talking for years.
c) She had been spending some time with her father.
d) He's left the kids with their nanny.
4. What form(s) of present tense does the following sentence use?
"I can't believe that he has lost his keys again!"
a) Present Simple
b) Present Continuous
c) Present Perfect

d) Present Perfect Continuous

e) A & B

f) A & C

g) A & D

Present Simple Tense

Definition

The **present simple tense** (also called the **simple present tense**) is used when

we speak about habits, general facts, and timetables. However, just because

something is *true* does not necessarily mean it takes the present simple tense, nor

does something have to be occurring in the present moment in time for it to be in

the present simple tense.

It is called the present "simple" because its basic form consists of one word only

—that is, it does not require an **auxiliary verb** to achieve its meaning. Most verbs in the present simple tense are in the same form as the infinitive

verb. However, if it is in the **third-person singular form**, then it usually takes

the ending *-(e)s*.

For example:

• "I **live** in London." (Fact: I live permanently in London.)

• "Hans **comes** from Berlin." (Fact: Hans is originally from Berlin.)

• "Mary **has** breakfast every morning." (Habit)

Now let's see how the form and meaning of the verbs change if we add the

auxiliary verb "be:"

• "I **am living** in London." (Still a fact, but it now highlights that I am only living in London temporarily—this wasn't always the case, and it might change

in the future.)

• "Hans **is coming** from Berlin." (Hans is currently travelling from Berlin.)

• "Mary **is having** breakfast." (Mary is currently in the process of eating breakfast.)

These are examples of the **present continuous** tense. As you can see, their

meaning is altered in comparison to those in the **present simple** tense. (To learn
more about this tense, please refer to the chapter section on **Present Continuous
Tense**.)
Present simple can also be used for future events that are fixed to happen, such
as in timetables. For example:
• "The train **leaves** at 7 PM."
This is a fixed timetable where the present simple is used to indicate a future
event. We can also say: "We leave for Berlin tomorrow at 7 PM," as the speaker
sees this as a fixed event similar to a timetable.
Normally we use **stative verbs** (also called **state verbs**) to express a fact. Here
are some examples of common stative verbs:
Like
Dislike
Love
Enjoy
Hate
Have
Know
Need
Want
Seem
Of course, some **action verbs** (also called **dynamic verbs**) used for habits can
also be seen as a state or general truth. For example:
• "I **play** tennis." (State/fact/general truth)
• "I **play** tennis *every week*." (Habit)
However, verbs with a stative meaning cannot be used to indicate habit. For
example:
✔ "I know John." (correct – state/fact)
✖ "I know John *every week*." (incorrect – can't be expressed as a habit)
Some stative verbs can also function as action verbs in different contexts:

- "I **enjoy** soup." (Stative verb—expresses a state/fact.)
- "I **enjoy** soup once in a while." (Action verb—expresses a habit. "Enjoy" in
this sense means to actively consume.)

We also use the present simple with the **zero conditional**, which means something is always true. For example:

- "If you **drop** an egg, it **breaks**." (Any egg will break if it is dropped.)

Present simple can be used in a variety of sentence formations, such as **positive**,
negative, **interrogative**, and **negative interrogative**. We'll briefly explain each
and provide examples with the present simple tense.

Positive sentences

Simply put, positive sentences indicate what **is** the case, as opposed to what is
not. In the present simple tense, they look like this:

- "I **jog** every day."
- "He **lives** in Chicago."
- "Dogs **bark**, while cats **meow**." (Third-person plural.)
- "Janet **writes** songs for a living."

Negative sentences

The opposite of a positive sentence, a negative sentence describes what
is **not** (or
no longer) the case. We form these by adding the auxiliary verb *do* (or *does* in
the third-person singular) and the word *not* after the subject of the sentence.
These can also be contracted to *don't* or *doesn't*. For example:

- "I **don't jog** every day."
- "He **doesn't live** in Chicago anymore."
- "Dogs **do not meow**, and cats **do not bark**."
- "Janet **does not write** many songs these days."

Interrogative sentences

Interrogative sentences ask a question. They are marked by the question mark
punctuation ("?") at the end instead of a period. Simple interrogative questions
also use the auxiliary verb *do* (or *does* in the third-person singular), but before

the subject instead of after. Generally speaking, it is uncommon to use a firstperson
subject in an interrogative sentence in the present simple.
• "**Do** you **jog** every day?"
• "**Does** he still **live** in Chicago?"
• "**Do** dogs **bark**, or **do** cats?" (The second "bark" is implied.)
• "**Does** Janet **write** songs anymore?"
Negative interrogative sentences
Negative interrogative sentences also ask a question, but they imply that the
speaker expects the answer to be (or believes the answer *should* be) "yes." We
form these by adding the auxiliary verb *do/does* before the subject of the
sentence and the word *not* after the subject. Again, these can be contracted to
don't or *doesn't*; if they are, the contraction comes before the subject:
• "**Do** you **not jog** every day?"
• "**Does** he **not** still **live** in Chicago?"
• "**Don't** dogs normally **bark**?"
• "**Doesn't** Janet **write** songs for a living?"
Unlike the interrogative sentences, **negative interrogative sentences** are much
more likely to be used in the first-person, with *do* and *not* typically contracted:
• "**Don't** I look **good** in this dress?"
(For more information about different types of sentences, go to the chapter about
Sentences in the part of the guide on **Syntax**.)
Exercise

1. Which of the following sentences is **not** in the present simple tense?
a) "I walk home each day."
b) "He always reads good books."
c) "She will talk to her mother at 5 o'clock."
d) "I go jogging every morning."
2. The following sentence is in present simple tense. What **kind** of sentence is it?
"Does he not have a car of his own?"
a) Interrogative sentence.

b) Positive interrogative sentence.

c) Negative sentence.

d) Negative interrogative sentence.

3. What kind of verb (usually) cannot be used to indicate **habit**?

a) Stative verbs.

b) Action verbs.

c) Passive verbs.

d) Sense verbs.

4. Which of the following sentences **is** in the present simple tense?

a) "We are leaving tomorrow on the 10 AM bus."

b) "We will leave tomorrow on the 10 AM bus."

c) "We leave tomorrow on the 10 AM bus."

d) "We are going to leave tomorrow on the 10 AM bus."

**Present Continuous Tense
(Progressive)**

Definition

We create the present continuous tense by using the **present participle**
(-*ing*
form) of the verb after the present-tense form of the **auxiliary verb** *be*.
Unlike the **present simple tense**, which is used to express things that
are **always**
the case or are at a fixed time in the future, we use the **present
continuous** (also
called the **present progressive**) **tense** to speak about actions that are
currently
happening, whether generally or at the exact moment of speech. It can
also be
used to describe actions or events that are planned for the future (but
are not
definitively fixed in time, such as a timetable).

**Actions happening at the moment of
speech**

The most common occurrence of the present continuous is when
someone or
something is performing an action at the very moment being described.
In this
case, the object of the verb is usually in the presence of or very near to
the
speaker. For example:

• "I **am going** home now."

- "He **is crying** because of the movie."
- "We **are heading** to the park."
- "It **is raining** outside."

Actions happening currently, but not at the moment of speech

The present continuous can also indicate something that is currently happening
but which is not at the exact moment of speech. It generally refers to something
that the person or thing is currently engaged in doing that is taking place
continuously over a longer period of time, but which is not (necessarily)
permanent. For example:

- "John **is working** in telemarketing."
- "She is **running** for president."
- "I **am living** in London."

Actions or events planned for the future

Like the present simple tense, the present continuous can also describe future
events. However, unlike the present simple, it describes that which someone is
planning or **expecting** to do, as opposed to that which is at a fixed point in time
in the future. The formation of the verb does not change to reflect this; rather,
information from the rest of the sentence informs the future intention.

- "She **is running** for president *next year*."
- "I **am taking** my driving test *after the Christmas break*."
- "We **are watching** a movie *later*."

With adverbs

We can also add **adverbs** relating to time between *be* and the present participle
to specify or clarify *when* or *how frequently* something happens or occurs.

- "I **am *already* leaving**." (I am leaving sooner than I expected.)
- "She **is *still* living** next door." (She continues to live next door, perhaps longer
than was expected.)

The adverb *always*

There is also a special usage when the adverb *always* is used between *be* and the
present participle. Rather than literally meaning that the action *always* happens
(as you might expect), it instead means that that action *very often* happens. We
use this as a means of adding hyperbolic emphasis to how frequently something
happens or occurs, and it usually implies that the action or event is questionable
or undesirable to some degree. For example:
- "My husband **is *always* leaving** dirty dishes in the sink!"
- "The used car I bought **is *always* breaking** down."
- "You **are *always* losing** your phone!"

Negative sentences

A negative sentence in the present continuous describes what is **not** currently
happening. We form these by adding the word *not* after the auxiliary verb *be*. For
second-person, third-person, and first-person plural (but not first-person
singular), *be* and *not* can also be contracted.
For example:
- "I **am *not* watching** the movie."
- "He **is *not* crying**."
- "You **aren't leaving** until the house is clean."
- "She **isn't going** home for Thanksgiving this year."
- ✖ "I **amn't reading** that anymore." (incorrect)

Not can also be replaced with the **adverbial phrase** *no longer* to indicate that
someone or something *was* doing something, but that is not the case now. For
instance:
- "She **is *no longer* living** in New York."

Interrogative sentences

Interrogative (question) sentences in the present continuous tense are formed by
reversing the verb *be* and the subject. If adverbs are used to clarify or specify the
time, they come before the main verb or at the end of the sentence.

- "**Is** she **sleeping**?"
- "**Are** you **seeing** this?"
- "**Are** they **going** home *already*?"
- "**Is** it *still* **raining** outside?"

The present continuous can also be used with the **question words** *who,* *what,*
where when, why, and *how*:

- "*When* **is** she **taking** the exam?"
- "*What* **are** you **watching**?"
- "*Why* **is** he **leaving**?"
- "*Who***'s talking**?"
- "*How* **are** they **getting** to the station?"

Negative interrogative sentences

Negative interrogative sentences also ask a question, but they imply that the
speaker expects (or expected) something to be the case. They can be used to
express surprise if something is no longer happening.

We form these by inverting *be* and the subject, and then adding the word *not*
after the subject. Again, *be* and *not* can be contracted; if they are, the contraction
comes before the subject. This can serve to make the sentence sound less formal
and stuffy. And adverbs can still be used to specify or clarify time. For example:

- "**Is** she ***not* painting** *anymore*?"
- "You want to play outside? ***Isn't*** it **raining**?"
- "Wait, ***aren't*** they *still* **dating**?

Like the negative sentence, *no longer* can be used instead of *not*. Just note that
you do not use other adverbs in this case:

- **Are** Tim and John *no longer* **living** together?
- **Is** it *no longer* **raining** outside?

Negative interrogative sentences in the present continuous can also be used with
the **question words** *why* and *how*. Again, it expresses the speaker's surprise (and
sometimes dismay) that something is not the case:

- "*Why* **is** she **not leaving** today?"

- *"How* **are** you **not watching** the match on TV?"
- *"Why* **are** we **not abandoning** this foolish enterprise?"
- "It's the middle of December. *How* **is** it **not snowing** yet?"

(For more information about different types of sentences, go to the chapter on

Sentences in the part of the guide on **Syntax**.)

Exercise

1. Which auxiliary verb is used in the **present continuous** tense?
a) Do
b) Will
c) Be
d) May

2. Which of the following sentences is in the present continuous tense?
a) "She will walk home alone."
b) "She walks home alone."
c) "She has walked home alone."
d) "She is walking home alone."

3. In the present continuous tense, which **question word** or **words** can be used
in negative interrogative sentences?
a) Who
b) Where
c) Why
d) How
e) A & B
f) B & D
g) C & D
h) All of the above
i) None of the above

4. In which grammatical person (first person, second person, third person) is it
not correct to contract "be" with "not"?
a) First-person singular
b) First-person plural
c) Second person
d) Third-person singular
e) Third-person plural

5. What **kind** of action is the following sentence describing?

"My brother William is always talking about his great political ambitions."
a) An action happening at the moment of speech.
b) An action or event planned for the future.
c) An action happening currently, but not at the exact moment of speech.
d) An action that happens very often, especially something questionable or
undesirable.
6. Which of the following questions is **not** in the present continuous tense?
a) "Is she still living in San Francisco?"
b) "Will we be seeing you tonight?"
c) "Aren't we meeting them later?"
d) "Sorry, John is working right now."

Present Perfect Tense
Definition
The **present perfect tense** (sometimes referred to as the **present perfect simple
tense**) is formed by using the present tense of the auxiliary verb *have* (or *has*, if
used with third-person singular pronouns) along with the *past participle* of the
"main" verb. Despite its name, the present perfect is used to give general
information about something that happened in the past (anytime "before now"),
but which did not occur at a definitive point in time.
For example:
• "I *have seen* that movie already."
• "She *has been* to Prague."
• "*They've decided* where they want to go for their honeymoon."
• "*John's lied* to us too many times."

Present Perfect vs. Past Simple
The present perfect tells us about something that occurred at some indefinite
period in the past. However, if something happened at a specific point in time in
the past ("last night," "two years ago," "yesterday," etc.), then we must use the

past simple tense.

For example:

✖ "I have seen *Titanic* on TV last night." (incorrect)

✔ "I **saw** *Titanic* on TV last night." (correct)

✖ "She's been to Prague when she was a little girl." (incorrect)

✔ "She **went** to Prague when she was a little girl." (correct)

If the focus moves to *when*, then we cannot use the present perfect anymore

because the attention shifts to that particular point in time.

When we say "I have seen *Titanic*," we are giving general information about

something that happened anytime "before now." The focus is on the fact that "I

saw *Titanic*" and not on *when* I saw it.

The same applies to the second example from above:

• **Present perfect**: "She**'s been** to Prague." (Generally, at some point in her

lifetime.)

• **Past simple**: "She **went** to Prague when she was a little girl." (We say *when*

because the exact point in time is specified.)

True in the past and still true now

In English, we use the present perfect simple with the prepositions *for* and *since*

when we speak about something that started in the past and is still true now. *For*

is used to specify the duration of time leading up to the present; *since* clarifies

the point in time at which something began. Let's look at some examples:

• "I can't believe Jenny **has lived** in Dubai *for 10 years*!"

• "He**'s had** that car *since he was in high school*."

• "We**'ve known** each other *(for) our whole lives*, but we**'ve only been** friends

since 2006."

Even though a point in time is being specified in these cases, we still use the

present perfect because the information in the sentence is **still true now**. The

"for" and "since" join the past situation to a present one. If we were to use the
past simple tense for any of the above, "for" would change to mean the duration
of the event before it *finished*, and we would be unable to use "since" at all:
• "I can't believe Jenny **lived** in Dubai for 10 years!" (Jenny no longer lives in
Dubai.)
• "He **had** that car in high school." (He owned it then, but does not now.)
• "We **knew** each other for our whole lives, but we only **became** friends in
2006." (The two people are no longer acquainted; perhaps the other person is no
longer living.)
Present Perfect vs. Present Perfect
Continuous Tense
There is another, very similar tense that is used to talk about something that has
been happening in the past and which is still happening now. It is called the
present perfect continuous (or **progressive**) **tense**, and it is used to emphasize
the *action* of the sentence (as opposed to the *result*).
It is formed by using *have/has* along with *been* (the past participle of *be*) and the
present participle of the main verb. For example:
• "I **have been writing** many letters." (This emphasizes the action of writing, in
which the speaker is still engaged.)
This is slightly different from "I have written many letters" (present perfect),
which emphasizes the result of many letters having been completed.
In some cases, either the present perfect or present perfect continuous can be
used with almost no difference to the meaning of the sentence:
• "I can't believe Jenny **has lived** in Dubai for 10 years!" (*present perfect*)

• "I can't believe Jenny **has been living** in Dubai *for 10 years*!" (*present perfect*
continuous)

However, though quite similar to present perfect simple, the usages of present

perfect continuous *can* be a bit different. See the chapter section **Present Perfect**

Continuous Tense to learn more.

Before now or not long ago

Let's compare "I lost my keys" with "I've lost my keys."

Taken on its own, the first sentence is less correct because we are expecting the

speaker to say when he or she lost the keys; for example, "I lost my keys **yesterday**."

"I lost my keys" *can* be correct on its own, but only if it answers a question.

For example:

• A: "Why are you late?"

• B: "(Because) I lost my keys."

Otherwise, if there is no question or no specification of time, we say: "I've lost

my keys." This carries the meaning that the keys were lost just before now or not

long ago.

Let's take a look at another example:

• A: "Would you like a coffee?"

• B: "No, thanks, *I've had* one."

This refers to not long ago. We don't say *when* because the time is not important

—we understand that the person had the coffee a short while ago. Again, if the

time *is* being specified, then you have to put the sentence in past simple tense

(i.e., "No, thanks, I **had** one an hour ago").

Here are some more examples:

• "I'm not hungry, **I've had** lunch."

• "**He's taken** the dog to the park."

• "She **has left** the kids with her sister."

Remember, when the time becomes more important than the fact or the event,

we need to use the past simple tense:
- **Present perfect**: "I**'ve had** lunch." (Meaning just now or not long ago.)
- **Past simple**: "I **had lunch** at 12 o'clock." (Referring to exactly *when* the speaker had lunch.)

It is incorrect to say: "I've had lunch at 12 o'clock."

Negative sentences

You can also make the present perfect negative by simply adding *not* (or, in

certain uses, *never*) between *have/has* and the main verb:
- "I **have** *never* **seen** *Titanic*."
- "I'm so hungry; I ***haven't* had** lunch yet!"
- "He **has** *not* **been** home since he finished high school."
- "I regret that we**'ve** *never* **traveled** to Paris."

Interrogative sentences

If an interrogative (question) sentence is in the present perfect tense, the subject

and the auxiliary verb *have* are inverted. For example:
- "**Have** you **seen** this movie?"
- "**Has** she **heard** any news?"
- "**Have** they **started** the movie yet?"

Negative interrogative sentences

Negative interrogative sentences also ask a question, but they imply that the

speaker expected the answer to be (or believes the answer *should* be) "yes."

Negative interrogative sentences in the present perfect have the same form,

simply with the negative word (usually *not*, but also *never*) placed after the

subject.
- "**Have** you *never* **seen** this movie?"
- "**Has** she *not* **heard** any news?"

Not can also come after *have/has*, but it is almost always contracted:
- "**Haven't** they **started** the movie yet?"
- "***Hasn't*** his license **expired**?"

However, *never* cannot be used in this way.

With a question word

Interrogative sentences using question words (*who, what, where, when, why, which*, and *how*) maintain the same structure. *Have/has* can also be contracted

with the question word:

- *"When **have** you **been** to Italy?"*
- *"Where **has** she **gone**?"*
- *"**What've** they **done**?"*

They can also be negative, but then they are straightforward questions of who,

what, where, when, why, which, or how something is **not** the case:

- *"Which* book **have** you ***not* read**?"
- *"Why **haven't** you **eaten** your dinner yet?"*

have got and has got

There is one tricky phrase that defies the normal form: *have/has got*. We would

expect it to be in the present perfect, because it is in the form *have/has* plus the

past participle of *get*. However, even though it is in the present perfect tense in

form, in *meaning*, *have got* is actually in the present tense. It is used to indicate

possession, in nearly the same manner as the verb *have* (especially in more

informal speech or writing); *got* simply adds a certain level of emphasis to the

possession.

For example, the following pairs of sentences mean almost exactly the same

thing.

- "I **have got** three classes on Monday."
- "I **have** three classes on Monday."
- "I hear she**'s got** lots of money."
- "I hear she **has** lots of money."
- "You**'ve got** a lot of nerve coming here."
- "You **have** a lot of nerve coming here."

However, we can never use *have got* interchangeably with *have* when it is used

to describe an action. For example:

- ✔ "I **have** breakfast every morning." (correct)
- ✖ "I**'ve got** breakfast every morning." (incorrect)

To create the past perfect *meaning* of *get*, we use its *other* past participle
—**gotten**. We use this form to describe a *process*, such as receipt or acquisition,
or some other action. For example:
• "I **have gotten** word that my father is ill."
• "**He's gotten** a lot of positive feedback about his play."
• "Those dang kids **have gotten** a Frisbee stuck in our tree again."
Note, however, that *have/has gotten* is **not** used to describe possession:
• "I hear she **has gotten** lots of money." (Implies acquisition or receipt of lots of
money, rather than outright possession.)
Gotten is almost exclusively used in American English. It very rarely used in
British English, where *have got* **is** sometimes used as the past perfect
(informally). One such example is:
• "You**'ve got** taller." (British English)
• "You**'ve gotten** taller." (American English)
Regardless, *have/has got* and *have/has gotten*, though correct, are often seen as
being less formal or professional sounding, so depending on what you're
writing, you may be better off rewording the sentence to avoid the phrases
altogether.
Exercise

1. Which of the following sentences uses the **present perfect tense**?
a) "I worked in the factory for a few months before I quit."
b) "She has been living with her father until recently."
c) "I hear he has left his wife."
d) "I had written to her years ago, but I never expected a response."
2. Which preposition is used with the present perfect to talk about something that
was true in the past and is still true now?
a) For
b) In
c) At
d) Since
e) A & B

f) A & D

g) B & D

3. When is the present perfect **not** used?

a) For something that happened just before now.

b) For something that happened at a specific point in time in the past.

c) For something that was true in the past and is still true now.

d) For something that happened at some general time in the past.

4. Which **auxiliary verb** is used to form the present perfect tense?

a) Have

b) Be

c) Can

d) Do

Present Perfect Continuous Tense

Definition

The **present perfect continuous tense** (sometimes called the **present perfect progressive tense**) is formed by using the present tense of the auxiliary verb *have* (or *has*, if used with third-person singular pronouns) along with *been* (the *past participle* of the auxiliary verb *be*) and the present participle (*-ing* form) of
the "main" verb. For example:

• "I **have been living** in New York City."

The present perfect continuous is very close in meaning to how we use the
present perfect tense. However, there are some key differences that distinguish
when and how the present perfect continuous is preferable.

Generally, we use the present perfect continuous to talk about that which began
in the past and is still happening in the present; the focus is on something that
continues to happen, as opposed to something which happened (finished)
sometime in the past. We can also use the present perfect continuous to
emphasize the length of time that has passed while something is happening, or
that something is only temporary. We can also use it to talk about something that
has been happening lately or only finished very recently.

That which began in the past and

continues in the present

The present perfect continuous is often used to talk about something that began

happening in the past (anytime "before now") and which is still happening

(unfinished) in the present. We usually specify the duration of time involved,

especially using the prepositions "for" or "since." Sometimes we can use different adverbials; sometimes we don't have to specify the duration at all. For

example:

- "I have been living in New York City."
- "I have been living in New York City *for three years*."
- "I have been living in New York City *since I was 18*."
- "I have been living in New York City *all my life*."

In each of the above examples, it is understood implicitly that the speaker *still*

lives in New York City; the only thing that changes is the duration of time. In

this usage, the present perfect continuous is nearly identical in meaning to the

present perfect tense, and, indeed, most of these examples would make perfect

sense either way:

- "I *have lived* in New York City for three years."
- "I *have lived* in New York City since I was 18."
- "I *have lived* in New York City all my life."

The only sentence that changes in meaning is the very first example: to say "I

have lived in New York City" without any further elaboration gives the impression that the speaker used to live there, but no longer does.

This distinction between something being completed as opposed to still happening is important, because it highlights when you might choose to use the

present perfect continuous instead of the present perfect simple in certain

instances.

Let's look at the very first example again, but this time using a different adverbial:

✔ "I have been living in New York City *while I finish my Ph.D.*" (correct)

✖ "I have lived in New York City *while I finish my Ph.D.*" (incorrect)
We can see that this sentence does not make sense at all in the present perfect
simple tense, because the adverbial "while I finish my Ph.D." requires the action
to still be taking place. In cases like this, we must use the present perfect
continuous tense to get across the meaning correctly.
This distinction can also be particularly useful when we are giving a response to
someone:
• Person A: "Let's take the longer trail when we're hiking back down."
• Person B: "But we *have walked* for three hours!" (*present perfect*)
• Person B: "But we **have been walking** for three hours!" (**present perfect continuous**)
We can see that the response is more appropriate in the present perfect
continuous, because it lays emphasis on the continuous action of walking. It also
puts emphasis on the amount of time that the speaker has been doing something.

Emphasizing length of time
The present perfect continuous is especially useful for putting emphasis on the
length of time that has passed while something is happening. This is particularly
true when the meaning of the sentence could otherwise be expressed in the
present perfect simple. Here are some examples:
• "They *have studied* for three weeks for this exam." (*present perfect*)
• "They **have been studying** for three weeks for this exam." (**present perfect continuous**)
• "The girl *has worked* for five hours." (*present perfect*)
• "The girl **has been working** for five hours." (**present perfect continuous**)
The difference between these is slight, but noticeable. In both sets of examples,
the present perfect continuous puts the emphasis on how long the action has

taken, as well as the fact that it is still happening. The present perfect is simply
reporting the completed result and how long it took.
Let's look at another example:
• "He *has talked* on the phone for almost an hour."
• "He **has been talking** on the phone for almost an hour."
The first sentence is merely reporting how long the person was talking. With the
present perfect continuous, the focus naturally shifts to the fact that an hour is a
rather long period of time—and that he might continue talking for even longer!

That which is happening temporarily
Another subtle difference between the two tenses is that the present perfect is
better at indicating that something is permanent, while the present perfect
continuous is better at suggesting something is only temporary. For example:
• "I *have worked* in the shop for three years."
• "I **have been working** in the shop for three years."
The first sentence simply reports the length of time the speaker has been
working in the shop. It does not suggest that he or she intends to stop working
there at any point. The second sentence, however, makes the situation sound
much less permanent. We can see the difference more clearly if we add a bit
more information:
• "I *have worked* in the shop for three years, *but I hope to find something else
soon.*"
• "I **have been working** in the shop for three years, *but I hope to find something
else soon.*"
The first sentence sounds less natural than the second, because the new
information specifically relates to the situation being a temporary one. In this
case, the present perfect continuous is preferable.

**That which has been happening lately
or finished very recently**
The present perfect continuous can also be used to express that which has been
happening lately, but is not necessarily happening at the present moment in time.
For example:
• "Bill **has been coming** into work late a lot."
• "Don't you think Mary **has been spending** too much time on the computer
lately?"
It can also be used without an adverbial to indicate that something was
happening until only recently:
• "My neighbors are angry because my dog **has been barking**."
• "Sorry I'm so sweaty! I**'ve been exercising** all morning."
The action is not taking place at the exact moment of speech (in which case we
would just use the **present simple tense**), but we can infer that it had been
happening until very recently.
Negative sentences
Present perfect continuous sentences can be made negative by using the word
not. It appears after *have/has*, and the two can be (and very often are)
contracted.
• "I **have *not* been writing** much recently."
• "She ***hasn't* been trying** to find work since her divorce."
• "I need to get up earlier, because I ***haven't been making*** it to work on time
lately."
We generally do not use *never* with the present perfect continuous.
Interrogative sentences
Like the present perfect tense, an interrogative (question) sentence in the present
perfect continuous has the subject and the auxiliary verb *have* inverted. For
example:
• "Where **have** you **been living** lately?"
• "**Has** she **been feeling** OK?"
• "Why **have** you **been lying** to me?"

We can also make negative interrogative sentences in the present perfect
continuous by adding *not* between the subject and *been*. We can also contract
have/has and *not*:
• "***Haven't*** you **been writing** a new book?"
• "**Has** she ***not* been feeling** well?"
• "Why ***haven't*** they **been working** on their homework?"
As we see in the first example, the meaning of the question can become rhetorical, implying that the speaker expected the answer to be "yes."
Exercise

1. The past participle of which **auxiliary verb** is used to form the present perfect
continuous tense?
a) Have
b) Be
c) Can
d) Do
2. The **main** verb of the present continuous tense is in what form?
a) Present participle
b) Past participle
c) Continuous participle
d) Future participle
3. Which of the following is something the present perfect continuous tense can be used for? (Choose the answer that is **most** correct.)
a) Talking about something that is always the case.
b) Talking about something that finished sometime in the past.
c) Talking about something that began in the past and is still happening.
d) Talking about something that is happening right now.
4. Which of the following sentences uses the **present perfect continuous** tense?
a) "I am writing to my sister in New England."
b) "She has spoken to her boss in the hopes of getting a raise."
c) "The train usually arrives at 3 PM, but it was late yesterday."
d) "I have been leaving earlier than usual this week."
e) "He hasn't seen the results of the test yet."

Answers

Tense: 1-b, 2-d, 3-c, 4-a, 5-c
Present Tense: 1-g, 2-a, 3-c, 4-f
Present Simple Tense: 1-c, 2-d, 3-a, 4-c
Present Continuous Tense (Progressive): 1-c, 2-d, 3-g, 4-a, 5-d, 6-b
Present Perfect Tense: 1-c, 2-f, 3-b, 4-a
Present Perfect Continuous Tense: 1-b, 2-a, 3-c, 4-d

***

Worksheet 4
***

Worksheet 5
***

Worksheet 6
***

Worksheet 7
***

Worksheet 6
***

Worksheet 7
***

Worksheet 8

***

Worksheet 9

***

Worksheet 10

***

* 9 7 9 8 8 8 9 3 5 2 9 0 7 *